English Plants
for your Garden

English Plants for your Garden

JILL DUCHESS OF HAMILTON
PENNY HART &
JOHN SIMMONS

PHOTOGRAPHY BY DON BERWICK

 PUBLISHED IN ASSOCIATION WITH
THE NATIONAL TRUST

FRANCES LINCOLN

For Dame Miriam Rothschild, whose early work with native plants paved the way for this book.

Invaluable support for this book has been given by Osborne & Little plc

Frances Lincoln Ltd
4 Torriano Mews
Torriano Avenue
London NW5 2RZ

English Plants for your Garden
Copyright © Frances Lincoln Limited 2000
Text copyright © Flora-for-Fauna 2000
Photographs copyright © Don Berwick 2000, except for those listed on page 176
Foreword copyright © Miriam Rothschild 2000
Preface copyright © John Brookes 2000

First Frances Lincoln edition: 2000

British Library Cataloguing in Publication data
A catalogue record for this book is available from the British Library.

ISBN 0 7112 1435 2

Set in Garamond MT
Printed in Hong Kong

Authors' note: Taking plants from the wild is often illegal and always immoral. It robs future generations of their national heritage and cheats animals of food and support. Native species can be obtained from a growing number of specialist nurseries, usually run by committed and knowledgeable growers (see page 172).

PAGE 1 *Iris pseudacorus*
FRONTISPIECE Native orchids at Great Dixter, Sussex
ABOVE Antony Little's garden in Wiltshire
CONTENTS PAGE *Quercus robur*

CONTENTS

Foreword

Wild and garden flowers, mixed together, grow all over the walls and roof of my house. Dog-roses are planted alongside the climbing roses *Rosa* 'Kiftsgate' and 'Etoile de Hollande'. *Clematis montana* competes with our native clematis species, old man's beard (*Clematis vitalba*). When visitors arrive at my house, they look around at the tangle of creepers that completely hides the stonework from view and they pause, puzzled – surely no one can live amid such disorder?

It is not really a muddle, but what Alfred, Lord Tennyson called 'a careless, ordered garden', which I favour. To me, at least, this confusion of the wild and the tame seems completely natural. My garden shows how exotic and cultivated flowers can mix with English native plants in perfect harmony. My greatest triumph came one evening when a nightingale visited the courtyard.

Although many of our garden flowers and vegetables have been improved and altered by selection, crossing and grafting, they still are – in some parts of the world – wild flowers. This was brought forcibly home to me when I first saw clumps of black-eyed Susans adorning the verges in Texas.

If you want to learn how to combine local wild flowers with exotic plants and take advantage of your local trees, wild flowers, ferns and grasses, you should consult this book.

Miriam Rothschild
Ashton, December 1999

Miriam Rothschild's garden at Ashton

Preface

Although there is an increasing number of writers who seek to bridge the gap between the horticulturist and the environmentalist, there are many who still see the merit of a garden as the number of exotica it includes. But this view is beginnning to be questioned, along with the issues of how plants are used in the garden and how they are cultivated. And as this happens, native plants are becoming more appreciated.

Many of us were raised with the Edwardian tradition of feeding the garden annually – for there was plenty of muck from the stables – in the manner of the walled garden. But this precedent has nothing to do with the use of native plants, for they need no sweat and tears: they are happy with their lot, or rather your lot, if you select only the right subjects for it, and more importantly do not cultivate or feed your ground. For nobody either mows or blows in nature, surely? The trick to achieving a natural effect is to select those plants which would grow naturally in your situation had the ground not been fed – cleared of pernicious weed certainly, but little more, although you may improve the soil's water-holding capacity. That should please the 'no maintenance' addict.

But I live in Bromley, Burnley or Bromsgrove, you say; what is my native plant association? The natural plant – right for your soil, its moisture, the sun or shade the garden receives and so on – would be roughly (apart from brambles and sycamore) what would grow if you left your lot alone for five years. But you need not wait five years: you know these conditions anyway and therefore you can make your own selection of suitable native plants, using this book.

And see how native plants grow! They drift and flow; they are not in tight little bundles of three, five or seven in tidy prepared borders – the effect is far looser. And of course you may mingle introduced species as well. The effect can be quite startlingly different, and quite beautiful too. *English Plants for your Garden,* I say – there is an amazing range and we are lucky to have them.

John Brookes
Denmans, November 1999

In my own garden at Denmans, West Sussex, I use gravel as a ground medium, allowing the plants to associate in a natural way.

Gardening with Native Plants

Swathes of dazzling sapphire-blue flowers regularly draw gasps of admiration from visitors to Norfolk's Breckland in summer. Many assume this is a new and exciting exotic, but on the contrary, it is one of England's oldest indigenous plants, the stunning viper's-bugloss (*Echium vulgare*).

Such plants are enjoying something of a renaissance, and viper's-bugloss is just one of the treasures of the English flora that have been rediscovered by enlightened gardeners. The newest finds are, in fact, some of the oldest inhabitants of this land, and although indigenous favourites such as the fritillary, columbine, foxglove, lily-of-the-valley, hazel, yew, holly, daffodil and harebell have long been grown in garden beds and borders, there are legions of fascinating natives that have been unfairly overlooked.

In the beginning it may have been a case of familiarity breeding contempt. For hundreds of years the lanes and hedgerows, the parks and cottage plots of England were filled mainly with indigenous flowers and trees. It was not until the nineteenth century, the era of the great plant-hunters, that these were gradually displaced by novel and exciting

The breathtaking blue of viper's-bugloss (*Echium vulgare*) is a wayside joy on the light, dry soil of the Norfolk Breckland. A magnet for bees and butterflies, it makes a spectacular garden plant, particularly in dry soils.

vegetation from overseas. The original, unimproved native species were then relegated to a minor league, becoming the Cinderellas of English horticulture.

Now, however, tiring of the flamboyance and uniformity of the hothouse flower, many gardeners throughout the world are appreciating anew the virtues of their local plants. No longer classed as mere weeds, native species are once again being admired for what they are: the successful fruit of the earth. They became so by adapting themselves perfectly to the conditions of their particular area. Unlike rare and imported plants, they need little help in the way of artificial heat and fertilizers, and no international transport. Their chief demand on the gardener may be the occasional sortie with the secateurs in order to curb their vigorous growth.

Appreciating English native plants may call for some visual adjustment on the part of the admirer. The colours are often understated in comparison with the harsher tones of flowers from sunnier climates, but then they are better suited to the soft light of the British Isles: think of the dog-rose (*Rosa canina*) in summer, its pale pink petals and golden stamens shining against a deep green backdrop of yew. They have their own surprising charms. Autumn brings the drama of the bold scarlet berries of stinking iris or the dark purple sloes of blackthorn; winter chill is made cheerful by the shining evergreen growth of holly and ivy. In the main, English flowers are smaller and more delicate in appearance than imported blooms such as peonies and magnolias. The largest indigenous English flower is the white water-lily (*Nymphaea alba*), usually only 10cm/4in in diameter, followed by the purple foxglove (*Digitalis purpurea*) and the yellow flag iris (*Iris pseudacorus*). But their scale fits the English countryside, and closer inspection will reveal the ingenious devices native flowers have developed in order to survive.

Survival, of course, is the key, because plants do not provide beauty and fragrance simply for our aesthetic pleasure. They are wonderfully well-devised weapons in the drive for propagation, and what were once known as 'common' plants are simply the most efficient in adjusting to their environment. The lives of people and animals depend on plant life, but whereas people can adapt to varying types of diet and shelter, many animals cannot. This is why the cultivation of native species is so important: many English creatures need specific plants for food and reproduction, or they will die.

ABOVE Foxglove (*Digitalis purpurea*)

RIGHT Arching branches of dog-rose (*Rosa canina*) display pale pink flowers in summer and scarlet hips in autumn. Here it makes an attractive specimen plant, but it is equally effective when grown over a building or hedge.

Unfortunately, with the spread of urbanization and new methods of agriculture, whole tracts of native plants have gone under the bulldozer and the plough. Gardens now collectively create an increasingly important reserve for local species and their dependent animals, and the aim of the charity Flora for Fauna is to encourage gardeners to include as many native flora as possible in their planting plans. If local plants are encouraged – and chemicals avoided – gardens can play a major part in conservation.

Including native plants in the garden is an idea with a respectable pedigree. William Robinson (1839–1931) and Gertrude Jekyll (1843–1932), those great influences on the English garden, both recommended the use of native plants: as a linking thread throughout a mixed border, in hedging, or as a feature in a part of the garden where few imported plants would flourish. To help gardeners follow their example and explore the rich variety of English flora, this book describes some exciting and relatively unknown indigenous plants for gardens, alongside the already tried and tested.

Wild strawberry (*Fragaria vesca*), with an emperor moth

Local heroes

As the world becomes more and more homogeneous, so there is a need to establish a local identity. Place names, languages, dialects, food, architecture and pride in landscape are all becoming increasingly precious to people. Now, at last, the very essence of a region – its local flora – is just beginning to receive its true recognition.

Local plants are the unsung heroes of the British landscape. They convey a sense of place. They are often a source of communal pride. They are suited to immediate soil and climate conditions. They have low maintenance requirements. And, after generations of cumulative adaptations, they can usually withstand long periods of dryness or spells of cold and wet.

The constant battle against the tendency of gardens to return to the wild could be one reason why gardeners have tended to shun native plants, perhaps associating them with the uncontrolled and the unruly. While it is true that some native plants in a garden such as brambles or nettles may look unkempt or be invasive, the same faults occur in a number of imported plants. Native plants can be just as much at home in gardens as they are in woodlands or fields: they may be interwoven with existing exotics, or they can form their own native plant section within a garden.

Even relatively formal gardens may be composed entirely of plants that predated the Roman invasion. By incorporating local plants in garden schemes it is possible to combine ornamental gardening with benefits to wildlife and the preservation of Britain's plant heritage.

Before the Rhododendron

To the great English poets, a true garden contained familiar English natives mixed with a few favoured imported plants, such as lilies, red roses, lavender, peonies, crocuses, crown imperials and marigolds. William Shakespeare (1564–1616) never saw a rhododendron. Neither did Geoffrey Chaucer (*c.* 1345–1400) before him, or John Milton (1608–74) or John Bunyan (1628–88), who came after him. In Chaucer's time the simple English daisy was regarded as a flower of some beauty, not a weed to be removed.

Poppy (*Papaver rhoeas*)

> *Of alle the floures in the mede,*
> *Than love I most these floures whyte and rede,*
> *Swiche as men callen daysies in our toun.*
> *The Legend of Good Women*, 'The Prologue'

The bright hues of a petunia, a fuchsia, a dahlia or a zinnia would have been startlingly exotic at that time. Over the last 300 years these and thousands of other ornamental plants were collected from mountain slopes, valleys and plains by explorers and traders, who brought them back to the British Isles. Now English gardens – the most renowned, the most lovingly tended in the world – are crammed with alien plants and new varieties from all corners of the earth. So dominated are they by imports and ever more elaborate flowers that the description 'English gardens' no longer means gardens growing English plants.

Even the words 'English' or 'London' in a name are no indication of origin. The London plane tree is a hybrid of the American and Oriental planes; English lavender came from the Mediterranean, and the English walnut tree from Asia Minor. The garden perennial London pride is a hybrid of species from the Pyrenees.

New introductions have added beauty to gardens at the price of neglecting native species. The numbers of garden plants known to be introduced in Britain were, according to the late botanist Anthony Huxley (1920–92), only 84 in the sixteenth century, leaping to 940 in the seventeenth century and 8,938 in the eighteenth century. The Victorian

marjoram (*Origanum vulgare*), a perennial with a similar flavour to the culinary variety and bright magenta flowers, which last well into autumn.

However, deciding on the desired shrubs or flowers is only part of the process of creating a truly English garden. Of course, they must never be taken from the wild, but buying native plants can be bewildering, and much of what is sold comes from mainland Europe where plants are cheaper. Thirty ton(ne)s of Dutch acorns alone are brought into England each year – part of the total annual importation of around £200 million worth of horticultural plants. Until recently there was no simple way of finding out what is native to England (as opposed to the entire British Isles). To guide gardeners, this book contains the first easily accessible checklist of English native plants (see pages 162–71).

What is a native plant?

Native plants in England are those that arrived independently of man and were here for several millennia before people and their buildings, farms, commerce and roads transformed the landscape. In its botanical sense, the word 'native' refers to plants indigenous to a particular place, while the term 'alien' indicates a plant introduced from another country or region. In a pluralist society the use of these terms is often considered highly offensive and smacking of imperialism, but for scientists and gardeners there is no alternative terminology, apart from the word 'indigenous'.

Dr Jim Dickson, Reader in Botany at Glasgow University, defines a native plant as one which 'in the studied area has arrived by natural means of dispersal, that is without being transported by man, either intentionally or unintentionally'. Centuries ago the invading Romans brought seeds with them, some deliberately and some accidentally in sacks of grain or even on the soles of their sandals. Confusion may arise where a plant has cousins in mainland Europe. Take the English bluebell (*Hyacinthoides non-scripta*): carpeting woodland floors with a luminous blue, it is one of the chief glories of English woodlands. But introductions from Spain, *Hyacinthoides hispanica* – though lacking the strong scent, slender stems and intense colour of the English species – are now widely grown as garden bluebells, sometimes escaping from cultivation to hybridize with their English counterparts, and also becoming naturalized in hedgerows and woods.

People often confuse native plants with naturalized plants, such as the now common horse chestnut, evening primrose and cornflower.

Some wild flowers, especially those like Oxford ragwort and buddleia which flourish on waste ground, are imports that have escaped from gardens. The Pontic rhododendron was brought to England from Turkey in the 1763 and has become so rooted in the landscape that it is often thought to be native, despite its propensity to spread through woods, choking young trees and casting a barren shadow where bluebells and wood anemones might have flourished.

Before the seas rose at the end of the Ice Age and cut off what are now the British Isles, England was on the fringe of continental Europe and the Thames was a tributary of the Rhine. It follows, then, that most English plants are relatives of European species. But in the 8,000 years since complete separation, many English plants have evolved in different ways according to local conditions. Even plants that do not appear to be distinct, such as certain species of birch or dog-rose, vary minutely in chemical composition in different regions.

Sixteen plant species, including the Lundy cabbage (*Coincya wrightii*) and a sea lavender (*Limonium logicanicum*), are native only to England and do not occur naturally anywhere else in the world. They are known as endemics. Some, like the two mentioned, have a very restricted range. Others are much more widely distributed. The early gentian (*Gentianella anglica*), for example, though rare, is found in isolated spots from Cornwall to as far north as Lincolnshire. Many endemic plants have close relatives on the Continent – for instance, the Isle of Man cabbage (*Coincya monensis*) is little more than a subspecies or variety of its continental relation – whereas other endemic plants are so distinct as to be considered different species.

Recent advances in specialized fields of archaeology and fossils have enabled botanists to distinguish with great precision between native and naturalized flora. Dr Max Walters, former director of Cambridge University Botanic Garden, says: '… we now have incontrovertible evidence, in many cases from peat and pollen studies, that a particular plant is "truly native". If we can show that the plant was growing wild in what is now England at least 10,000 years ago, then even the most stringent criterion for native status would be satisfied. A native plant would be one which arrived independently of man, and has been here for at least 2,000 years.'

An idea taken from nature – the shimmering blue carpet of native bluebells (*Hyacinthoides non-scripta*) in spring can be recreated in any neglected corner of the garden, transforming a dull patch into a stretch of glorious colour.

Changing the face of nature

A flower is not simply a pretty accident of nature, blooming to please the onlooker. It is a set of sexual organs wrapped in lovely robes, bent on survival and propagation of the species. Gaily coloured petals, intriguing markings, enticing fragrance, sweet nectar – all these are cunningly contrived to entice insects, the flower's often unwitting agents in the deadly earnest business of reproduction. The sole aim is to produce seed and disperse it as widely as possible. To achieve this, male pollen must first be conveyed to female ovaries. Male and female organs may be in the same flower or in separate flowers on the one plant; they may even be on separate plants. Whatever the arrangement, plants are unable to go courting, and a go-between is required in order to effect a union. This envoy might simply be gravity, as pollen drops on to the female part; or it might be wind, as the pollen is blown from male to female; but by far the most important of flowers' co-conspirators are pollinating insects, often lured by patterns which only they can see. Bees, for instance, are attracted by coloured petals before landing on a perfectly constructed lip and following the marked guide lines to reach their prize, a feast of nectar and pollen. On the way in, they cannot avoid a coating of sticky pollen from the anthers. They then fly off to feed on the next plant, where the pollen brushes off on the female parts to ensure fertilization. The trade-off is complete: food for the insect, reproduction for the plant. One thing is clear – the flower is exquisitely designed for its purpose.

Then along comes the plant breeder, eager to improve the flower: to enlarge the petals, double the bloom, increase their number, brighten the colour. For centuries gardeners and plant-breeders have been crossing and selecting flowers to transform the simple original into a showy double. This has added immeasurably to richness and variety in gardens and to the pleasure of the new, but it is as if a plastic surgeon had taken his scalpel to fresh-complexioned country girls and turned them into Hollywood sirens. Now it is not so easy to find the plant equivalent of the girl-next-door. The majority of plants available in most garden centres have been altered in some way by breeders.

Few gardeners realize that many of the hybridized varieties that they select and cherish represent the equivalent of a famine for birds, butterflies and other wildlife. Old-fashioned, single-flowered varieties are a valuable source of nectar for flower-visiting insects such as bees and butterflies. Conversely, the more elaborate blooms of many modern hybrids provide

Hazel (*Corylus avellana*)

24

meagre fare, because the sex organs are often altered, sacrificed in order to create more petals. Some have little or no nectar. Others produce nectar but insects cannot reach it, obstructed by double petals or 'improvements' in the bloom. Many exotic flowers are completely sterile – a facelift at the expense of fertility.

Revulsion against gaudy, highly bred and crossed flowers has a surprisingly long history. In a book on botany that was partly written during his eighteen months in England, the eighteenth-century French philosopher Jean-Jacques Rousseau (1712–78) condemned double flowers as 'nature disfigured by man'. 'Should you find double flowers, waste no time in examining them,' he wrote, 'they are deformed, or, if you prefer, we have embellished them according to our whim: nature is no longer there; she refuses to be reproduced by such deformed monsters; for while the most arresting part, the corolla, is reduplicated, it is at the expense of our more essential organs, which disappear beneath this splendour.'

While acknowledging the attractions of garden doubles such as carnations, Watson cautions: 'Let us never be so far dazzled as to forget that they are for the most part highly artificial products. Much of their beauty is produced at the expense of native character.' Gardeners, he said, could become so preoccupied with breeding 'improved' flowers that they come to dislike 'every form of that wild looser sort of vegetation which is wholly excluded from the garden'.

Earlier still, in his poem 'The Mower, against Gardens', Andrew Marvell (1621–78) made a scathing reference to plant breeding, and grafting in particular:

Wild cherry (*Prunus avium*)

> *No plant now knew the stock from which it came;*
> *He grafts upon the wild the tame,*
> *That the uncertain and adulterate fruit*
> *Might put the palate in dispute.*
> *His green seraglio has its eunuchs too,*
> *Lest any tyrant him outdo;*
> *And in the cherry he does Nature vex,*
> *To procreate without a sex …*

A vital food source

Garden plants are important to people, and they are becoming more and more important to English wildlife. Many animals, especially birds, rely on

Herbaceous Flowers

The flowers appear on the earth;
The time of the surfacing of the buds is come ...

The Song of Solomon, 2:12

With herbaceous plants the scale of planting is important. If sizeable clumps are needed for effect, then a border by a house should be at least 2m/6½ft wide – twice that size for beds in grass. Shrubs (see page 119) and spring bulbs can add structure and early interest to herbaceous borders. A border might be based around guelder-roses and coppiced hazel, while on lighter, more acidic soils, broom and heather could be substituted, as could dogwood in moister soils and daphne in basic soils, all with bulbs underneath and flowers between them. The taller teasel, ornamental thistle, willowherb, foxglove and campanula at the back may be graded into mallow, columbine, goldenrod, campion, oxeye daisy, valerian and hemp-agrimony. In the middle of the border there might be lords-and-ladies, spiked speedwell, Jacob's ladder, toadflax, viper's-bugloss and scabious; while at the front, meadow crane's-bill, thrift, thyme, mountain avens and marjoram would be appropriate.

Drifts of daffodils can be planted under deciduous shrubs and any gaps filled with primrose, lily-of-the-valley and field pansy. Hellebore and bold clumps of grass, chosen for a long season of flowering, form pleasing shapes.

Drifts of white oxeye daisy (*Leucanthemum vulgare*) lend light and elegance to the garden, well suited to meadow or border as long as the soil is well drained.

Spring bulbs and anemones flower early and their dying foliage can be hidden by summer perennials. As in cottage gardens, free-seeding summer annuals live happily among perennials but usually need thinning out if they threaten to crowd out weaker plants. In late summer the dead remains of annuals may have to be removed. For many of the abundant seed producers, such as poppies, this should be done before the seeds are distributed. But always leave plenty of seeds for birds on plants such as knapweed.

Though a fully furnished border suppresses weeds, attention still needs to be paid, at least fortnightly, to weeding and training branches and stems. Taller plants may need staking to stop them falling over and smothering their neighbours. Each year, in late summer or winter, a proportion of plant clumps should be divided so that their vigour is maintained. Owing to the diverse nature and particular requirements of most indigenous plants there may not be as high a rate of seed germination as from, say, a packet of commercial vegetable seed.

Cultivating native plants calls for straightforward gardening crafts and often very little maintenance once they are established. There are plants to suit just about every condition, from dry shade to boggy ground, from a woodland corner to an exposed clifftop. Finding the right plant for the right place is the key, a task that should be made easier with the help of the following profiles of a selection of the most garden-worthy native plants.

White and pink-tinged flowerheads of yarrow (*Achillea millefolium*) make perfect feeding platforms for the lovely peacock butterfly (*Inachis io*).

It grows in sun or semi-shade and prefers moist but well-drained soil. Columbine self-seeds freely to produce dozens of seedlings, but can be raised from seed collected from the ripe pods and either planted immediately in a cold frame or in the open in May or June.

Thrift
Armeria maritima   PLUMBAGINACEAE

The cheerful, rounded, rose-pink flowerheads of thrift have long been a garden favourite. In fact, the flowers featured on the pre-decimalization threepenny-bit. A low-growing, cushion-forming perennial, up to 25-30cm/10-12in tall, it has numerous long, narrow, grasslike but fleshy leaves arising from a woody rootstock. From this arise the leafless, hairy, grooved stalks, ending in dense hemispherical heads of five-petalled pink, or occasionally white, flowers surrounded by a ring of chafflike bracts. The central flower in each head is the first to open. Thrift continues to bloom from April to October. The oblong fruit capsule is enclosed by sepals.

It grows on cliffs, rocks and in salt marshes all round the coast of England, and up to 850m/2,790ft on mountains inland in the Lake District. An inland form, *A. m.* subsp. *elongata*, which is more robust and has hairless flower stalks, occurs on lime-rich soils in Lincolnshire.

The flowerheads can be dried and used in flower arranging.

The plant is good for attracting wildlife, with flowers producing both nectar and pollen for bumble bees; it is also attractive to hoverflies and gall-midges. The nectar is the main food of the Granville fritillary butterfly, but this occurs only on the Isle of Wight. It is the food plant of the annulet and feathered ranunculus moths.

With a long flowering season, thrift is a reliable performer at the front of a well-drained herbaceous border, in a rock garden or tucked into crevices between stone paving slabs. It prefers an open situation in full sun and will tolerate poor soil, as long as it is free-draining. It is easily propagated by dividing the rootstock in spring, or from seed grown either in a cold frame in autumn or in a sandy soil in spring. In comfortable, cultivated conditions, thrift appears to produce fewer seeds than it does when struggling in the wild.

Lords-and-Ladies
Arum maculatum   ARACEAE

The intriguing, hooded cream-coloured flowerheads of the perennial lords-and-ladies never fail to excite a second glance as they unfurl in April and May. The pointed, ribbed cowl (the spathe) shelters a purple column (the spadix), and both are part of a complex construction to trap pollinating insects. Warmth and a slight rotting smell from the spadix lure small flies towards the base, past a ring of male flowers to the female flowers beneath. Backward-pointing hairs capture the departing, nectar-drugged insects long enough to ensure that they are well covered with pollen before they can escape to pollinate another plant. Lords-and-ladies has a stout stem and grows up to 25cm/10in, with arrow-shaped, glossy green, net-veined leaves, often with dark purple blotches. After the spathe shrivels, the fruiting spike develops into a club of shining orange-red berries, each containing ridged seeds.

Lords-and-ladies is found throughout England, in deciduous woods and hedgerows, often on lime-rich soils, from lowlands to foothills.

Beware: the berries are very poisonous.

Lords-and-ladies is pollinated by small flies of the *Psychoda* family.

Its dramatic form and bright berries will add interest to any garden when grown in a wooded corner, a shrubbery or hedgebank. It will grow in sun or semi-shade in well-drained soil and is useful in alkaline soil. Propagate it from seed sown in a cold frame in autumn – but wear gloves when removing the flesh from the berries – or, better still, divide the clumps by carefully separating the white tubers. Again, wear gloves, because the tubers contain toxins that can harm the skin.

Sea Aster
Aster tripolium   ASTERACEAE

A handsome, maritime plant with bluish-purple flowers with yellow centres, the sea aster (or sea starwort) is similar in appearance to the North American Michaelmas daisy. Indeed, both are members of the daisy family. But the fleshy leaves of this biennial (sometimes annual) mark it out as a coastal plant because they are designed to retain essential fresh water in the salty conditions of their favoured shoreline sites. This perennial grows up to 60cm/24in high, with upright, sparsely branched

stems and succulent, lance-shaped alternate leaves. Blooming from August to October, the flowerheads are composed of clusters of tiny florets: the tubular, inner disc-florets bright yellow and the straplike outer ray-florets bluish-purple. These ray-florets are sometimes missing in plants in the south. The flat, nutlike fruit has a silky parachute to aid dispersal.

Sea aster is found all round the coast, in salt marshes and tidal estuaries, and sometimes on cliffs and rocks.

It has been grown in gardens since the sixteenth century, and was cultivated to aid the healing of wounds.

Sea aster is visited by bees and other insects.

A natural for seaside gardens, it will flourish in a salty atmosphere, and when grown in drifts in a sunny border it provides an impressive splash of colour from summer right through autumn. Propagation is from side-shoots taken in summer or by careful division of the rootstock in spring. The seed has low viability and is best sown in quantity in autumn.

The related goldilocks aster, *A. linosyris*, sadly now very rare, is found on sea cliffs in western England from south Devon to Cumbria. Its leaves are longer and borne on slightly shorter stems than those of the sea aster, and its flowers (which lack ray-florets) form a tight golden head in later September.

Daisy

Bellis perennis ASTERACEAE

Well by reason men call it maie
The Daisie, or els The Eye of the Daie.
The Empresse and floure of floures all.
Geoffrey Chaucer (*c.* 1345–1400)

Taking its common name from the Old English for 'day's eye', the dainty daisy opens its petals in the morning light and closes its pink-fringed lashes at dusk. It is a beautiful perennial familiar to all gardeners, but too frequently regarded as an enemy because of its habit of growing in grass. The daisy is readily recognized by its neat rosettes of bright green, spoon-shaped, slightly toothed leaves, which are rounded at the top and narrow abruptly into a broad stalk. Hairy, upright flower

Often banished from lawns, the dainty English daisy (*Bellis perennis*)
holds childhood memories of summer days spent making daisy chains.
It should be valued as an attractive garden flower in its own right and
can be effective when grown in containers.

40

obviously not a problem when it is naturalized in a wilder area. It is best propagated by saving the seed and keeping it dry in winter before sowing in April or May, transferring seedlings to a shady holding bed in July and planting in their final position in autumn.

Teasel
Dipsacus fullonum DIPSACACEAE

The tall, sculptural form of the biennial teasel has long been a favourite of flower arrangers, but increasingly the merits of this robust, prickly plant are being appreciated by gardeners. In the first year it appears as a rosette of oblong basal leaves with prickles. The second year brings the stout, branched, angled flowering stem, up to 2m/6½ft tall, with spines on the angles. Its pairs of opposite, lance-shaped stem leaves are joined at the base round the stem, forming cups that collect rainwater. The egg-shaped flowerheads rise on long stalks from the upper leaf-axils, each surrounded by long, curving, spiny bracts that grow upwards from the base. Masses of rosy-purple, four-lobed, tubular flowers, each with four protruding stamens, appear in July and August; flowering begins with a central band around the head and continues upwards and downwards until the flowerhead is covered. Each flower develops into a ribbed fruit topped by a persistent, hairy calyx, and the many spiny bracts between the flowers persist through the winter.

Teasel grows on damp wood margins, stream banks and roadsides and in scrub and grassy places on disturbed, heavy soils throughout lowland England. It is common south and east of a line joining the Humber and Severn estuaries, but scattered elsewhere.

After flowering, the heads can be shaken to release the seeds, before being dried and kept for flower arrangements. The heads of the closely related but introduced Fuller's teasel, *D. sativus*, are used in the woollen trade to raise the pile on woven cloth.

Bees, butterflies (including the brimstone, common blue and small copper) and other long-tongued insects visit the flowers to collect the nectar, and the heads may be infested with the caterpillars of a tortricoid moth. The ripe seeds are relished by goldfinches, which work in groups to harvest the food. Birds drink from the rainwater collected in the cuplike leaf bases, but small insects sometimes become trapped in the tiny pools and drown.

Its height and sturdiness make the teasel a good plant for

the middle or back of a herbaceous border, but it would equally suit a woodland feature, particularly one on damp ground. It grows in sun or semi-shade and tolerates a wide range of soils, including clay, as long as there is some moisture. It is best propagated by sowing seed in the open in May or June, thinning out the seedlings and planting to permanent positions in September, where they will flower the following year. The plant will self-seed once it is established, the seeds sometimes taking two years to germinate, but the seedlings are rarely prolifically produced and can easily be removed.

Mountain Avens
Dryas octopetala ROSACEAE

The delightful, evergreen mountain avens is a low-growing perennial, which forms a dense mat of narrow, dark green, oaklike leaves with silvery undersides – a perfect foil for the lovely large, delicate white flowers with clusters of golden stamens at the centre. The many-branched, woody stem, up to 50cm/20in long, has masses of oblong, round-toothed leaves on alternate sides, each with a coating of dense white hairs underneath. In June and July each single, upright, 2–8cm/¾–3in stalk carries an eight-petalled flower cupped by long green sepals. Later, the fruit appears as a large silvery head with long, feathery styles, described thus by Dr John Lindley (1799–1865) in his book *Ladies' Botany*: 'as it waves about in the wind, one might fancy it a tuft of feathers accidentally fastened to the flower stalk'.

Mountain avens is an alpine plant, a relic of the last Ice Age, found in the north, mainly on mountain ledges and rock crevices, and sometimes near sea-level, on base-rich soil.

Infusions of the plant were once used as a stomach tonic and to treat mouth and throat infections.

Small insects pollinate the plant while seeking nectar at the base of the stamens. The leaves may be mined by the larva of the small *Stigmella dryadella* moth.

Its hummock-forming evergreen foliage makes mountain avens an ideal plant for the rock garden, the edge of a border or for trailing from gaps in a stone wall. It could also be used

PREVIOUS PAGES The straight lines of a trimmed privet hedge enclose a free-growing abundance of native and cottage-garden plants including mallow, teasel and tansy (in bud).

at the edges of containers, and will grow in sun or semi-shade, preferably in humus-rich, free-draining soil. It is propagated by taking summer cuttings of procumbent rooted stems for autumn planting. Plants can also be raised from seed sown thinly in a pan or box, damage to delicate seedlings being most easily avoided by transferring larger seedlings straight to pots or a nursery bed.

Viper's-bugloss
Echium vulgare BORAGINACEAE

There poppies, nodding, mock the hope of toil;
There the blue bugloss paints the sterile soil;
Hardy and high, above the slender sheaf,
The slimy mallow waves her silky leaf;
O'er the young shoot the charlock throws a shade.
The Village, George Crabbe (1754–1832)

Its brilliant blue, trumpet-shaped flowers with protruding purplish-pink stamens make this the most dazzling English member of the borage family. In its first year the biennial produces a rosette of hairy, strap-shaped leaves up to 15cm/6in long. The following summer the tall, erect stem (up to 90cm/36in) appears, with reddish-tinged bristly hairs and unstalked, pointed leaves. Grape-like clusters of reddish-pink flower buds clothe the flower spike to its tip, opening from June to August into funnels of vivid blue, round-lobed petals enclosing four long stamens. After pollination, the flower produces four ridged nutlets said to resemble the head of a viper, hence its common name.

The plant is found on open grassland, rough ground, cliffs, dunes and shingle, usually on light (often calcareous) soils, throughout England, especially in the south and east.

Beware: contact with the leaves may irritate the skin.

Viper's-bugloss is important for wildlife because the alluring colour and scent of the nectar-filled flowers attract large numbers of bees, hoverflies, butterflies and moths. The roots are the food plant for the orange swift moth.

Viper's-bugloss is a spectacular plant for a herbaceous border or wildflower garden; useful in dry, sandy soils; and impressive when planted in drifts. Its bold splash of blue will remain through September. It is propagated by sowing seed in summer and sheltering seedlings over the winter before planting out.

Sea Holly
Eryngium maritimum   APIACEAE

*I came on that blue-headed plant
That lovers ate to waken love,
Eryngo; but I felt no want,
A lovesick swain, to eat thereof.*

'Eryngo', Andrew Young (1855–1971)

The sculptural sea holly (eryngo) is an outstandingly attractive seaside perennial, with bright, glaucous foliage covered with a sea-green bloom and its lustrous, metallic-blue, oval flowerheads. Although it resembles a thistle, it is a member of the carrot family and has a thick, fleshy tap root to prove it. Growing to about 60cm/24in tall, it has hollow, upright, branched stems with thick, wavy, spiny-edged leaves that are variously lobed. The stalked basal leaves are almost round, often heart-shaped at the base, while the stalkless upper leaves clasp the stem. From July to September many pale blue, egg-shaped flowerheads appear, each up to 3cm/1¼in long and with a ruff of shiny, leaflike bracts. They are composed of tightly packed, five-petalled flowers with purplish-pink stamens, the flowers being interspersed with spines. The bristly, egg-shaped fruit has two seeds and splits in two.

Sea holly is found on coastal sand and shingle round most of the English coast, but is now absent from most of the north-east.

The fleshy, aromatic roots were once peeled and candied to make sweetmeats called eryngoes, which were reputed to have a tonic effect.

The nectar is attractive to bumble bees, short-tongued flies and various other pollinating insects. On the south-east coast leaves may be damaged by caterpillars of a tortricoid moth.

This is a striking plant for the herbaceous border, particularly when grown in large clumps, where its colour and shape will contrast dramatically with other flowers. It can also be naturalized on a dry bank. Sea holly is an obvious choice for the seaside garden because it is adapted to poor soil and salt spray. It needs full sun and light, well-drained soil. Taking root cuttings in winter is the best method of propagation, but it may also be raised from ripe seed sown in containers in a cold frame.

Hemp-agrimony
Eupatorium cannabinum   ASTERACEAE

In sunny weather the downy pink flowerheads of this tall, erect perennial are magnets for swarms of butterflies. Growing up to 1.2m/4ft with a woody rootstock, it is the only common member of the daisy family to have opposite leaves. These are downy and almost stalkless, divided into three (rarely five) lance-shaped, toothed leaflets. They give the impression of whorls around the red-tinged stem. From July to October branches at the stem top carry broad, flattish flowerheads composed of many smaller heads of five to six tiny tubular, whitish-pink or mauve florets, each with a long, forked style. Each head is surrounded by about ten purple-tipped bracts. The blackish nutlet has a parachute of white hairs.

Hemp-agrimony is widespread in wet woods, fens and marshes and on damp sea cliffs throughout lowland England.

Despite its name, it is in fact related neither to hemp nor to agrimony. Sometimes known as raspberries and cream, it is a valuable homeopathic herb prescribed for liver, spleen and gall-bladder disorders.

The nectar, which attracts hosts of butterflies, moths and hoverflies, is eagerly sought by honey bees, which also take away pollen. The seedheads may be infested by caterpillars of a tortricoid moth.

This is a colourful late-summer and autumn-flowering species for a woodland garden, a border, a bog garden or pond margin. It grows in sun or semi-shade and likes moist but not acid soils. It is easily propagated by splitting in autumn and planting out in a rich soil.

Wood Spurge
Euphorbia amygdaloides   EUPHORBIACEAE

*From perfect grief there need not be
Wisdom or even memory;
One thing then learnt remains to me,—
The woodspurge has a cup of three.*

'The Woodspurge', Dante Gabriel Rossetti (1828–82)

An unusual, slightly primitive-looking plant, the striking wood spurge is worthy of a place in any garden. The matt, dark green leaves of this softly hairy, semi-evergreen perennial are visible most of the year, and in spring they contrast with the tall clusters of vibrant lime-green flowerheads. In winter it forms a low shrub with stout, tufted, reddish stems up to 30cm/12in tall, and lance-shaped, spoon-shaped or narrowly elliptical, dark bluish-green leaves. From March to June the plant produces tall, flowering biennial stems, up to 80cm/32in, with slender branches bearing many pairs of pale green bracts, joined at the base to form an almost circular disc. The upper ones form shallow, yellow-green cups with yellow, horned glands around tiny greenish flowers at the centre. Each flower cluster consists of one three-styled female surrounded by several attendant males. The smooth, three-celled capsule contains a few smooth seeds.

Wood spurge grows in damp woods and shady hedgerows throughout the southern half of England and is especially conspicuous when its yellow glow lights up recently coppiced areas in spring.

Beware: as with all spurges, the stems contain a poisonous, milky latex that can irritate the skin.

The horned glands round the cups secrete nectar on their upper surface, which attracts a wide range of flies (such as sawflies, craneflies and March flies) as well as ants, bees, beetles and wasps. In moving around the inflorescence, they transport pollen from the male to the female flowers.

This is an impressive species when grown in light shade, where it provides focal colour for most of the year. It can be used in the woodland garden or in the border, where its strong yellow-green flowers provide an effective counterpoint to other colours, particularly deep blue and purple. It will cope with dryish, shady conditions at the base of a hedge, and will grow in sun or shade, and in most soils apart from the very acid. Wood spurge can be propagated by division in spring. Ripe seeds may be sown in a cold frame.

Meadowsweet
Filipendula ulmaria ROSACEAE

Shall I strew on thee rose or rue or laurel,
Brother, on this that was the veil of thee?
Or quiet sea-flower moulded by the sea,
Or simplest growth of meadow-sweet or sorrel?
'Ave Atque Vale', Algernon Charles Swinburne (1837–1909)

The fragrant, frothy, creamy-white blossom of meadowsweet has made it a long-established favourite. The erect stems of this handsome herbaceous perennial grow up to between 70cm and 1m/28in and 3½ft high, bearing strongly veined, dark green basal leaves with whitish hairs beneath. These are divided into two to five opposite pairs of toothed, ovate leaflets with tiny leaflets in between. The terminal leaflet is usually three-lobed. From June to September masses of tiny,

LEFT On moist soils the vigorous meadowsweet (*Filipendula ulmaria*) quickly makes a striking specimen clump in the flower bed or border. In a garden meadow it competes successfully with coarse grasses and if mown in summer it may produce a second flowering.

RIGHT With its decorative leaves and arching runners, the wild strawberry (*Fragaria vesca*) is ideal for the smaller garden or for growing in a container. Its small, white flowers will be followed in midsummer by tiny, intensely flavoured scarlet strawberries.

cream-coloured, five-petalled flowers with protruding stamens appear in dense, irregular-shaped heads. The five sepals are bent back, and the clusters of fruits are twisted spirally.

Meadowsweet is widespread throughout England in damp places, in marshes, fens and meadows, and by rivers and streams, ascending to over 550m/1,800ft in the Pennines.

When she visited houses, Queen Elizabeth I liked to have this sweet-smelling flower, known in the sixteenth century as mede-sweet or Queen of the Meadowes, strewn among the rushes on the floor. Not only are the flowers scented, but the crushed leaves emit an aroma of oil of wintergreen, providing a natural air freshener. The flower was also used to flavour mead, a drink made from fermented honey.

The numerous stamens produce abundant pollen, which attracts many insects, including craneflies, midges and short-tongued flies. The leaves are the food plant for various moth caterpillars including the spectacular emperor moth, the glaucous shears moth, the Hebrew character moth and the powdered Quaker moth.

This is a most attractive species for a damp, partially lit corner of the garden or for planting in drifts in the bog garden or round the margin of a pond or lake. It grows in sun or semi-shade in most soils. It is propagated by division from autumn through to spring, or by sowing seeds in a cold frame as soon as they have ripened in autumn.

Wild Strawberry
Fragaria vesca ROSACEAE

Every part of the perennial wild strawberry is as sweet and enticing as its scarlet fruit. The bright green leaves are composed of three oval, toothed leaflets with strongly marked veins and silky hairs on the underside. Graceful, arching, reddish-coloured runners stretch from the low-growing plant,

carrying little daughter-plants, complete with leaves and root. From April to July the simple white flowers, with five petals and a central yellow boss, stand proud of the leaves in branched heads at the top of stems up to 30cm/12in high. Then in midsummer the miniature red strawberries ripen, each up to 2cm/¾in long and dangling from a curved stem. The fleshy part is actually derived from the swollen base of the flower and the real fruits are the tiny, golden pips on the surface.

Wild strawberries may be found in scrub, open woods, grassland and hedgebanks throughout England, ascending to 500m/1,640ft in the Pennines and the Lake District.

The delectable, slightly scented fruit is sweet enough to eat straight from the plant, and the dried leaves make an excellent tea substitute. Although the name strawberry may refer to the practice of growing the plants in straw to prevent the fruit rotting, it is just as likely to be derived from 'straw berry', referring to its habit of spreading by long, strawlike runners.

This is a valuable food for wildlife; if humans do not eat the berries first, then other mammals, birds and the strawberry snail surely will. The flower buds are relished by weevils, and pollen-seeking beetles help with fertilization. The leaves are food for the caterpillars of grizzled skipper butterflies and may be mined by the larvae of small moths.

Decorative, edible and easy to grow, the wild strawberry is an asset in any garden. It can be grown at the front of a sunny border, but it will cheerfully root itself in a neighbouring lawn and makes attractive ground cover. It may be better suited to a bank or rock garden where its cascading runners can be seen, and it is effective when used at the edge of container plantings. It grows in sun or light shade, and although it prefers alkaline soils, it will generally grow on all but the most acid and waterlogged. It is easily propagated by detaching the long runners, which root at the nodes, and planting them out in autumn. The naturalist Gilbert White (1720–93) noted that the seeds are viable for many years when the conditions are suitable: 'When old beech trees are cleared away, the naked ground in a year or two becomes covered with strawberry plants, the seeds of which must have lain in the ground for an age at least.'

Fritillary
Fritillaria meleagris LILIACEAE

I know what white, what purple fritillaries,
The grassy harvest of the river-fields,
Above by Eynsham, down by Sandford, yields,
And what sedg'd brooks are Thames's tributaries.
'Thyrsis', Matthew Arnold (1822–88)

The unique, chequered purple markings on the nodding, bell-like flowerheads of this beautiful perennial make it one of our most idiosyncratic plants. Its curious, almost reptilian aspect gives the flower its other name, snake's head. The erect, hairless stems rise up to 30cm/12in from a small, poisonous bulb and carry three to six narrow, straight-sided, alternate grey-green leaves, the uppermost rising like a curved spire behind the single flowerhead. From April to May the 3-5cm/1½-2in flowerheads appear, drooping from the stem tip with their six translucent, petal-like segments boldly chequered with light and dark purple and cream. Later an oblong capsule develops, which splits into three to release dozens of flattened brown seeds.

The fritillary grows in damp soil and grassy places, particularly in old, wet meadows. Once scattered throughout central and southern England, it rapidly declined after 1940 owing to drainage and ploughing and is now confined to the Thames Valley and a few meadows elsewhere.

Beware: the bulb is poisonous.

The nectaries at the base of each bell, as well as the pollen, are a valuable source of food for pollinating bumble bees.

No garden should be without this exquisite flower where, in spring, it will add colour and grace to a woodland corner, rockery or raised bed, a large container or, best of all, naturalized in grass. It grows in sun or light shade and likes moisture-retentive soil. It will sparkle in grass, if the grass is left unmowed until the seed is shed in midsummer. It is best propagated by separating the bulbs in late summer or autumn and planting immediately, but the bulbs are delicate and should be handled carefully. The fritillary may also be raised from seed sown in a cold frame immediately after collection. Seedlings transplanted after two years should flower three to four years later.

LEFT Sunlight picks out the beautiful chequered patterns on massed ranks of fritillaries (*Fritillaria meleagris*) flourishing in one of their last strongholds, the Thames-side water meadows in Oxford.

OVERLEAF A designer's eye shows how well the flowing nature of native plants such as woodruff (*Galium odoratum*) and Solomon's-seal (*Polygonatum multiflorum*) can be integrated into formal gardens.

Woodruff
Galium odoratum RUBIACEAE

A fragrant perennial with long creeping rhizomes, woodruff forms large patches from which arise simple, square stems, up to 45cm/18in, which are vanilla-scented when crushed. Like a series of ruffs up the stem, the leaves are in whorls of six to eight bright, shining green, elliptical leaves with forwardly directed marginal prickles. In May and June the stems are topped by a loose cluster of tiny white, trumpet-shaped, scented flowers (up to 6mm/¼in across) with four splayed petals. The small, globular fruit is covered with hooked, black-tipped bristles.

Woodruff is found in damp woods and on hedgebanks, and also in dry southern beech woods, mainly on calcareous soils, throughout most of England, ascending to over 350m/1,150ft in the Lake District. It is infrequent in East Anglia.

The dried flowers and foliage smell strongly of new-mown hay and were once used for scenting linen. The flowers add a delicious flavour to a cooling wine-cup.

The scent attracts many pollinating flies, bees and sawflies, which feed on the easily accessible nectar, while the leaves are food for the caterpillars of various species of hawk and dart moths.

As a garden plant, woodruff must be carefully sited because of its penetrating rhizomes, but it makes ideal ground cover for a shady woodland corner or hedge-bottom. It grows in sun (but not strong sunlight), or in semi-shade in well-drained but moist, humus-rich soil. It is easily propagated by division in autumn or early spring.

Lady's Bedstraw
Galium verum RUBIACEAE

Hung on his faded back a hone,
He slowly, slowly, scythes alone
In silence of the wind-soft air,
With ladies' bedstraw everywhere,
With whitened corn, and tarry poles,
And far-off gulls like risen souls.
'The Coast: Norfolk', Frances Cornford (1886–1960)

A multitude of bright yellow flowers carried on numerous frail, square stems are the hallmark of this perennial, with its sprawling or upright growth, up to 80cm/32in in height. It has whorls of eight to twelve dark green, single-veined, narrow, needle-like leaves with rough, downturned margins, and from June to September the upper parts of the stems are covered with dense clusters of tiny, golden yellow, four-petalled flowers. The smooth, dry, two-lobed fruit turns black and splits in half.

Lady's bedstraw grows in grassland, hedgebanks, sand dunes and heaths, especially on calcareous soils, throughout England, from sea-level to 600m/1,970ft in the Pennines.

The sweet-smelling dried flowers were once added to bed straw, hence its common name, and fresh leaves were used for curdling milk to make cheese or junket.

This is one of England's most important plants for insects. The honey-scented flowers attract flies and many other small insects, while the leaves provide food for several types of carpet, rustic and hawk moths, as well as the red chestnut and flame shoulder moths. The tip of the stem may be surrounded by a ring of galls induced by a midge; each of the four to five segments contains one larva.

Lady's bedstraw is a wonderful, long-flowering addition to a meadow or gravel bed, spreading rapidly if given the chance, and it can be used with vigilance in the border. It requires a sunny site and grows on well-drained to dry soils, except the most acid. It is raised from seed collected in early autumn and sown outdoors in April, or by division in spring or autumn.

CRANE'S-BILLS
Geranium species GERANIACEAE

England is rich in wild geraniums, and at least ten are recognized as distinct species. They are all beautiful plants with their fine, decorative, lobed and toothed leaves and their delicate colouring, and these – combined with their good-natured habits – make them an asset to any garden. The name comes from the Greek word *geranos*, meaning 'crane-bird', referring to the resemblance of the mature seedhead to a bird with a long beak. Crane's-bills have an ingenious mechanism for dispersing their seeds. When the outer surface of the ovary dries it becomes taut and elastic, splitting into five strips that suddenly roll upwards individually, ejecting the underlying seed some considerable distance from the parent plant. These geraniums are good value in the garden, the majority easy to grow and free-flowering, particularly if old flowering stems and leaves are cut back to encourage fresh ones. The true geranium must not be confused

ABOVE, TOP TO BOTTOM

Herb-robert (*Geranium robertianum*)

Bloody crane's-bill (*Geranium sanguineum*)

Wood crane's-bill (*Geranium sylvaticum*)

RIGHT Meadow crane's-bill (*Geranium pratense*)

with the popular cultivars of the South African pelargoniums: for the English species, see the Directory (page 166).

Meadow Crane's-bill
Geranium pratense GERANIACEAE

The perennial meadow crane's-bill with its large, showy, saucer-shaped violet-blue flowers is probably the most beautiful of the English geraniums. Growing in clumps from 30 to 80cm/12 to 32in in height, its upright, branched stems are covered with silky hairs and the leaves have seven to nine deeply dissected and toothed radiating lobes. From June to September dense clusters of veined, bright blue flowers appear, each long-stalked, usually in pairs, with broad, oval petals, 3–4cm/1¼–1½in across, pale purple anthers and hairy, beaked sepals. The seeds have ridges that help anchor them to the ground.

Meadow crane's-bill is widespread in meadows and open woodland, and on banks and roadsides throughout England, although absent from parts of the south.

Bumble bees and honey bees are the main visitors to the flowers, guided to the concealed nectar by dark, radiating veins on the petals. On the way, their bodies are brushed by the pollen-filled anthers, thus assisting pollination. Butterflies also seek the nectar, and meadow crane's-bill is the food plant of the brown argus.

This is one of the most popular native flowers in gardens, especially when grown in large clumps in herbaceous borders. It does well in ordinary garden soil with some moisture and prefers a sunny spot. Later in the season the leaves turn red and tawny, providing autumn colour. It is easily propagated by division in spring or autumn, or by raising from seed sown in a cold frame or in the open in early spring. Regular division encourages free flowering.

Herb-robert
Geranium robertianum GERANIACEAE

Herbe Robert bringeth foorth slender, weake and brittle stalkes, somewhat hairie, and of a reddish colour, as are often-times the leaves also, which are jagged and deepely cut, like unto those of Chervile, of a most lothsome stinking smell.

The Herball, John Gerard (1545–1612)

With its fragile red stalks, deep red sepals and attractive, bright green filigree leaves, which often turn to blazing red in autumn, the annual or biennial herb-robert is a far more attractive plant than Gerard's description suggests. The much-branched stems, up to 50cm/20in tall and often reddish, are cut to the midrib, with three to five very deeply divided leaflets. The hairy plant does give off a very strong geranium smell, which is not unpleasant to some. Purplish-pink flowers, up to 1.4cm/⅝in across, appear in loose clusters from May to October, each with wedge-shaped, round-edged petals. The ten stamens are orange or purple and the fruit is the characteristic long-beaked capsule with smooth, oblong seeds.

Herb-robert is found scattered throughout England in woods, hedgebanks, waste ground, rocky places and on shingle by the sea, mostly on calcareous soils.

The flower's name probably comes from its link with St Robert of Salzburg.

The plant is visited by bees, long-tongued hoverflies and small insects.

This is an ideal plant for the rock garden, or for growing in gravel or the crevices in stone walls where drier, more exposed conditions will encourage the red autumn leaves. Herb-robert is a good choice for a seaside garden, but is just as content among deciduous trees, in the cracks of an old tree trunk or in the moist, shady corner of a border. It can self-pollinate when the flower droops at night or in wet weather. It grows in sun or semi-shade and most well-drained soils. Once it is established, there is no need for propagation, since it regenerates freely and seedlings can easily be transplanted.

Bloody Crane's-bill
Geranium sanguineum GERANIACEAE

The word 'bloody' may refer to the colour of the petals of this geranium, which are a deep magenta to purplish-crimson, but it is just as likely to refer to the red colour of the stalk joints. This creeping, low-growing, clump-forming perennial (up to 30 cm/12in high) has deeply dissected, dark green leaves with five to seven narrow lobes, each with three segments. Masses of solitary, cup-shaped, five-petalled red flowers on long, slender stems appear from June to August, each up to 3cm/1¼in across and usually with notched petals. In this and other crane's-bills the ten stamens ripen first, and the pollen is shed before the stigma opens to expose five pollen-receptive lobes.

Bloody crane's-bill is found in grassland, open woods and rocky places, and in a more prostrate form on sand dunes, mainly on calcareous soils in scattered localities in the north and west of England.

As with all crane's-bills, the veins on the petals act as honey guides, directing visiting bumble bees and honey bees to the source of nectar. Sawflies are also pollinators.

Its bushy habit allied to the delicate foliage and bright flowers of this delightful plant mean that it is well suited to a rock garden or to a herbaceous or shrub border. After a long flowering season the leaves develop autumn tints. It grows in sun or light shade and well-drained soil, preferably alkaline. It is propagated by division or by sowing seed in the same way as that described for meadow crane's-bill.

Wood Crane's-bill
Geranium sylvaticum GERANIACEAE

This perennial is similar to meadow crane's-bill, but taller, and the large, rounded leaves on the erect stems, up to 80cm/32in in height, are more finely toothed although not as deeply dissected. The flowers, which appear in June and July, are smaller and bluish-purple or purplish-pink and white at the centre.

Wood crane's-bill is found in lowland woods and hedges and in upland meadows and rock-ledges, but apart from outlying localities in Worcester and Gloucester, it is confined as a native to the northernmost counties of England, ascending up to 650m/2,130ft in the Lake District.

Hairs on the petals act as weather shields for the nectar, preventing it being diluted by rain. Even after a storm the bees find sustenance in the flowers. Each petal has dark veins guiding insects down towards the nectaries.

A suitable plant for a damp, shady border or hedgebank, it prefers slightly moist soils. It is propagated by division or by sowing seed, as for other perennial crane's-bills.

Water Avens
Geum rivale ROSACEAE

The demure, drooping blooms of water avens vary from orange-pink to purplish-pink and are largely hidden by a bonnet-like, reddish-brown calyx. This downy perennial, up to 50cm/20in tall, has long-stalked, pinnate basal leaves, the large terminal leaf and upper pair of toothed leaflets being wedge-shaped and the rest much smaller. The short-stalked stem leaves usually have three lobes. From May to August loose groups of long-stalked, nodding flowers, up to 1.5cm/⅝in across, appear at the stem tip, each with five broad petals. The one-seeded fruits make a raspberry-like cluster, each fruit being hooked at the tip. It will hybridize with its wood relative, *G. urbanum*.

Water avens (*Geum rivale*)

Yellow horned-poppy (*Glaucium flavum*)

Water avens is found in marshes, wet woods and on damp rock ledges, mainly on base-rich soils, throughout most of England, except the extreme south-west and south-east, and rising to over 800m/2,620ft in the Lake District.

The genus name *Geum* comes from a Greek word meaning 'I taste'.

Nectaries, hidden by the large number of stamens, and pollen attract honey bees and bumble bees, which are the main pollinators. The leaves are eaten and may be mined by the caterpillars of a number of small moths.

This makes an agreeable and not too aggressive species for pond margins, the rock garden or a wooded corner. It grows in sun or semi-shade and likes humus-rich soils that are not waterlogged. Propagation is by division in spring or autumn, or from seed sown out of doors in April and May.

Yellow Horned-poppy

Glaucium flavum PAPAVERACEAE

Yes, I have brought to help our vows
Horned poppy, cypress boughs …
'The Witches' Song', Ben Jonson (1572–1637)

Splashes of sunny yellow on shingle at the seashore mark the natural sites of the striking yellow horned-poppy, which blooms even in the most unpromising ground. According to Greek mythology, Glaucus was amazed when some fish he had caught nibbled a marsh plant and flew back into the sea. Intrigued, he followed their example and leapt into the ocean, where he became a sea-god; hence the word 'glaucous', which is used by botanists to describe pale, sea-green-coloured foliage such as that of this handsome plant. From a basal rosette of fleshy, bristly, pinnately lobed leaves, the tall, branched stems rise up to 90cm/36in in height, clasped by similar (but smaller) bluish-grey stem leaves. Above the waxy-looking foliage are held the large, clear yellow, four-petalled flowers, 6–9cm/2½–3½in across, which brighten parts of the coast from June to October. When the flower opens, the two concave sepals that protected the wrinkled bud simply fall off. This biennial, or short-lived perennial, is anchored by a deep, stout tap root, which enables it to survive in the thinnest soils. 'Horned' in its name refers to the strange, narrow, sickle-shaped seedpods, which can reach up to 30cm/12in long when ripe.

They split open lengthways from the top to release small, black seeds.

The magnificent yellow horned-poppy is now almost entirely confined to shingle banks around the coast of south and west England, and is absent north of the Wash on the east side.

Beware: yellow sap oozes from the cut stem and all parts of the plant are poisonous.

Like other poppies, this is a 'pollen-plant' attracting small solitary bees, bumble bees and beetles to its copious supply of food. As the insects scramble about in the forest of stamens they smother themselves with pollen, which they then carry to other flowers, a process known as 'mess and spoil' pollination.

With its large flowers and attractive foliage, this is a useful plant for a herbaceous border or for covering a dry bank. Obviously suited to seaside gardens, it also adapts easily to inland areas, flourishing in a sunny spot and tolerating dry conditions and sandy soil. It is propagated from seed sown in a gritty compost or by division in spring or autumn.

Ground Ivy

Glechoma hederacea LABIATAE

Ground ivy is not related to ivy, although it shares ivy's habit of trailing along the ground. This perennial has square, softly hairy stems that root as they grow, throwing up more flowering branches. Long-stalked, heart- or kidney-shaped opposite leaves have netted veins and rounded teeth. Clusters of bluish-violet tubular flowers appear from March to May, borne in loose whorls of about two to four in the leaf axils. Each flower is up to 2cm/¾in long, with a notched upper lip and a larger, three-lobed lower lip decorated with reddish-purple spots. The clusters sometimes include much smaller female flowers. The egg-shaped fruits split into four nutlike parts.

Ground ivy is found in woods, hedgebanks, grassland and waste places throughout England, from sea-level to 400m/1,310ft in the Pennines.

It was once used in brewing to flavour ale, and it makes a somewhat bitter tea.

Mainly pollinated by bumble bees, ground ivy is also visited by bee-flies, which take the hidden nectar, although they are too small to pollinate the wide-throated flowers. The leaves may be attacked by a gall-midge and their response is to produce light-coloured cylinders known as 'lighthouse galls'. Other, pea-sized lumps are caused by a gall-wasp.

This is an excellent, showy ground-cover plant for naturalizing in an orchard or a sunlit, wooded corner where it can form paths of colour in spring. It will tolerate light mowing. Ground ivy also makes a good trailing plant for containers. It grows in sun or semi-shade in moist but well-drained soils. It is easily propagated by separating pieces of the creeping stem, complete with roots and soil, in spring or autumn and transplanting.

Common Rock-rose
Helianthemum nummularium CISTACEAE

Opening its large, flimsy, golden-yellow flowers with the first warm rays of the sun and dropping its petals by sunset, the rock-rose was once called the sun-flower. Indeed, its botanical name comes from two Greek words meaning 'sun' and 'flower'. A delightful, dwarf trailing perennial, usually around 25cm/10in tall, it produces a tangle of wandering, wiry stems bearing paired, narrow, oblong leaves with whitish hairs underneath and pairs of narrow stipules at the leaf bases. From June to September the flowers appear in loose clusters of between one and twelve at the tips of the upward-growing stems. Each is up to 2.5cm/1in across, with five sepals – three large and green-veined and two tiny ones – and six crinkly, oval petals like tissue paper, which close when the weather is overcast. They last no longer than a day and the ground around the plant becomes littered with yellow confetti. The globular fruit splits into three.

Lighting up the shade where little else will grow, the striking green leaves of the stinking hellebore (*Helleborus foetidus*) give year-round pleasure while the unusual, pale green flowers brighten the winter garden.

Rock-rose is widespread in calcareous grassland and on base-rich rocks and sea-cliffs in England, except Cornwall, ascending to 640m/2,100ft in the Pennines.

Each pollen-rich flower has numerous stamens, and visiting bees attracted by the colour become coated with the copious pollen. The leaves form the food of the caterpillars of the green hairstreak, silver-studded blue and brown argus butterflies, as well as several moths, including the annulet, cistus forester and silky wave.

No sunny garden is complete without this prostrate little shrub, which produces a blaze of colour in summer but remains green and compact for the rest of the year. It can be used in the rock garden or raised bed, to cover walls and dry banks, and it can also be grown around the edge of containers. It can be propagated from cuttings of the current season's growth taken in summer, or from ripe seed sown in a cold frame in autumn or spring. Rock-rose generally resents transplanting.

Stinking Hellebore

Helleborus foetidus RANUNCULACEAE

Helleborus foetidus … all over the High-wood and Coney-crofthanger: this continues a great branching plant the winter through, blossoming about January, and is very ornamental in shady walks and shrubberies …

Gilbert White (1720–93) in a letter

This evergreen perennial is a close relative of the introduced Christmas rose, *H. niger*, but its bell-shaped clusters of pale yellow-green flowers with purple-tinted rims do not usually bloom until February. However, the handsome, radiating, dark green lower leaves of the sturdy stinking hellebore last right through the winter. These are long-stalked and divided into three to nine lance-shaped, coarsely toothed segments, and nearer the branched, upper part of the long stem (up to 80cm/32in high) there are smaller, pale green, smooth-edged bracts. The clusters of drooping, almost globular flowers, up to 3cm/1¼in across, appear from late winter through to April, each cup being formed by five petal-like sepals containing masses of stamens. The follicles split when ripe to release smooth black seeds.

Stinking hellebore is found in woods, scrub, hedgebanks and scree on shallow chalk or limestone soils, but is a rarity now in woodlands and is confined to a few parts of southern England, in areas such as the Cotswolds and along the border with Wales.

Stinking hellebore was once cultivated as a medicinal herb, and has been used in gardens for centuries. When bruised, the plant gives off an odour that may be unpleasant to humans but is a powerful attractant to pollinating insects.

Its nectar is a source of food in early spring for bees and other insects, and later for ants, which take seeds away unless a fungus, *Coniothyrium hellebori*, has attacked the overwintering stems before the seed has set.

Stinking hellebore is an ornament to the winter border, particularly when grown in groups, and it can also be grown among trees or by a hedge. It thrives in light shade on neutral to alkaline soil and is a useful plant for the often difficult combination of dry, chalky soil and partial shade. It is propagated from ripe seed collected before it has been eaten by mice, and sown in containers in a cold frame, or by potting up self-sown seedlings.

Bluebell

Hyacinthoides non-scripta LILIACEAE SUBFAM. SCILLOIDEAE

Dark bluebells drenched with dews of summer eves –
And purple orchises with spotted leaves –
But none has words she can report of thee.

'The Scholar Gypsy', Matthew Arnold (1822–88)

Carpeting spring woodlands with a scented, shimmering violet-blue just as the trees above them break into fresh new leaf, bluebells are among the great glories of the English countryside. In fact, the flower was considered so quintessentially English that it was reputed to bloom on 23 April, St George's Day, and a bluebell was sometimes worn in honour of the patron saint. A graceful perennial, up to 50cm/20in high, it has long, linear, keeled leaves that are a glossy dark green and rise from the bulb with arching growth. The smooth, juicy, leafless flowering stem also arches at the tip, and from April to June bears a raceme of bright blue (occasionally white) flower bells, which hang

Native plants meet introduced species in a woodland garden where a bank of grasses and bluebells (*Hyacinthoides non-scripta*) flows down to a valley, thickly planted with moisture-loving species.

from the lower side. Six segments joined at the base form the narrow flower tube, 1.5–5cm/⅝–2in long, and the pointed lobes curl back to reveal six stamens with cream-coloured anthers. The dried brown stalks persist throughout summer, carrying the large, three-angled capsules that ripen to shed their black seeds.

Bluebells are found throughout England in woods, shady banks and in damp grassland, usually on light, slightly acid soils, on hedgebanks and even on sea cliffs in western areas, ascending to 600m/1,970ft in the Lake District. The native bluebell can be confused with the Spanish bluebell, *H. hispanica*, which escapes from gardens and may be recognized by its wider leaves, blue anthers and more erect, paler, not one-sided flowers.

The sap of the plant was used during the Middle Ages to set feathers on arrows, and the Elizabethans used it both as a laundry starch and as glue.

As well as giving copious nectar to butterflies, bumble bees, honey bees and other insects, plus pollen for hoverflies, bluebells form homes for miniature thrips, which lay their eggs inside the dangling bells. Mites arrive on the hairs of bees' bodies. Honey bees sometimes 'steal' the nectar by biting a hole near the bottom of the bell rather than entering via the mouth. The leaves are consumed by the caterpillars of

autumnal and six-striped rustic moths, and the bulbs occasionally make a meal for hungry badgers.

This frost-hardy, bulbous plant is particularly effective when naturalized in drifts in a wooded corner or in grass. It can also be used to underplant shrubs, since the native bluebell does not spread as rapidly as the Spanish bluebell. Growing in sun or light shade, it likes moist but well-drained soils. The bluebell is easily propagated by division of large clumps of bulbs and replanting about 10cm/4in deep in the autumn. The seeds will take four to five years to grow into flowering plants.

Stinking Iris
Iris foetidissima IRIDACEAE

Stinking iris forms flattened sprays of long, flat, pointed leaves that are tough and evergreen and grow up to 75cm/30in high. From May to July each tall, branched stem bears up to five purple-violet flowers, up to 7cm/3in across, each delicately marked with darker veins and tinged with pale yellow. Its most dramatic offering comes in autumn when the oblong, 4.5cm/1¾in-long, fruit capsule ripens from green to brown and splits wide into three segments revealing large, bright orange seeds. The decorative, fleshy seeds persist into winter, often until the following spring.

Stinking iris is found in dry woods, hedgebanks and sea cliffs, mainly on calcareous soils, in south and central England.

When bruised, its evergreen leaves give off a slightly meaty smell, hence the common name, but that should not detract from the virtues of this plant. Another common name, gladdon, is derived from the Latin word *gladiolus*, meaning 'little sword', referring to the leaf shape.

Beware: the leaves and roots are poisonous to livestock, although in the past stinking iris was used as a purgative.

The freshly opened flowers are pollinated by bumble bees or long-tongued flies, which can crawl into any of the flower's three nectar-containing tubes.

This is a splendid species for the border, its pointed evergreen leaves providing contrasting form with other foliage and its orange seeds giving autumn and winter colour. It suits seaside gardens and can also be naturalized in a

Large, clear yellow flowers and sword-like leaves distinguish the stately yellow iris (Iris pseudacorus).

wooded corner or hedge-bottom. Stinking iris grows in sun or semi-shade and likes well-drained, preferably alkaline soil. Large clumps can be renewed by splitting. Given enough moisture in the soil, seedlings will occur naturally round a mature plant, increasing the stock.

Yellow Iris or Flag
Iris pseudacorus IRIDACEAE

Thou art the Iris, fair among the fairest,
Who, armed with golden rod
And winged with the celestial azure, bearest
The message of some God.

Thou art the Muse, who far from crowded cities
Hauntest the sylvan streams,
Playing on pipes of reed the artless ditties,
That come to us as dreams.

O flower-de-luce, bloom on, and let the river,
Linger to kiss thy feet!
O flower of song, bloom on, and make for ever
The world more fair and sweet.
'Flower-de-Luce', Henry Wadsworth Longfellow (1807–82)

With its beautifully shaped, clear yellow flowers and its architectural bluish-green, swordlike leaves, the yellow iris is a strikingly attractive perennial of water and wet ground. It has a fleshy, creeping underground stem and the narrow, straight-sided, pointed leaves with parallel veins are stiff and sharp enough to cut the unwary gardener. At the base they sheathe the erect, flattened stems, which grow up to 1.5m/5ft tall and from May to July carry the bright yellow flowers at the top in groups of two or three, held in papery-edged bracts. The iris flower is a complex structure, 8–10cm/3–4in across, with six petal-like parts. The three outer segments are broad, roughly oval and curling down at the tip, with a deeper yellow patch and orange and purple markings at the base. The small ones are narrow and upright. Above each of the three stamens are three arching styles, which look like petals. The large, oblong, three-angled green capsule, 4–8cm/1½–3in long, lasts into the autumn and splits to release the brown seeds.

Yellow irises are found in wet meadows, fens and ditches,

marshes, and on river and lake margins, throughout England from sea-level to about 300m/985ft.

The yellow iris's alternative name, flower-de-luce, is from *fleur de lis*, or lily-flower.

Beware: like stinking iris it is also poisonous.

The whole plant gives shelter to frogs and newts and the leaves are food for the caterpillars of several species of moth. Freshly opened flowers hold their petal-like styles well above the true petals and are pollinated by bumble bees, but a day later the styles lie flat on the petals and only long-tongued hoverflies can reach the nectar.

As fine as any introduced iris, this is a magnificent plant for a pond or stream margin, or for a bog garden; it is particularly impressive when grown in large clumps. It is also effective in a damp border. It grows in sun or semi-shade and needs deep, moist soil. In ideal conditions it can form clumps 2m/6½ft across in under ten years, and the floating seeds will germinate on muddy pond margins. It can be readily divided into separate plants in spring and will then probably only require lifting and dividing again every three years.

Bitter-vetch (*Lathyrus linifolius*)

Field Scabious
Knautia arvensis DIPSACACEAE

The outstanding feature of this tall, elegant perennial is the clear, bluish-lilac colour of its broad flowerheads, with their pink stamens standing proud like pins in a pincushion. It grows up to 90cm/36in, with stalked, undivided, spear-shaped basal leaves that remain in winter. In contrast, the opposite-paired upper leaves are stalkless, deeply pinnately divided and with variable outlines, all the foliage being hairy and a dull green. Round, slightly domed flowerheads, up to 4cm/1½in across, are carried on long stalks from July through September. Each comprises around fifty lilac flowers with protruding stamens, the outer flowers having larger, more blue and unequal petals than the more regular four-lobed inner ones. The oval bracts beneath the flowerheads are shorter than the flowers. The cylindrical, nutlike fruit has a crown of bristles.

Field scabious is common in dry, ungrazed grassland, on scrubland and in hedgebanks, mainly on calcareous soils throughout England from sea-level to 350m/1,150ft in Derbyshire.

An infusion of the flowers was once used for purifying the blood and curing various skin disorders, including scabies, hence its common name.

This is an invaluable wildlife plant. The nectar in the flowers attracts a succession of butterflies, bees, beetles and hoverflies, while the leaves are eaten by the caterpillars of several moths and butterflies, including the shaded pug, narrow bordered bee hawk, marsh fritillary and chalkhill blue.

Field scabious is a splendid plant for naturalizing in a wild meadow area, where it competes well with vigorous grasses and gives a colourful display well into autumn. It can also be useful in a dry, alkaline border. It grows in sun and needs well-drained, preferably alkaline soil. It can be propagated by sowing seed in a cold frame in spring, or by division in March.

Yellow Archangel
Lamiastrum galeobdolon LAMIACEAE

Throughout its late spring and early summer flowering period, the perennial yellow archangel creates a glorious splash of gold. Similar to a white dead-nettle in shape, it has upright, square stems up to 60cm/24in high and opposite pairs of toothed, nettle-like leaves, although these do not have the heart-shaped bases of the dead-nettle. From late April to July the whorls of large, bright-yellow, two-lipped flowers appear in the axils of the upper leaves. The large upper lip is hooded, while the lower lip is divided into three smaller lobes that are marked with reddish-brown lines. The triangular brown nutlets are smooth.

Yellow archangel is common in damp, open woodland, thickets and hedgebanks, on neutral to calcareous soils in most of England, ascending to 350m/1,150ft in Derbyshire. However, it is almost absent from northernmost counties, Cornwall and the Fens.

In the past the plant was regarded as protection against evil spirits and it may be that its weapon was the unpleasant smell given off by its crushed stems and leaves. Its botanical name comes from the Greek *galen*, meaning 'a weasel', and *bdolos* 'stench'.

Yellow archangel is a valuable flower, providing both nectar and pollen for bumble bees. Seeking nectar at the base of the flower tube, the bees land on the lower lip and, while entering and leaving the flower, their backs become dusted with pollen from anthers hidden under the upper lip. The leaves are eaten by caterpillars of the speckled yellow moth.

This striking plant creates splendid ground cover in light woodland, or it could be allowed to colonize a rough bank. It can also be grown in the herbaceous border, and although it can be invasive it needs little attention, apart from occasional replanting. It is easily propagated by separating rooted pieces from the spreading clumps and replanting.

Bitter-vetch
Lathyrus linifolius FABACEAE

A dainty, creeping perennial with blood-red, pea-like flowers (later fading to blue), bitter-vetch has a wing on either side of its slender stems, giving it an almost quatrefoil shape in cross-section. It grows up to 40cm/16in high and the blue-green leaves have two to four pairs of leaflets, each ending in a short point and usually elliptical, although narrow forms also occur. Long-stalked racemes of two to six flowers appear from April to July. The pod, up to 4cm/1½in long, has a curved beak and contains several rounded seeds.

Bitter-vetch is found in woodland margins, hedgebanks and scrub, on acid soils, throughout most of England although it is absent from East Anglia. It is mainly found in the lowlands, though it rises to 550m/1,800ft in the Lake District.

It was formerly cultivated for its tubers, which were eaten in the north and west of England; the flavour is said to resemble that of chestnuts.

Brushlike hairs below the stigma collect pollen, which is shed before the flowers open. This pollen dusts the bodies of visiting bumble bees while they collect nectar, and they then transfer it to the next flower. The leaves are food for the caterpillars of wood white butterflies.

This is a useful species for naturalizing in a shady corner at the bottom of a hedge or wooded bank. It grows in sun or semi-shade in well-drained, preferably neutral to acid soil. It can be propagated by soaking the seeds and sowing in a cold frame in spring, or by separation of the tubers in spring.

Meadow Vetchling
Lathyrus pratensis FABACEAE

Although the curling tendrils of this delicate perennial look as though they are made for climbing, they are more often used to grab nearby grasses or neighbouring stems for support. The

Rough hawkbit (*Leontodon hispidus*)

71

spindly, angled stem grows to 1.2m/4ft, either climbing or trailing, and bears leaves that have two rigid, lance-shaped leaflets, 1–3cm/½–1¼in long, with marked parallel veins. There are broad, arrow-shaped stipules at the base of the leaf and a tendril, sometimes branched, at the tip. From May to August the yellow flowers with greenish veins are carried in clusters of five to twelve on stalks up to 8cm/3in long. Each five-petalled flower has a large upper petal and a joined lower pair overlapped by the side pair. The flattened, pea-like pod is up to 3.5cm/1⅜in long and contains up to ten seeds.

Meadow vetchling occurs in rough grassland and hedgerows on moderately acid to neutral, somewhat damp soils throughout most of England, ascending to over 450m/1,475ft in the Pennines.

The flowers are visited mainly by bumble bees, which are strong enough to force their way into the petals and have tongues long enough to reach the nectar at the bottom of the lengthy flower-tube. The leaves are eaten by the caterpillars of wood white butterflies and the pods may be invaded by the larvae of tortricoid moths.

This is a valuable species for naturalizing in a meadow or for adding broad masses of sunny yellow to grassy banks. It can also be used as a trailing plant in containers. It grows in sun or semi-shade and likes moist but well-drained soil. Like other members of the pea family, it has bacteria in nodules on its roots which fix nitrogen and increase soil fertility. Propagation is as for bitter-vetch.

Rough Hawkbit
Leontodon hispidus ASTERACEAE

The sunny, deep-yellow flowerhead of the perennial rough hawkbit resembles that of its relative the dandelion; it also has a similar basal rosette of wavy-margined or segmented leaves. But the hawkbit is easily recognized if it is examined with a hand-lens because the hairs on the surface are forked at the tip in a Y shape. Roughly haired unbranched stalks (dandelion's are hairless) arise from the middle of the rosette to a height of 60cm/24in, and from June to September they carry a single head of golden-yellow strap-like florets. These are usually orange-red underneath, on the outside, and surrounded by densely hairy bracts. The rough, slightly curved fruit has a parachute of feathery hairs.

Rough hawkbit is common in grassland, especially on chalk and limestone, and on sand dunes, throughout England from sea-level to 600m/1,970ft in the Pennines.

Like the dandelion, its leaves can be used to flavour a salad.

It is visited by a wide range of pollinating insects, especially bumble and honey bees, which feed on the nectar and pollen. Rough hawkbit growing on dunes may have its heads damaged by the larvae of a tortricoid moth.

This is a compact but strongly growing plant that is equally at home in an alkaline rock garden and in a meadow, where its low-growing leaves help it to survive mowing after it has flowered in the summer. It likes a sunny spot and well-drained, preferably alkaline soil. Propagation is by division of the rootstock in March or April, or by sowing the pale brown seeds in a free-draining soil out of doors in April, about 1cm/½in deep, then thinning to 10cm/4in apart.

Oxeye Daisy
Leucanthemum vulgare ASTERACEAE

The tall, graceful oxeye daisy has long been a favourite cottage-garden perennial, being one of the most appealing of English flowers with its solitary, large, daisylike head composed of white rays and a golden central boss. Rising to 75cm/30in, but normally half that height, the upright, almost hairless, sparsely branched stem has stalkless, oblong, roughly toothed or lobed leaves, whereas the basal leaves are spoon-shaped with long stalks. The single flowerhead, up to 5cm/2in across, appears from June to September with a central disc of tiny, yellow tubular florets and an outer ring of strap-shaped white florets. The base of the flowerhead is enclosed by close-set green bracts with dark margins. The oblong, ribbed fruit has no parachute.

The oxeye daisy grows in meadows, on roadsides and in other grassy places on moderately acid to calcareous soils throughout England, ascending to 500m/1,640ft in the Pennines.

The young leaves may be added to salads or sandwiches, in moderation, as the taste is strong. The flowerheads can be used for wine-making. Extracts of oxeye daisy were once used to treat a variety of ailments from chest diseases to watery eyes.

More delicate in appearance and more accommodating than the introduced shasta daisy (*Leucanthemum* × *superbum*), the oxeye daisy (*Leucanthemum vulgare*) gives a fine display through high summer and once established the plant will last for many years.

The flowers are an important source of food for a great variety of butterflies, moths, bees, wasps, beetles, soldier flies and hoverflies. The leaves may be eaten by caterpillars of the heath fritillary butterfly, while those of tortricoid moths first mine the leaves and then fold them together to make shelters.

A showy, vigorous, long-flowering summer plant, the oxeye daisy is especially attractive when growing among grasses in a meadow area. In heavy soils, however, the strong grass growth can overpower the oxeye daisy and it is better on light soil with weaker grasses. It also makes a fine border plant, although it can be invasive unless kept in check and regularly divided. It grows in sun or semi-shade and in a wide range of well-drained soils. It is best propagated by division in spring or autumn, but is also easily raised from seed.

Common Sea-lavender

Limonium vulgare PLUMBAGINACEAE

A frothy mass of pale lilac-coloured flowers are carried above the robust, dark green, slightly fleshy foliage of this handsome maritime perennial. Large, lance-shaped leaves, each with a prominent midrib, pinnate veins and a spine at the tip, grow up to 20cm/8in high from the woody, creeping rootstock. From the centre rises the leafless, widely branched flower stem, up to 40cm/16in tall, carrying lacy blooms composed of clustered spikelets of scentless, five-petalled, bluish-purple flowers with bracts and yellow anthers. The plant has a flowering period from late June through to October, and the fruit is a single-seeded nut.

Common sea-lavender is found in salt marshes around the coast of England.

It is 'everlasting' when dried and can be used in flower arranging.

The flowers are visited by bee-flies.

This is a plant that will flourish in gardens, particularly seaside gardens. Grouped in a border, it will provide a drift of colour until late autumn and it can be effective in the gravel garden. It likes full sun and light, free-draining soil and protection from cold winds. Sea-lavender can be kept in check by dividing it in spring every four years. It can be propagated by division also, in spring, or from seed sown outside in early spring.

Common Toadflax

Linaria vulgaris SCROPHULARIACEAE

And thou, Linaria, mingle in my wreath
Thy golden dragons; for though perfumed breath
Escapes not from thy yellow petals, yet
Glad thoughts bring'st thou of hedgerows foliage, wet
With tears and dew.
'Toadflax', Anne Pratt

Despite its unattractive name, the common toadflax is a pretty plant with a lovely spire of yellow flowers with rounded orange lips, rather like those of a miniature snapdragon. Spreading freely with a creeping rhizome, this perennial has sturdy, upright, branched stems rising to 75cm/30in, and narrow, pointed, greyish-green leaves, resembling flax leaves, growing spirally around the stems. From June to October the stem tip is crowded with a raceme of up to thirty flowers. Each is tubular, up to 3.5cm/1⅜in long, with five petals: two making the upper lip and three forming the lower lip, which has a bright orange swelling on the inside. A long, pointed spur at the base contains nectar and there are five oval, pointed sepals. The oblong capsule contains many flattened seeds, each surrounded by a distinctive black frill.

Common toadflax grows in rough grassland, on field edges and railway banks, along roadsides and on waste ground throughout lowland England, ascending to 320m/1,050ft in Derbyshire.

The plant is used in homeopathy for treating diarrhoea and cystitis, and it was formerly used to make an ointment for skin complaints. The flowers provide a yellow dye.

Common toadflax is an important bee flower, with the spurs full of nectar being reached only by long-tongued bees, which alone are strong and heavy enough to force open the petals; with their long tongues, they are then equipped to reach the nectar at the base of the tube. On its way to the nectar, the bee pollinates the flower. The capsules may become infested with the larvae of the toadflax pug moth.

This is an excellent flower for the border, provided its tendency to spread can be curbed, or for a dry bank or gravel bed. It grows in sun on light, well-drained soil and is useful in dry or sandy ground. Cutting it back after the first flowering will produce fresh blooms, and it can be controlled by cutting away seed stems before they mature. It can be propagated by division in spring, or by sowing seed in a cold frame in early spring.

Common Bird's-foot-trefoil
Lotus corniculatus FABACEAE

This is a low-growing, hairless, creeping perennial, with a woody rootstock that produces trailing, branched stems, which are solid, not hollow, and up to 40cm/16in long. Its alternate leaves, despite the implication of the name trefoil, have five lance-shaped or almost round, pointed leaflets, but the upper three are more prominent. The lower pair is further down at the base of the leaf. From June to September long flower stalks from the leaf base carry clusters of two to seven large, pea-like yellow flowers, up to 1.5cm/⅝in long. Three or four straight pods, 2–3cm/¾–1¼in long, usually develop on each stalk and spread out like the toes of a bird's foot, containing mottled grey seeds.

Common bird's-foot-trefoil is found on grassland, heaths, bare ground and dunes, on free-draining soils throughout England, from sea-level to 700m/2,300ft in the Pennines.

As the yolk-yellow of the petals is occasionally streaked or tinged with red, and the buds are also red, the plant is sometimes known as bacon-and-eggs.

The leaves, which become blue when dried, are the food plant of the common blue, small blue, dingy skipper and green hairstreak butterflies, as well as many moths, including the six-spot burnet. This is an extremely important insect plant, for apart from the value of its foliage, the nectar of its flowers is high in sugar and attracts butterflies, bumble bees, honey bees and solitary wasps, which 'rob' the flowers by biting through the base of the petals.

Common bird's-foot-trefoil is ideal for naturalizing in a meadow area, but can also be grown in the rock garden, as ground cover in the border or in a container. It likes a sunny site and thrives on most well-drained soil. It can be propagated from seeds; scarify them before sowing in autumn or spring.

Ragged-robin *(Lychnis flos-cuculi)*

Ragged-robin

Lychnis flos-cuculi CARYOPHYLLACEAE

Some went searching by the wood,
Peeping 'neath the weaving thorn,
Where the pouch-lipp'd cuckoo-bud
From its snug retreat was torn;
Where the ragged-robin stood
With its piped stem streak'd with jet,
And the crow-flowers, golden hued,
Careless plenty easier met.

John Clare (1793–1864)

The call of the cuckoo in May heralds the appearance of the perennial ragged-robin with its attractively fringed, bright pink petals, which look as though they have been snipped to shreds with a pair of scissors. Its Latin species name *flos-cuculi* means 'cuckoo-flower'. The slender, reddish stems, upright or spreading, grow up to 50cm/20in high, with hairless, lance-shaped leaves in opposite pairs, the lower ones being stalked and the narrower stem leaves stalkless. Purplish-pink (sometimes white) flowers appear in loose terminal clusters from May to July, each having five petals, which are deeply cut into four, narrow, straplike lobes with white scales at their base. The reddish-brown calyx-tube has marked veins and five pointed teeth, and the oval capsule contains many kidney-shaped seeds.

Ragged-robin is widespread in damp woods, meadows and marshes, on river banks and lake margins throughout England, ascending to over 600m/1,970ft in the Lake District.

The plant attracts bees, hoverflies and butterflies, such as the green-veined white, orange-tip and wood white. It is the food plant of the lychnis moth and caterpillars of the campion moth feed on the ripening seeds from July to September.

Its colourful stems and flowers will brighten a damp corner of the garden, a bog garden or the edge of a pond or meadow. It grows in sun or semi-shade and likes moist soils. Cutting back after flowering will encourage a second flowering. In less than ideal conditions it tends to be short-lived and may need to be raised each year from seed sown outside in spring. It self-seeds readily and plants may be increased by division in spring.

Compared with the introduced *Lysimachia punctata*, the native yellow loosestrife (*L. vulgaris*) is a less competitive plant which is easily accommodated in a mixed border.

76

Creeping-jenny

Lysimachia nummularia PRIMULACEAE

The cheerful, bright yellow, cup-shaped flowers of creeping-jenny, and its long perennial trailing stems with little rounded leaves, are familiar to many gardeners. Spreading vigorously with prostrate stems that can reach 60cm/24in in length, it has leaves in opposite pairs. In June and July short stalks rising from the base of the leaves carry the deep yellow, five-petalled flowers, up to 1.8cm/¾in across, each overlapped by broad, pointed sepals that later hide the fruit capsule, although it rarely produces ripe fruit.

Creeping-jenny is found in damp hedgebanks, ditches and meadows scattered throughout most of lowland England, but is almost absent from the south-west peninsula and northernmost counties.

The shape of its leaves prompts its other names of herb twopence and moneywort: the Latin species name *nummularia* means 'coinlike'. An infusion of fresh stems was once used as a remedy for various internal disorders.

The flowers produce no nectar but are full of pollen, which attracts bees and other pollen-eating insects.

This is a useful, long-flowering plant, bringing a glow to damp and slightly shady areas, although its fast-spreading habit and propensity to form a dense mat mean that it needs controlling. It makes good ground cover, and is effective grown on the edge of a pond or stream. It grows in sun or semi-shade and needs moist but well-drained, preferably slightly acid soil. It is easily propagated by division in spring or autumn.

Yellow Loosestrife

Lysimachia vulgaris PRIMULACEAE

With its upright, leafy stems packed with bright yellow, starry flowers, yellow loosestrife is a tall, handsome perennial, reaching up to 90cm/36in in height. The bright green, downy, lace-shaped leaves are bluish underneath, up to 10cm/4in long, either in opposite pairs or in whorls of three or four. Tiny orange or black glands speckle the upper surface of the leaves, and the sepals have orange margins. From June to August the short-stalked, five-petalled, golden-yellow flowers, 1.5cm/⅝in across, appear at the stem tops. Unlike the garden escapee *L. punctata*, which has petals with hairy edges, yellow loosestrife has smooth-edged lobes. The fruit capsule is spherical.

Yellow loosestrife is found in marshes, on river banks and along lake margins, scattered throughout lowland England.

The plant was useful to both man and beast, being used by the herbalist Nicholas Culpeper (1616–54) to treat nosebleeds and stomach complaints, and to keep flies away from draught animals. The genus name *Lysimachia* is derived from Greek words meaning 'loosing strife', hence its common name.

The flowers are nectarless and scentless, but several species of wasp and a tiny solitary bee, *Macropis labiata*, are attracted to the abundant pollen. The leaves comprise food for the caterpillars of dentated pug and white ermine moths.

This strongly growing species is ideal for the edge of a garden pond, alongside a stream or for naturalizing in a damp hollow. It is suitable for the border, as long as it is controlled by regular division. It is best propagated by dividing the clumps of rhizomes in early spring or autumn.

Purple-loosestrife

Lythrum salicaria LYTHRACEAE

There is a willow grows aslant a brook,
That shows his hoar leaves in the glassy stream;
Therewith fantastic garlands did she make
Of crow-flowers, nettles, daisies and long purples …
Hamlet, William Shakespeare (1564–1616)

The tall, reddish-purple spires of the stately purple loosestrife, which is not related to yellow loosestrife, conceal interesting variations among the flowers, for each plant has one of three different flower forms. The position and length of the stamens and stigmas vary in each type, to ensure that pollinating insects fertilize different plants, thus maintaining the vigour of the species. The stout, square, upright, branched stems of this perennial grow up to 1.2m/4ft tall, sometimes taller, and the stalkless, lance-shaped leaves are in whorls of three. From June to September the large, rich purple flowers, up to 2cm/¾in across, appear clustered in whorls in the axils of the leafy bracts. Each flower usually has six free, oblong petals and twelve stamens. The egg-shaped capsule splits into two.

This plant is common in marshes, swamps, fens, river banks and lake margins throughout most of England, though it is only scattered in the north-east; it reaches 380m/1,250ft in the Pennines.

Its tannins act as a coagulant and were formerly used in

medicine, while the juice was sometimes used as an alternative to oak bark in the process of tanning leather.

Both nectar and pollen are available for visiting honey bees, hoverflies and summer-flying brimstones. They have to be clever to reach the nectar, which is hidden in narrow tubes. Flowers and seeds may be spoilt by the larvae of a tortricoid moth, and the leaves provide food for elephant hawk-moth caterpillars.

A showy, long-flowering species, this plant is best suited to damp areas, such as pond or stream margins and bog gardens, or a damp border. It grows in sun or semi-shade and needs moist soils. The woody, annually produced stems persist for two or three years unless cut down. It can be propagated by division in spring; it also self-seeds freely, but the seeds need careful handling when transplanting.

Musk Mallow
Malva moschata MALVACEAE

The sitting down, when school was o'er,
Upon the threshold of the door,
Picking from Mallows …

John Clare (1793–1864)

This is the most handsome of our native species of mallow, its bright, saucer-shaped, rose-coloured flowers borne in abundance on sparsely hairy upright stems up to 60cm/24in in height. The long-stalked basal leaves of this perennial are kidney-shaped, whereas the decorative stem leaves are deeply divided, with narrow lobes. In July and August the five-petalled, pink (rarely white) flowers appear, either singly from a leaf-base or crowded at the top of the stems. Each is wedge-shaped, up to 3cm/1¼in across, with darker veins and jagged margins and a central column of clustered stamens, rather like those of its relative the hollyhock. After fertilization they develop a ring of one-seeded fruits, resembling small wedges of cake, which are hairy at the back and become black and smooth when ripe.

Musk mallow grows on woodland margins, in hedgebanks, rough pasture and other grassy places throughout lowland England, and ascends to 330m/1,080ft in the Pennines.

The fruits are edible and taste like peanuts. Its name comes from its slightly musky scent.

The plant is visited by solitary bees, bumble bees and

For gardeners in soft-water areas the beautiful, fringed bogbean (*Menyanthes trifoliata*) is the most desirable, fragrant perennial for the bog garden or pond margin.

many other insects in search of nectar and pollen. The leaves are food for the caterpillars of painted lady butterflies.

As one of our most beautiful native wild flowers, musk mallow is a joy to have in any sunny, well-drained herbaceous border. It can also be grown in areas of longer grass or on a bank, and it will thrive on fairly mean soils. Cut it back after flowering. It is easily raised from seed sown in a sandy soil in spring and planted out to flower the following year.

Common Mallow
Malva sylvestris MALVACEAE

Common mallow is a showy, easy-to-grow perennial with tall, bushy groups of upright or spreading stems bearing rose-purple flowers from early summer through to autumn. Growing to 90cm/36in in height, these robust, sparsely hairy stems are woody at the base and bear crinkly, deep green, broadly rounded or heart-shaped leaves, palmately veined and with three to seven shallow, toothed lobes. The short-stalked upper leaves have more ivylike lobes. Numerous wide-open flowers, up to 4cm/1½in across, appear in clusters in the upper leaf axils from June to September, each having five heart-shaped, pinkish-purple petals with darker purple stripes. At the centre many stamens are joined in a club-shaped head. The fruit is a disc of cake-like nutlets, which differ from that of musk mallow in that they are hairless, brown and have a rough surface.

Common mallow is abundant throughout lowland England on roadsides, hedgebanks, field edges and on waste ground, rarely ascending above 250m/820ft.

Owing to its round shape, the edible fruit is often called a 'cheese', giving the plant alternative names such as fairy cheese, lady's cheese or bread and cheese. The leaves can be cooked like spinach, but they are full of mucilage and may be more palatable in a soup. Common mallow was formerly a valued medicinal plant, its juices being used in cough-mixtures, soothing ointments and poultices.

The flower is a valuable source of nectar and pollen for bees, and the leaves form the food plant of the painted lady butterfly and the mallow and least yellow underwing moths. Leaves and stems may have been damaged by the fungus hollyhock rust, *Puccinia malvacearum*, which also infests other members of the mallow family.

Its handsome form and long flowering period make this an ideal plant for the herbaceous border or shrub border, or for growing in front of a fence or along a bank. Common mallow likes an open site and will withstand dry conditions and lean soil. It may need staking. It is a relatively short-lived plant, but self-seeds readily. It can be propagated by sowing seed *in situ*, or by rooting basal cuttings in spring.

Bogbean
Menyanthes trifoliata MENYANTHACEAE

Bogbean's rather basic name belies the fact that this sweet-smelling aquatic perennial is one of England's most beautiful native plants, admired throughout the ages by naturalists and gardeners, from John Gerard to William Robinson. From its creeping underground or underwater rootstock come smooth stalks, each bearing three large, upright, shining, rich green oval leaflets with thick midribs and wavy margins. From May to July racemes of star-shaped white flowers with a short tube are carried on leafless stems up to 30cm/12in tall. Each funnel-shaped flower is up to 2cm/¾in across with five curved-back, fleshy lobes, flushed pink on the outside and pure white inside, and fringed with a froth of white, cottony hairs. The five stamens have reddish anthers. Until it is ripe, the globular fruit is topped with a single style.

Bogbean grows on the edge of streams and lakes, and in bogs, fens and shallow muddy places, often on peat, and is local in England; it is rare in the south-east and the Midlands.

It was once used as a blood purifier and general tonic, and when hops were scarce the bitter-tasting bogbean leaves were used to flavour beer.

As the nectar is deep-set its chief visitors are bees, because only they have tongues long enough to pass between the hairy filaments on the petals. Smaller insects attempt to crawl in to the flower, but often become entangled in the barrier of hairs.

This plant deserves a place by every pond or water garden, where it will send out a dense growth of matted roots into the mud in search of food and anchorage. It flowers best in full sun and prefers slightly acid conditions. Propagate it by dividing rhizomes in late spring or summer and immediately setting the pieces in mud or shallow water and pegging them down. Seed may be sown in winter in wet soil or in containers standing in shallow water.

Wood Forget-me-not

Myosotis sylvatica BORAGINACEAE

And simple small Forget-me-not
Each with a pinshead yellow spot
I' the middle of its tender blue
That gains from poets notice due.

'May', from *The Shepherd's Calendar*, John Clare (1793–1864)

The jaunty, sky-blue flowers of wood forget-me-not seldom fail to lift the spirits in late spring and may explain why it is the most widely cultivated of our wild forget-me-nots. Clothed with soft, spreading hairs, this perennial has upright, branched stems up to 50cm/20in tall with alternate, narrowly oblong or lance-shaped grey-green leaves. The numerous dense clusters of flowers appear in May and June, and occasionally through the summer, each flower bud – usually pink – opening to reveal a light blue, wheel-shaped flower up to 8mm/¼in across, with five rounded, flattened-out petal lobes and a yellow eye. The style is longer than the calyx tube and clearly visible when viewed from the side after the petals have fallen. The glossy, black-brown nutlets appear in the calyx after pollination.

Wood forget-me-not is found in woods and on rock ledges and scree, mainly in the Midlands and the north, and very locally in the south, ascending to 380m/1,250ft in the Pennines. It also occurs widely as an escapee from gardens.

The genus name *Myosotis* comes from the Greek for mouse-ear, referring to the shape and soft hairs of the leaves.

The nectar at the base of the very short tubular flower attracts butterflies, long-headed flies and bee-flies, but if pollinators do not visit the flowers they are usually self-pollinated.

Despite its tendency to wander, wood forget-me-not is a faithful and persistent species for edging the front of the border or for naturalizing in a woodland corner, although here the white-flowered form, *M. s. alba*, may be preferred. It grows in sun or semi-shade and on most moist but well-drained soils. In suitable conditions the plant regenerates freely and the seedlings can be transplanted in early autumn.

Wild Daffodil

Narcissus pseudonarcissus

LILIACEAE SUBFAM. AMARYLLIDOIDEAE

Fair Daffodils, we weep to see
You haste away so soon:
As yet the early-rising sun
Has not attained his noon.
Stay, stay,
Until the hasting day
Has run
But to the even-song;
And, having prayed together, we
Will go with you along.

'To Daffodils', Robert Herrick (1591–1674)

The glorious, two-toned yellow trumpet flowers of the wild daffodil are bright harbingers of the English spring and have been an inspiration to poets for centuries. The nodding blooms may be smaller than those of the cultivated varieties, but their elegance is unsurpassed. This perennial has an onionlike bulb from which arises a long, slightly flattened leafless stem and narrow, straight-sided, bluish-green leaves up to 35cm/15in long, the inner sides being slightly grooved. In March and April the bud bursts from its papery brown protective wrapping and a solitary flower appears, up to 6cm/2½in long and held horizontally at the stem top. A whorl of six pointed, twisted, pale yellow tepals frames the central golden-yellow trumpet tube, the corona, which flares out slightly towards the frilled margin. Inside the tube are six stamens and a long style with a swollen, three-lobed stigma. The fruit is a three-celled globular capsule, which splits to shed its many egg-shaped seeds.

Wild daffodils grow in damp woods and grassland, often on heavy soils, throughout the lowlands of England, but they are more often found in the south and west and are absent from most parts of the east and north-east. 'Common yellow Daffodilly', wrote John Gerard at the end of the sixteenth century, 'groweth almost everywhere through England'; but today many of the plants seen in wild places are escaped garden hybrids and not the true native English daffodil.

Beware: the bulb is poisonous to eat, although it was once used in making embrocations and wound dressings.

The flower is pollinated by early flying, short-tongued

bumble bees, which push past the anthers surrounding the single style to reach the nectar at its base. It is also visited by long-tongued bees and droneflies.

This should be the chosen species for growing beneath deciduous trees or naturalizing in grass, being more delicate and less blowsy than most of the cultivated hybrids, which have its genes but not its gentility. Wild daffodil grows in sun or light shade in most well-drained garden soils, as long as the ground is moist during the growing season. Dead-head spent flowers and allow the leaves to die down naturally. When grown in grass, cutting must be delayed until the seeds have been dispersed. The plant will increase naturally by seeding and breeds true, if there are no other daffodils near by. It is better to leave clumps undisturbed for a few years, before lifting and dividing the bulbs in late summer, planting the offsets immediately.

Yellow Water-lily
Nuphar lutea NYMPHAEACEAE

Floating on the surface of still or slow-moving water, the leathery, heart-shaped leaves of the perennial yellow water-lily are the largest of the native aquatic plants and soon form an attractive, mid-green covering contrasting with the dark water beneath. These leaves, up to 30cm/12in in diameter, have a narrow cleft at the base and a waxy surface and are carried on very long, flexible stems, which rise from the fleshy, creeping rootstock that grows in the mud. Cunningly constructed air-canals in the leaves and stalks give the plant buoyancy and convey oxygen to the underwater parts, including the thinner, cabbage-like submerged leaves. Smooth stems hold the large, rather unpleasantly scented, bowl-shaped yellow flowers above the surface from June to the end of August. Each is up to 6cm/2½in across with five or six concave sepals, greenish-yellow outside and bright yellow inside. These are cupped around an inner circle of about twenty narrow yellow petals and many large stamens. The fascinating flask-shaped seed capsule is topped with a ring of stigmas and floats for a while, to allow birds or current to move it to a new site; then the air goes out of the capsule and it sinks, to seed in the mud.

The yellow water-lily is common in lakes, ponds and slow-moving streams and rivers throughout lowland England, except the south-west and parts of the north.

Both the carafe shape and the slightly alcoholic smell of the ripe fruit gave the plant its old name of brandy bottle.

The alcoholic smell attracts small pollinating flies, which crawl about among the stamens seeking nectar, which lies at the base of the petals. During their search they unwittingly collect pollen, which is transferred to the many radiating stigmas on the upper surface of the ovary.

This is a handsome plant for a large pond where its glossy leaves, green-gold flowers and shapely fruits add distinction from summer to autumn. It is propagated by division of the massive rhizome in March, then planting about 60cm/24in deep in pond baskets filled with rich loam.

White Water-lily
Nymphaea alba NYMPHAEACEAE

Now folds the lily all her sweetness up,
And slips into the bosom of the lake:
So fold thyself, my dearest, thou, and slip
Into my bosom and be lost in me.
'The Princess', Alfred, Lord Tennyson (1809–92)

The lakes and ponds of England are host to some of the loveliest and most luxuriant of our native flowers, but the queen of the aquatics is surely the perennial white water-lily. With its white, floating flowers (the largest in the native flora) and its glossy, bright green leaves, it is a magical sight. From the stout, creeping underwater rhizome come smooth stems, up to 3m/10ft long, carrying almost circular floating leaves with a deep cleft. These are dark, glossy green on the surface and often reddish underneath. Borne from June to August on equally long stalks, the showy, scented flowers, up to 20cm/8in across, open completely only in full sunlight. As the day draws in, they close, dipping slightly below the surface of the water. Each bloom has four spear-shaped sepals, green on the outside, white inside, and between twenty and twenty-five spirally arranged, oval, pointed white petals. After flowering, the spongy, globular fruit capsule sinks to ripen underwater. The seeds have a spongy, air-filled coating and when the fruit rots they float to the surface, drifting away before the air escapes and then sinking into the mud to germinate.

White water-lilies are found in lakes, ponds and slow-moving rivers throughout lowland England, and rising to over 450m/1,475ft in the Lake District.

The underwater stems are sometimes eaten in parts of

northern Europe and, in the past, distillations of the plant were used to treat skin blemishes, sunburn and baldness.

The flowers, which produce a curious, boron-containing nectar, are fragrant when first open and attract bees, flies and beetles to assist in pollination.

The white water-lily adds unmistakable glamour to a lake or large garden pond. It needs full sun and still water and is best planted just under the surface of loamy soil in a pond basket, covered with coarse gravel or small pebbles. Submerge the basket until it is covered with about 50cm/20in of water; once the water lily is established it can go deeper. The plant grows vigorously, forming a dense circle of leaves up to 3m/10ft across, but it can be controlled by keeping it in smaller baskets and dividing regularly. It is propagated by dividing the thick rhizome in spring.

Marjoram
Origanum vulgare LAMIACEAE

With margeran gentle,
The flower of goodlihood,
Embroidered the mantle
Is of your maidenhood.

John Skelton (c. 1460–1529)

Marjoram is the aromatic home-grown version of the related Mediterranean marjorams, *O. onites* and *O. majorana*, which are more commonly planted in herb gardens. A bushy, vigorous perennial with a woody, creeping root, it has thin, downy, branched stems up to 60cm/24in high, and rounded to ovate, dark green leaves with smooth or slightly toothed margins. These are strongly scented when crushed. From July to the end of September the roundish flowerheads at the tips of stems and branches are composed of dense clusters of pinkish-purple flowers with purple, leaflike bracts. Each five-petalled flower has a flat, two-lobed upper lip and a short, three-lobed lower lip, with four protruding purple stamens; the tube is longer than the calyx. The fruit splits into four one-seeded nutlets.

PREVIOUS PAGE Wide skies and luminous red poppies of the field – one of the most glorious sights of the English summer and one that can be echoed in the garden by growing the common poppy (*Papaver rhoeas*) threading through the border or in a garden meadow where the ground is cultivated each year.

Marjoram grows in dry grassland, and on hedgebanks and scrub, usually on calcareous soils throughout England, from sea-level to 400m/1,310ft in North Yorkshire.

Fresh or dried, the aromatic leaves add flavour to dishes such as stews and pasta.

The nectar at the base of the flower-tubes attracts many bees, long-tongued flies and butterflies, including such rarities as the Adonis blue and Lulworth skipper. The leaves are food for the caterpillars of the lace border and sub-angled wave moths.

This fragrant plant is a source of colour and culinary delight through summer into autumn. It is ideal for herbaceous borders, herb gardens, rockeries and window boxes, and it will thrive even on dry, sandy soil. It likes full sun and well-drained, preferably alkaline soil. It is propagated by sowing seeds in open ground on a light, warm soil in spring; by division of the rootstock in spring; or by taking cuttings in late spring.

Common Poppy
Papaver rhoeas PAPAVERACEAE

The common poppy with its dazzling, vivid red petals is one of the few truly scarlet flowers found wild in England. The others are the scarlet pimpernel, *Anagallis arvensis*, which is arguably salmon-red; the early marsh orchid, *Dactylorhiza incarnata* subsp. *coccinea*, although its colour is more crimson red; and the introduced pheasant's-eye, *Adonis annua*. The upright, branching stems of the common poppy, an annual, grow to 60cm/24in and have stiff, outward-pointing hairs. The downy, pinnately divided, light green leaves have toothed, lance-shaped segments. Held on slender, hairy stalks, the drooping buds open and shed their two bristly, concave sepals to reveal crimped single flowers, each turning upwards and quickly spreading to display four rounded, slightly crumpled scarlet petals; these often have a black blotch at the base. The large flower can be up to 10cm/4in across with a dark centre composed of a circle of masses of blue-black stamens surrounding the globular ovary with its radiating stigmas. Alas, the richly coloured, papery petals often fall after only one day, but then a healthy poppy may produce up to 400 blooms in succession during its June to September flowering. The smooth, almost globular, ripe seed capsule is known as a 'pepperpot' because the numerous black seeds are shaken from holes beneath the 'lid', formed by the disc of stigmas.

The common poppy is found on disturbed ground and waste places, and along roadsides and railway lines, on well-drained soils throughout lowland England, but is less common in the north and west where it may be replaced by the long-headed poppy, *P. dubium*. The scarlet and gold of poppies among ripe corn used to be a common sight before weedkillers were used on arable land.

Like all poppies, the stem contains a bitter, narcotic latex. A soothing syrup was once made from the petals.

The flowers lack nectar, but their brilliant red is visible to bumble bees and honey bees, which are attracted, along with beetles and hoverflies, and then discover abundant supplies of pollen.

With few rivals for its blaze of bright red, the plant is ideal for a 'hot'-coloured border or for growing among grasses in a flowering meadow. Common poppy prefers full sun and well-drained, preferably infertile soil. It can be propagated from seed, which is easily collected by putting ripe heads in a paper bag and shaking. The seeds can be sown outside in early autumn (preferable for a meadow) or in spring, their key requirement for germination being bare earth. They will regenerate freely in beds, but not in dense grass.

Common Bistort
Persicaria bistorta POLYGONACEAE

Common bistort forms large patches of broad, green leaves punctuated by spikes of attractive pale pink flowers. A vigorous, almost hairless perennial, it has long, oval, pointed leaves with untoothed margins and strongly marked veins, the stalks of the large lower ones being winged at the base. From May to August the tops of the numerous erect, straight stems, up to 80cm/32in high, carry cylindrical flowerheads densely packed with narrow, bell-shaped, rose (rarely white) flowers. Each is up to 5mm/⅛in long and has showy stamens, which give the flowerhead a brushlike appearance.

Common bistort is found in grassy places throughout England, but is common only in the north-west, ascending to 360m/1,180ft in the Pennines. It is introduced in much of the south.

Common bistort (*Persicaria bistorta*) spreads naturally to form dense clumps in moist soils, flowering freely in full sun and with sufficiently vigorous growth to crowd out less desirable plants.

The underground stems are contorted and the name bistort comes from the Latin *bis*, meaning 'twice', and *tortus*, 'twisted'. In the north it is called pudding dock, after the use of the young leaves in making Easter-ledge pudding. The young leaves can also be eaten like spinach.

The nectar in the small tubular flowers attracts St Mark's and feverflies, which find them full of pollen. It is the food plant of the small copper butterfly. The stamens ripen first and the stigmas are not receptive until the anthers have withered.

This is a useful, adaptable plant for the border, the rock garden, the edge of a pond or for naturalizing in a damp meadow or woodland. It grows in sun or semi-shade on most moist soils, but in a cool site will tolerate dry, sandy ground. It is propagated by division of the roots in spring or autumn, or by sowing seed outside in summer.

Mouse-ear-hawkweed
Pilosella officinarum ASTERACEAE

Mouse-ear-hawkweed is a neat little perennial, which spreads by producing long, slender white runners bearing small, well-spaced leaves, some rooting stems terminating in a rosette of leaves that lasts through winter. The thick leaves are rounded, broadest near the tip, and dark-green above but white felted underneath. From May to October the hairy, leafless flower stalks, up to 30cm/12in high, carry solitary, dandelion-like heads of pale yellow florets, the outer ones red striped underneath. The flowerhead is enclosed by grey-green bracts. The one-seeded, purple-black fruit has a parachute of hairs.

Mouse-ear-hawkweed grows in short grassland, on heaths, dry banks and rocks, both acid and alkaline, throughout England, rising to 725m/2,380ft in the Pennines.

'Mouse-ear' is a reference to the shape and hairiness of the leaves, which were once used to make an infusion for the treatment of enteritis, influenza and cystitis.

Mouse-ear-hawkweed is a small wildlife haven, producing abundant pollen that attracts pollen-eating beetles, and nectar that is reached by butterflies, bumble bees, bee-flies and hoverflies. The leaves may be host to a gall-wasp, which produces swellings on the midrib.

This is an enchanting plant for the rock garden, a dry sunny bank or wall, or for a flowering meadow. It grows in sun or semi-shade and in a wide range of well-drained soils,

tolerating poor, dry soils. It is readily propagated by division throughout the growing season, or from seed sown outside.

Spring Cinquefoil
Potentilla neumanniana ROSACEAE

Although yellow in colour rather than white, the perennial, mat-forming spring cinquefoil is so similar to wild strawberry that it has been called a tall strawberry. It has long, trailing, slightly woody runners with leaf-rosettes at the tips and the palmate basal leaves have five to seven toothed leaflets (hence the name cinquefoil), broader towards the top and usually hairy on both surfaces. Flowering stems up to 10cm/4in tall arise from the side of the main stems and from April onwards bear loose groups of flowers. Each is up to 1.5cm/⅝in across, with five deep yellow, notched petals with the sepals showing between, and a mass of stamens in the centre. The plant produces a head of dry, one-seeded fruits.

Spring cinquefoil grows in dry, open basic grassland and on limestone crags, but it is a declining species threatened by lack of grazing and is now found only in scattered localities in England, but reaching 300m/985ft in the Malvern Hills.

Nectar is secreted in a ring at the base of the petals and attracts pollinating insects, such as bees and wasps. Pollination is necessary to stimulate the production of seed, although the majority of seeds are produced apomictically – asexually and identical to the parent.

This is a neat, bright plant for the border or the rock garden, or for growing in a raised bed or container. It prefers a sunny, free-draining site. It is propagated by division in spring or autumn, or by sowing seed under glass in March.

Cowslip
Primula veris PRIMULACEAE

The cowslip's clusters of nodding, deep yellow, apricot-scented flowers were once a familiar sight in early summer meadows, but cultivation of their grassland habitat has made them a rarer pleasure. This cheerful perennial is closely related to the primrose and has similar oblong, wrinkly, toothed, fresh-green leaves, but cowslip leaves have fine hairs on both sides and narrow more abruptly into the leaf stem than those of the primrose. In April and May long, leafless, shortly hairy stems, up to 30cm/12in tall, carry abundant clusters of up to thirty tubular flowers, each wrapped in a downy, bluntly toothed, pale green calyx. The five-petalled flower has lobes much shorter than those of the primrose and curved inwards to form a cup, up to 1.5cm/⅝in across. Orange streaks decorate the interior of the cup with its throat of folded petals. The fruit is an egg-shaped capsule enclosed in the enlarged calyx and, as it ripens, the flower stalk becomes upright.

Cowslips are found in grassland and open woodland, especially on calcareous soils, throughout England, ascending to 600m/1,970ft in the Pennines.

The name cowslip is a polite form of cowslop or cowpat, referring to the way it grows in scattered clumps in grassland. It was once valued for its sedative properties, and a delicate wine can be made from the flowers – a practice now discouraged in order to conserve plants in the wild.

RIGHT Tolerating light shade or full sun and grown in moist soils, the unassuming cowslip (*Primula veris*) rewards close scrutiny of its little cup-like flowers marked inside with orange streaks.

BELOW North-facing borders or banks can be transformed in early spring by clusters of pale yellow native primrose (*Primula vulgaris*).

The flowers are a useful source of nectar and attract bee-flies, solitary bees, butterflies and moths, which effect the pollination of this heterostylous species (see definition under primrose below). It is the food plant of the Duke of Burgundy fritillary butterfly and of clay and northern rustic moths.

As one of our most delightful spring flowers, the cowslip is ideal for naturalizing in a wildflower lawn or meadow, but it is also a good plant for the herbaceous or shrub border. It grows in sun or semi-shade on reasonably moist but well-drained soils, preferably chalky; it dislikes acid soils. Once established, it will spread of its own accord, but is very selective of its site and in the drier east of the country may die out after a year or two. Naturally regenerating seedlings under the light shade of trees appear to last longer. It can be raised from seed sown in a seedbed in spring, but germination is erratic unless the seed is kept cold throughout the winter (and not in a plastic bag).

Selfheal (*Prunella vulgaris*)

Primrose
Primula vulgaris PRIMULACEAE

Aske me why I send you here
This sweet Infanta of the yeere?
Aske me why I send to you
This Primrose, thus bepearl'd with dew?
'The Primrose', Robert Herrick (1591-1674)

True to its botanical name, from the Latin *primula* meaning 'first', the large, pure, pale-yellow flowers and rich green leaves of the primrose are an early promise of the spring to come. This prized perennial has a whorl of inversely ovate or spoon-shaped, irregularly toothed, crinkly leaves, which narrow gradually into the leaf-stalk, hairless on the upper side and downy underneath. From the midst of this leaf-rosette in late February or March come hairy flower stalks, up to 12cm/5in high, each bearing a single wheel-shaped flower with five yellow petals, up to 4cm/1½in across; flowering continues through May. Faintly scented in sunshine, the flower has orange honey-guides at the base of the petals and thick folds in the throat of the flower tube, which is wrapped in a pleated, pale green calyx tube with five narrow teeth. Primroses are heterostylous: some plants have flowers with the style appearing at the top of the tube above the stamens (pin-eyed), while others have the style hidden below the stamens (thrum-eyed). Pollen of one flower type will only grow in the stigma of the other flower type and, according to Charles Darwin's experiments, this 'crossing' ensures the production of more seeds. The fruit is a capsule full of sticky seeds.

Primroses grow in woods, on hedgebanks and in open grassland, often on heavy soils, throughout England, ascending to about 600m/1,970ft in the Pennines.

In the Middle Ages the primrose was used to treat rheumatism, gout and nervous disorders, and for many years the flowers were candied and also made into wine.

The nectar at the bottom of the long flower tube is food for butterflies, moths, solitary bees, hoverflies and particularly bee-flies. It is the food plant of many moths, including the pearl bordered yellow underwing, double square spot, green arches and triple spotted clay. Duke of Burgundy fritillary butterfly caterpillars feed on the leaves and the sticky seeds attract ants, which help dispersal by carrying them away.

Few early plants can match the primrose in the garden. It is particularly effective when planted in large clumps at the front of a border, naturalized in a damp, spring-flowering meadow, in grass between trees or on a grassy hedgebank, or massed beside a pond or stream. It prefers semi-shade and grows on a fairly wide range of soils as long as there is constant moisture. It can be propagated by division of the dense crowns immediately after flowering. Rooted pieces should be pulled apart by hand and either replanted immediately or potted in moist compost before planting out in autumn. Seed can be sown in containers in a cold frame in autumn or spring.

Selfheal
Prunella vulgaris LAMIACEAE

Selfheal grows happily in partnership with grass, its densely packed, oblong flowerheads forming deep violet carpets on meadows and old lawns. This slightly downy, creeping perennial has upwardly curving or upright, square stems, up to 30cm/12in tall, with pairs of bright green, oval leaves, untoothed or shallowly toothed. At the stem tip, clusters of bluish-violet (rarely pink or white) flowers form dense heads from June to September, each in the axil of a small, purple-tinged bract. The 1-1.5cm/½-⅝in flower has a hoodlike upper lip and a convex, three-lobed lower lip. After flowering the purple-tinged, two-lipped calyx closes up and remains throughout winter. The fruit is made up of four smooth, oblong nutlets, each with a central ridge.

Selfheal is one of the commonest plants of grasslands, heath, scrub and woodland clearings, growing throughout England, from coastal dunes to over 750m/2,460ft in the Pennines.

It may be gathered and mixed with other wild plants and used in soups and stews. It was once widely used as a medicinal herb for soothing sore throats and, as its name suggests, for healing wounds.

Bees are the main visitors, and a ring of hairs in the throat of the flowers prevents small insects from stealing the nectar without pollinating them.

Too vigorous and spreading for the flowerbed, selfheal is ideal for naturalizing in grass or growing as ground cover in the light shade of a shrubbery or orchard, where it will provide large patches of colour from summer to autumn. It grows in sun or semi-shade and in most soils, although it prefers moist, rich loam. Self-seeding can be checked by dead-heading. It is readily propagated by division in spring or autumn, or by sowing seeds when the ground has begun to warm up in spring.

Common Fleabane
Pulicaria dysenterica ASTERACEAE

Common fleabane, with its bright, sunny yellow flowers, is a waterside perennial with spreading rhizomes and hairy, branching stems, up to 60cm/24in high, bearing a spiral of wavy leaves with dense, woolly undersides. The lower leaves are stalked and oblong while the upper ones are stalkless, heart-shaped at the base and clasping the stem. From July to September the tips of stems and branches carry the broad, daisylike golden-yellow flowerheads, up to 3cm/1¼in across, with narrow, hairy green bracts at the base. Each head consists of a tight cluster of tubular disc-florets surrounded by strap-shaped outer ray-florets. The oblong, ribbed fruit has a parachute of hairs.

The plant is widespread in marshes, wet meadows, ditches and streamsides, mostly on heavy soils, throughout most of lowland England, but is scarce in the northernmost counties; it ascends to 300m/985ft in West Yorkshire.

The Latin genus name *Pulicaria* is derived from *pulex*, 'a flea', referring to the old tradition of strewing the plant among rushes on the floor of the house to repel fleas and other insects. Common fleabane was also used to treat dysentery.

The nectar produces a regular supply of food in high summer for brown hairstreak and gatekeeper butterflies, but also attracts many other insects, chiefly flies. The woolly leaves are apparently too much of a mouthful for most caterpillars.

Late-flowering as it is, the common fleabane adds a splash of autumn colour to the side of a pond or stream, or to the bog garden, although it can spread with speed and needs controlling.

It is effective when naturalized in damp ground among grasses, where the previous season's growth can be mown off in winter. It is propagated by division of the rhizome in spring or autumn, but it seeds freely on bare, moist soil and seedlings can be transplanted.

Lesser Celandine
Ranunculus ficaria RANUNCULACEAE

They fuse themselves to little spicy baths,
  Solved in the tender blushes of the peach;
They lose themselves and die
  On that new life that gems the hawthorn line;
Thy gay lent-lilies wave and put them by,
  And out once more in varnish'd glory shine
  Thy stars of celandine.

'Progress of Spring', Alfred, Lord Tennyson (1809–92)

Suddenly illuminating shady places in early spring, the glistening, golden-yellow flowers of the lesser celandine are a visual tonic at the end of winter. This perennial often forms a great mass of green and gold on woodland floors or on grassy banks. Smooth stems, usually about 10cm/4in high, arise from a fibrous root with numerous white, fig-shaped tubers, and the long-stalked, glossy, dark green basal leaves are broadly heart-shaped, often with scalloped edges, sometimes with purplish-brown or silvery patches. Solitary, bright yellow flowers appear from March to May, up to 3cm/1¼in across, each with three oval green sepals and seven to twelve glossy, oval petals (narrower than those of other buttercups), which close in the late afternoon. The short-beaked fruits are clustered in a rounded head.

Lesser celandine is found in damp meadows, grassy places, hedgebanks, woods and stream sides throughout England.

The flower is a valuable source of nectar and pollen for bees, flies and other insects. It is the food plant of the flame brocade moth.

This beautiful, clump-forming plant will brighten a woodland corner or bank in spring. The leaves die down after flowering and have largely disappeared by summer. It prefers shade or semi-shade and moist soils. Lesser celandine seeds freely and spreads rapidly, needing plenty of space for its invasive habit. The tubers are well below the surface and difficult to weed out, but some gardeners believe that growth can be controlled by dressing the ground with wood or coal ash. Propagation is by division in spring or autumn.

Greater Spearwort
Ranunculus lingua RANUNCULACEAE

Towering above other marsh plants such as bog asphodel and marsh orchid, the greater spearwort is tall and spectacular, one of the loveliest members of the buttercup family with its large, gleaming yellow flowers and an attractive blue patina to its foliage. A perennial, it has thick, hollow stems growing up to 1.2m/4ft high from densely fibrous roots, and blunt, heart-shapes leaves at the base that wither before flowering. The long, lance-shaped stem leaves are leathery, spear-shaped and shallowly toothed with a bluish sheen. From June to September the hairy flower stalks carry glossy yellow cups, up to 5cm/2in across, each with five petals and numerous stamens. The single-seeded fruit has narrow wings and a short, curved beak.

Greater spearwort grows in marshes and tall herb vegetation at the edge of pools and lakes where the water is neutral to alkaline, in scattered localities throughout England, but is declining in many areas because of land drainage.

Beware: do not plant greater spearwort where cattle can reach it, as the sap is poisonous, as is that of most ranunculus. It can also cause skin irritation.

The plant is mainly cross-pollinated by insects attracted to the nectar and pollen, and visitors include butterflies, moths, thrips, hoverflies, feverflies, bees and small beetles. It may also be self-pollinated by rain, when pollen floats over the surface of water-filled flowers to receptive stamens.

This is a handsome species for the margin of a pond or lake, or for a bog garden, where its glossy leaves and golden flowers will delight throughout the summer. Greater spearwort prefers a sunny spot and dislikes acid conditions. As it spreads rapidly and can be very aggressive, it may be controlled by growing it in a container sunk into damp soil or about 20cm/8in below the surface of still water, although seedlings will still occur if the conditions are favourable. It can be propagated by removing clumps of stout shoots and planting them out in spring.

Wild Mignonette
Reseda lutea RESEDACEAE

Thus wandering o'er the cliffs one day, a wayside plant I saw,
Which from my unaccustomed lips did joyful welcome draw;
A gush of perfume, at the sight, around me breathed, – but when
I sprang and pluck'd the flowers, ah me! Where was the fragrance
    then?

'It is the Mignonette,' quoth I; 'yet odour there is none!'
Abundant o'er the chalky hills its blossoms met the sun;

A deeper yellow on them lay than clad my garden flowers,
And yet there was no soothing scent, the semblance only ours …

'Mignonette', Calder Campbell (1798–1857)

The conical flowerheads of wild mignonette are similar to those of the garden variety, *R. odorata*, although the flowers are smaller and scentless. The stems of this biennial or perennial are upward-turning or upright and well-branched, growing up to 60cm/24in in height, and the glossy leaves are deeply pinnately divided into linear segments with wavy margins. From June to September dense, spike-like racemes of little greenish-yellow flowers appear, each flower having six narrow sepals and six variously cut petals. The knobbly, short-stalked, open capsule, up to 1.8cm/¾in long, contains many ear-shaped, shiny black seeds.

Wild mignonette is found on disturbed waste and arable land, roadsides and quarries, especially on calcareous soils, throughout most of lowland England, but is rare in the west.

'Mignonette' comes from the French, meaning 'little darling', and was originally applied to the more fragrant *R. odorata*. It was once used as a dye plant.

Nectar in the flowers attracts many small bees, sawflies and other insects, and the leaves are food for the caterpillars of the Bath white, cabbage white and orange-tip butterflies.

This medium-sized plant is suitable for a herbaceous border or rock garden in full sun or semi-shade, preferring well-drained, alkaline soil. It is best raised from seed sown in a sunny situation, covered by a thin layer of fine soil and watered in spring. It does not transplant too readily.

Wild Clary
Salvia verbenaca LAMIACEAE

The violet-blue spikes of the perennial wild clary bloom throughout the summer, borne on sparsely branched, hairy, upright, square stems, which reach up to 80cm/32in in height. The pairs of long-stalked lower leaves are oblong or oval and coarsely toothed or lobed, with a 'blistered' and strongly veined surface. The opposite stem leaves are unstalked and almost triangular, reducing in size towards the stem tip. From

Grown in a mixed border, the greenish-yellow conical flowerheads of the wild mignonette (*Reseda lutea*) enhance the stronger colours of other summer flowers.

May to September the small, 6–15mm/¼–⅝in, violet-blue flowers appear in terminal spikes, arranged in whorls, each with tiny leaves at the base. These flowers are of two types: either large and open, with a hooded upper lip, three-lobed lower lip and two projecting stamens; or smaller and never opening properly. The large calyx is bell-shaped. The four nutlets swell and become surrounded by mucilage when wet.

Wild clary grows in dry grassland, on rough ground and roadsides, mainly on calcareous soils in the lowlands of south and east England, becoming rare in central England.

Mucilage from the soaked seeds was once used to treat sore eyes, and the plant's name thus became clear-eye. The flowers were also mixed with brandy and cinnamon to make a cordial called clary water.

Wild clary is attractive to bees, which unwittingly collect pollen while pushing past the two stamens beneath the upper lip as they seek nectar from the bottom of the flower-tube.

This is a useful, long-flowering plant for a border or gravel bed, or among grasses. It prefers a sunny site and well-drained or dry sandy soil. Propagate by division of the rootstock or by sowing seed in a cold frame in spring.

Meadow Saxifrage
Saxifraga granulata SAXIFRAGACEAE

This charming perennial adds sparkle to its natural habitat in early summer grass with its clean white flowers and attractive rosettes of kidney-shaped, lobed leaves. Straight, upright, hairy stems grow up to 50cm/20in high; they are branched, and at the base are long-stalked, kidney-shaped, coarsely toothed or lobed leaves, which in dry conditions may be tinted red or brown. The few upper leaves are smaller. From April to June the loose groups of large white flowers appear at the top of the stem, each up to 1.5cm/⅝in across, with five rounded, pure-white petals shading to greenish-yellow at the base and ten yellow stamens. A distinctive feature of meadow saxifrage is the cluster of tiny, brown, pea-like bulbs, which develop where the lower leaf stalks join the stem and last through winter. The egg-shaped capsule splits along the upper edge to release many rough seeds.

Meadow saxifrage grows in moist grassland on basic or neutral, free-draining soils throughout most of England (though it is absent as a native in the south-west peninsula), ascending to 550m/1,800ft in Yorkshire. It is much less frequent now because of the ploughing and reseeding of old grassland.

Like other saxifrages, it is a source of nectar and pollen for many insects, especially bees, wasps and sawflies. It is the food plant of the yellow-ringed carpet moth. Sticky hairs on the stem and calyx protect the flowers from robbery by wingless species.

This plant is excellent in the rock garden or at the front of a well-drained border. It grows in sun or light shade and in most free-draining soils, preferably neutral to alkaline. The Latin species name *granulata*, meaning 'knotted', refers to its bulbils, which are the main means of propagation. When the plant dies down in summer pieces of stem with bulbils attached can be removed and grown on. It may be divided in autumn or winter and planted out the following spring.

Small Scabious
Scabiosa columbaria DIPSACACEAE

The pretty, domed, bluish-lilac flowerheads of small scabious are freely produced in summer and a magnet for bees and butterflies. This downy, slender-stemmed, upright perennial grows up to 70cm/28in in height with stalked, broadly lance-shaped, entire or narrow-lobed basal leaves and pinnately divided stem leaves, which become more finely divided towards the stem tip. In July and August the rounded flowerheads, up to 3.5cm/1⅜in across, appear at the tip of long stalks, each cupped by narrow, pointed bracts. The outer, five-lobed flowers on the clustered head are larger and more irregularly lobed than the inner ones. The fruiting head is cone-shaped with a characteristic honeycomb appearance, and the oblong, furrowed fruit has a scaly, cup-shaped rim with five dark calyx bristles projecting from the top.

Small scabious is locally common on dry grassland, rocky places and banks, on chalk and limestone throughout England, from sea-level to 610m/2,000ft in the Pennines.

The name scabious comes from the Latin *scabiosus*, meaning 'rough or scurfy', referring to the use of some species as remedies for itching and other skin complaints. The slender segments of the divided stem leaves supposedly resemble a dove's foot, hence the species name *columbaria*, from the Latin *columba*, 'a dove'.

This is an important wildlife plant. The nectar in the flowers is attractive to many butterflies, including brimstone, comma, painted lady and peacock, as well as to bees, beetles, hoverflies and sawflies. Birds enjoy the ripe seeds. The terminal leaves and flowerheads are frequently swollen as a response to attack by a gall-fly.

Small scabious provides delicate colour for borders and rock gardens and combines well with grasses, preferring an open, sunny position on free-draining (preferably alkaline) soils. It is more compact, better behaved and less invasive than field scabious and can withstand dry conditions. It can be raised from seed sown in spring or by division of clumps in spring or autumn.

Skullcap

Scutellaria galericulata LAMIACEAE

Pairs of tubular flowers growing in the same direction, and a curious bump on the calyx, mark out the skullcap from other members of the mint family. The upright or ascending stems of this perennial grow up to 50cm/20in in height, carrying opposite pairs of broadly lance-shaped, almost stalkless, deep green leaves, heart-shaped or rounded at the base and with shallow, rounded teeth. Both stem and leaves are often tinged with violet. Solitary, bright violet-blue, tubular flowers, up to 1.8cm/¾in long, appear in the leaf axils from June to September, but look as if they are in pairs. The sparsely hairy, two-lipped calyx has a hollow bulge on top, which closes the upper lip over the four nutlets after the petals fall. When dry, the calyx splits to release the fruit.

Small scabious (*Scabiosa columbaria*) is one of the most important wildlife flowers in gardens where its fetching, bluish-lilac flowers are hosts to butterflies and many other insects.

Skullcap is found in marshes, fens and wet meadows and on the edges of ponds and streams, on moderately acid to base-rich soils. It is widespread throughout the lowlands of England, though it ascends to 360m/1,180ft in the Pennines.

Scutella is Latin for 'a small dish', after the bulge on the calyx, while *galericulum* means 'a small hood'. An infusion made from the dried plant was once used as a nerve tonic.

Two lateral petals form a bulge in the mouth of the flower, ensuring that even small visiting insects are covered in pollen from the anthers.

This is a valuable and not too vigorous species for the margin of a garden pond, the bog garden or for naturalizing in a marshy hollow. It grows in sun or light shade and moist soils. Propagation is from seed sown outside or by division in spring, but it will also readily root from cuttings taken during the growing season.

Biting Stonecrop
Sedum acre CRASSULACEAE

Abundant bright yellow, starlike flowers overlay a mat of succulent yellow-green foliage on this low-growing, evergreen perennial, which has a sweet appearance but bitter-tasting leaves. It forms a low-growing tangle of trailing stems, which spread outwards and upwards, rarely exceeding 10cm/4in in height, with smooth, fleshy, egg-shaped, pale-green leaves usually overlapping one another. In June and July yellow flowers smother the plant, carried in small, flat-topped, branched clusters at the end of the shoots. Each flower is up to 1.2cm/½in across with five free, spear-shaped petals and ten stamens. The starlike, follicular fruit splits to release numerous tiny seeds.

Biting stonecrop is widespread on walls, rocks, open grassland and on coastal shingle and sand dunes throughout England, ascending to 460m/1,510ft in the Lake District.

Its leaves have a hot and acrid flavour, hence its common name. Another English name, wall-pepper, aptly describes its habitat and taste.

The flowers are full of easily accessible nectar, an attraction for ichneumon-wasps, which also take the pollen. Perhaps not surprisingly, the acrid leaves are ignored by caterpillars.

This is a splendid species for the front of a border, for a rock garden, a dry wall or for growing in a container. It enjoys a sunny spot but will tolerate light shade and likes well-drained, neutral to alkaline soils. It spreads vigorously, but trimming

after flowering will help keep it in shape. A more suitable sedum for the seaside garden would be the English stonecrop, *S. anglicum*, which has tiny, fleshy, grey-green leaves, often tinged with red, and starlike, pink-tinged, white flowers. Both sedums can be propagated by separating small rooted clumps or rooted stems at any time of year and growing them on.

Orpine
Sedum telephium CRASSULACEAE

This handsome, fleshy, clump-forming perennial with broad, reddish-purple flowerheads and succulent leaves is the tallest of the native sedums and was a favourite in medieval gardens. Rising to a height of 30–60cm/12–24in from a thick rootstock, its upright stems are often tinged with red and carry alternate flat, fleshy, oblong to ovate leaves, which are glaucous grey-green and bluntly toothed. From July to September the rounded flowerheads, up to 12cm/5in across, appear at the tops of the stems, each crowded with small, five-petalled, rose-purple flowers. The cluster of five slender fruits contain numerous tiny seeds.

Orpine grows in woods, hedgebanks and rocky places throughout much of England, although it is uncommon in the north-east. It ascends to 450m/1,475ft in the Pennines.

The fleshy stems and leaves enable the plant to withstand spells of drought, hence its other common name, livelong.

Orpine is an extremely hospitable species for insects, providing nectar into September for butterflies such as peacocks and small tortoiseshells, and for many kinds of bees, sawflies and other small flies.

This is a good substitute for the more common exotic sedums, ideal for borders, rock gardens or a woodland corner. It will grow in sun or semi-shade and tolerates most soils, preferring the light and sandy. It is propagated by division of the rootstock in spring or autumn.

Saw-wort
Serratula tinctoria ASTERACEAE

Saw-wort is a wiry, thistlelike perennial with slender, grooved, upright stems. These are usually well-branched at the top, grow up to 80cm/32in tall, although they are much shorter in exposed sites. The dark green leaves are variably divided, the lower ones usually lobed almost to the midrib and some of the stalkless stem leaves not at all. The leaf lobes have sharp, bristle-tipped teeth. From July to September flowerheads up to 2cm/¾in across appear at the tips of the branches, each cluster of five-lobed tubular purple flowers sheathed tightly at the base by closely overlapping, purple-tinged bracts. The oblong fruit is crowned with a tuft of off-white hairs of unequal length.

Saw-wort is found in open woodland, grassland, scrub, heaths and clifftops, on well-drained soils. It is local throughout the southern half of England, usually in lowlands, but ascending to 560m/1,835ft on Dartmoor.

The genus name *Serratula*, which is Latin for 'little saw', refers to its leaves' pointed teeth. It was called *tinctoria* because it was the source of a beautiful, greenish-yellow dye for woollen cloth.

Nectar in the florets attracts butterflies, long-tongued moths and other winged insects. The leaves may be eaten by the caterpillars of tortricoid moths.

Providing colour through to autumn, this is a suitable plant for the border, for stony banks or for mixing with grasses. It prefers an open position and well-drained (preferably alkaline) soil. It is propagated from seed sown in spring or by division in spring or autumn.

Red Campion

Silene dioica CARYOPHYLLACEAE

He is English as this gate, these flowers, this mire.
And when at eight years old Lob-lie-by-the-fire
Came in my books, this was the man I saw.
He has been in England as long as dove and daw,
Calling the wild cherry tree the merry tree,
The rose campion Bridget in her bravery …
'Lob', Edward Thomas (1878–1917)

Red campion's generous display of delightful deep-pink flowers makes this one of the most attractive and easily recognized of Britain's native perennials. The downy, upright, loosely branched stems can grow to about 90cm/36in in height and may be slightly sticky at the top. The oval or oblong, downy stem leaves are in opposite pairs, the lower leaves having long winged stalks. From May to October the rose-pink flowers appear in the forks

With its fleshy leaves and stems, the clump-forming orpine (*Sedum telephium*) withstands drought, dry conditions and salt spray.

of the stems, each with five, two-lobed, deeply cleft petals and a reddish, ribbed, tubular calyx. Red campion is dioecious, having male and female flowers on separate plants. Male flowers have ten stamens, while the female flowers have five long styles above an ovary. The fruit capsule has ten curled back teeth at the top and contains numerous black, kidney-shaped seeds.

Red campion is common in lowland woods and hedgerows, and on upland cliffs and scree-slopes throughout most of England, but is almost absent from Cambridgeshire. It rises to 575m/1,885ft in the Pennines.

The nectar at the bottom of the long, tubular flowers can be reached by butterflies, long-tongued bumble bees and hoverflies. The leaves are food for caterpillars of lychnis and marbled coronet moths, and the seed capsules may be infested with 'maggots' of campion, rivulet or sandy carpet moths.

This is a rewarding plant for the border or for naturalizing in a hedge-bottom or wooded corner. It will grow in sun or dappled shade and likes moderately fertile, well-drained soils. Seedlings seem to regenerate best along moist, shaded hedge-bottoms and ditches where there is not too much competition from grass. They will overwinter as rosettes and produce dense clumps of pale leaves in early spring. There is a coastal-cliff form, with deep magenta flowers on more robust and hairier stems, which is even more attractive, and, like other forms, can be readily raised from seed sown in spring in pans placed in cold frames and planted out in autumn. Clumps may be divided in autumn.

Goldenrod

Solidago virgaurea ASTERACEAE

Reaching up through bush and briar,
Sumptuous brow and heart of fire,
Flaunting high its wind-rocked plume,
Brave with wealth of native bloom, –
Golden rod!

'Golden Rod', Elaine Goodale Eastman

The golden, daisylike flowerheads of goldenrod continue to glow through late summer and autumn. Growing up to 70cm/28in tall, this perennial has upright, often blackish, stems

Not only does the red campion (*Silene dioica*) give a long summer display of deep-pink flowers, it also enlivens the winter garden with its clumps of pale young leaves.

that branch at the top, and dark green alternate leaves, the basal ones ovate and toothed, the lance-shaped stem leaves slightly toothed. Dense, narrow clusters of bright yellow flowerheads appear on straight, erect branches from July to the end of September, each up to 1cm/½in across with darker yellow, tubular inner florets and a single row of straplike outer ray-florets. There are narrow green, overlapping bracts at the base. The downy, brown, nutlike fruit has a parachute of white hairs.

Goldenrod is found in woodland, grassland, hedgebanks, heaths and cliffs, on neutral to acid soils throughout England, although it is rare or absent from large areas of the Midlands and East Anglia. It grows up to around 725m/2,380ft in the Lake District, where there are compact forms with unbranched 'rods'.

Solidago comes from the Latin *solidare*, to make whole, referring to the plant's use in centuries past as a wound-healer.

Goldenrod is visited by several species of nectar-seeking bees, solitary wasps and short-tongued flies, as well as by less selective beetles, which eat the pollen and anthers and drink the nectar. The leaves are eaten by caterpillars of the peppered moth and several species of pug moth. The seedheads are a food source for seed-eating birds.

This plant will provide late summer and autumn colour in a woodland corner or in an area of rough grass. It grows in sun and prefers light, sandy soils. On warm, dry soil it seeds freely and can be invasive. Introduced North American species may hybridize with native species. It is easily propagated by division of the clumps in spring or autumn.

WOUNDWORTS
Stachys species LAMIACEAE

Woundworts, as the name suggests, were long valued for their medicinal properties. Some are slightly antiseptic and were used for treating wounds and digestive problems. Although betony is not called a woundwort, it belongs to the same genus as the woundworts, whose name – *Stachys*, Greek for 'spike' – describes the flowerheads, all of which come in varying shades of reddish-purple.

Betony
Stachys officinalis LAMIACEAE

This perennial was often grown in monastery gardens and is recognized by its almost leafless, square stems, which are upright, sparsely hairy and mainly unbranched. Growing up to 60cm/24in in height, it has a basal rosette of ovate to oblong long-stalked, wrinkled leaves, heart-shaped at the base, with blunt teeth. The few pairs of stem leaves are widely spaced, the upper ones being almost stalkless. From June to September bright, reddish-purple, tubular flowers appear in dense spikes, each flower with a flat upper lip and a lobed lower lip. The almost hairless calyx has narrow teeth, and the fruit splits into four nutlike, three-angled parts.

Betony is found in woods, hedgebanks, heaths and grassland, mainly on neutral to acid, lighter soils, throughout most of England, but locally in East Anglia, ascending to over 375m/1,230ft in the Pennines.

In the past betony was used as a remedy for fever and for making a bitter herbal tea.

The plant is mainly pollinated by long-tongued butterflies, moths, bees and hoverflies, which are attracted by the colour and are able to reach the nectar at the base of the flower tubes. The calyx and upper leaves may be swollen in response to attack by gall-midges.

The wine-coloured spikes, which last from midsummer to early autumn, make this a useful ground-cover species for the herbaceous border or for growing in a hedge-bottom or garden meadow. It grows in sun or light shade and prefers free-draining soil that is not too alkaline. It is propagated by sowing seeds in a cold frame in autumn or spring, or by separating rooted pieces in spring. It can also be grown from cuttings, taken in summer.

Marsh Woundwort
Stachys palustris LAMIACEAE

Marsh woundwort is a perennial of damp places, growing up to 1m/3½ft tall with softly hairy, stout, hollow, upright stems and opposite pairs of long, narrow, lance-shaped, finely toothed leaves, the middle and upper stem leaves being stalkless. The two-lipped, tubular flowers are a paler purplish-pink with white markings and appear from July to September in interrupted terminal spikes. The fruit is four nutlets.

Marsh woundwort is common by rivers, streams and ditches and in marshes and fens throughout most of England, ascending to over 450m/1,475ft in the north Pennines.

It was said to have been one of the most valuable of the *Stachys* species for healing wounds and was used by sedge-

Hedge woundwort *(Stachys sylvatica)*

Common comfrey *(Symphytum officinale)*

cutters in the past to treat gashes while they were harvesting.

The nectar at the base of the flower tubes attracts bees and numerous butterflies, including the meadow brown.

This plant will lend a splash of pink to a damp area of the garden, by a pond or in a bog garden. It will grow in sun or semi-shade as long as the soil is moist. It is propagated by dividing rooted sections in spring. Marsh and hedge woundworts hybridize and the resulting intermediate, *S. × ambigua*, appears to be better adapted to harsher climates than either parent.

Hedge Woundwort
Stachys sylvatica LAMIACEAE

Hedge woundwort is square-stemmed, but unlike the marsh woundwort, this perennial is bristly and has a foetid smell when bruised. Growing up to 1m/3½ft tall, it has opposite pairs of long-stalked, heart-shaped, pointed and coarsely toothed leaves. From July to September the attractive flower spike is made up of a series of loosely spaced whorls of deep magenta flowers, each with a hooded upper lip and a three-lobed lower lip, with dark red markings on a paler patch. The hairy calyx has long, pointed teeth and the four nutlets blacken as they ripen.

Hedge woundwort is commonly found in woods, hedgebanks and waste ground, mostly on rich soils throughout England.

The plant is pollinated by bees and forms the food plant of the rosy rustic, plain golden Y and sub-angled wave moths.

It is a useful plant for shady areas of the garden, for growing under trees or for adding colour to a grassy bank. It prefers heavy, moist soils. Propagation is as for the marsh woundwort.

Greater Stitchwort
Stellaria holostea CARYOPHYLLACEAE

This pretty, fragile perennial carries large white, starry flowers on delicate, threadlike stems, which lean on neighbouring plants and grasses for support. From a slender creeping root, the weak, quadrangular stems turn upwards, growing up to 60cm/24in tall, bearing opposite pairs of stiff, stalkless, blue-green leaves, which are lance-shaped and pointed, with rough margins. Loose, branched clusters of flowers appear from April to June, each white flower up to 2.5cm/1in across, with five deeply cleft, two-lobed petals (nearly twice as long as the sepals) and ten stamens in two whorls. When ripe, the globular capsule makes a popping sound when it splits to release numerous reddish-brown, kidney-shaped seeds.

Greater stitchwort grows in woods and hedgebanks on mildly acid to calcareous soils throughout most of England, from sea-level to 500m/1,640ft in the Pennines.

The name stitchwort comes from an infusion that was made from the leaves in order to treat pains in the side.

Greater stitchwort is visited for both its pollen and partially concealed nectar by a wide range of insects, including many butterflies and moths, bees, hoverflies, bee-flies and beetles. The leaves provide food for the caterpillars of various dart and yellow underwing moths.

Its glowing white flowers are ideal for brightening a shady corner of the garden and they show to advantage against a dark hedge, such as yew. It will grow in sun or semi-shade and prefers well-drained, fertile soil. It is not always easy to cultivate if there is competition from surrounding plants. Propagation is by division in spring or autumn, or by raising from seed sown in pans in the autumn.

Devil's-bit Scabious
Succisa pratensis DIPSACACEAE

... or scabious tall
That country children call
Pincushions, with their gift
of accurate observance and their swift
Naming more vivid than the botanist.
'The Garden', Vita Sackville-West (1892–1962)

Compact domed flowerheads of deep bluish-violet bloom on the devil's-bit scabious from midsummer through to late autumn. This softly hairy perennial grows up to 80cm/32in tall and differs from other scabious species by having all its leaves undivided. The majority of these long, oval, pointed, opposite pairs of leaves are at the base. From July through September the pincushion flowerheads, up to 3cm/1¼in across, appear at the tip of slender, branched stalks, each composed of up to fifty individual four-lobed tubular flowers, all more or less the same size. Some plants with smaller heads have only female florets, while others with larger flowerheads are hermaphrodite. The oval green fruit has four lobes and four or five dark spines at the top.

Devil's-bit scabious is common in grassy places and woodland rides throughout England, to over 700m/2,300ft in the Lake District.

Its common name comes from the abruptly shortened rootstock, believed to have been bitten off by the devil, who was infuriated by the plant's apparent success as a cure-all. The distilled juice and powdered root of this plant were used to treat many ailments, including coughs and fevers.

Devil's-bit scabious is important for insects – its nectar attracting clouds of late-flying butterflies, such as the red admiral, as well as mining bees and hoverflies, while the leaves are enjoyed by the caterpillars of marsh fritillary butterflies, and satyr pug and narrow-bordered bee hawk-moths.

This is a compact, not-too-vigorous species that lends itself to naturalizing in a garden meadow; it can also be effective in the water garden or around the margin of a pond, providing an intense blue sheen in late summer. It will grow in sun or semi-shade and prefers moist soils, although it will tolerate drier, alkaline soils. Propagation is by sowing seeds in a cold frame in spring or autumn, or by rooting basal cuttings in spring.

Common Comfrey
Symphytum officinale BORAGINACEAE

Common comfrey is a tall, bristly perennial with large leaves, wings on its stout stems and nodding sprays of tubular bells. The upright, well-branched stems grow up to 1.2m/4ft in height with hairy, broadly lance-shaped, pointed leaves; the lower ones have long stalks and the stalkless upper ones have broad wings, which run down the stem to at least the next leaf below. In May and June the curved, drooping flower clusters appear, each bell-like tubular flower having five short lobes and long, narrow calyx teeth. The colour of common comfrey flowers can vary from purplish to pink or pale creamy-yellow. The calyx swells in fruit enclosing four shining black nutlets.

Common comfrey grows on river banks and streamsides, in ditches, fens and marshes, and on roadsides and rough ground throughout lowland England and up to 320m/1,050ft in Derbyshire.

The leaves and stems are full of mucilage and were once used to pack around a broken limb, hence the plant's other common name, knitbone.

Common comfrey is extremely important for bumble bees, which – in order to reach the nectar – have to 'learn' to push their proboscis between the five scales that close the throat of the flower-tube. However, cunning bees often take a shortcut by biting through from the side.

This is a handsome and vigorous species, which can make a brave display in a shady border, in a woodland corner or the larger bog garden. It will grow in sun or semi-shade and needs moist soil, and if it is cut down after flowering it will bloom again in the autumn. Common comfrey can be an aggressive colonizer, regenerating from any part of the rhizome or even from the root, but that can be an advantage in shade under trees where it makes a fine ground-cover plant. The foliage makes excellent plant food, either composted or steeped in water in summer and used diluted. Common comfrey is easily propagated by division of the massive rootstock at almost any time of the year.

Wild Thyme
Thymus polytrichus LAMIACEAE

I know a bank whereon the wild thyme blows
Where oxlips and the nodding violet grows …
A Midsummer Night's Dream, William Shakespeare (1564–1616)

This delightful, sprawling, low-growing perennial forms dense mats of rosy-purple and green, which are slightly aromatic when crushed underfoot. The slender, trailing, rooting stems have ascending flowering stems, up to 7cm/3in long, with hairs on just two opposite sides. Small oval, dark green untoothed leaves with short stalks are found in opposite pairs, with oil glands dotted on the undersides. From June to August the pinkish-purple flowers appear in dense whorls at the tip of the stems, each with four lobes and a two-lipped, five-toothed calyx. The smooth, egg-shaped fruit splits into four nutlets.

Wild thyme is found in short grass, heaths, rocks, dunes and clifftops on acid to base-rich soils throughout most of England, except on heavy clay, ascending to over 800m/2,620ft in the Lake District.

This plant was once valued medicinally for its strong antiseptic qualities. The leaves have a milder flavour than the herb garden species, *T. vulgaris*, which comes from the Mediterranean.

The flowers are packed with nectar and attract hosts of butterflies and moths, bees, solitary wasps and bee-flies. It is the food plant of the large blue butterfly and of moths, including the light-feathered rustic, thyme pug and transparent burnet.

No rock garden, gravel bed, paved area, trough or wall should be without some covering of wild thyme, which provides a pleasing touch of colour throughout the summer. It needs full sun and free-draining soil to thrive, and is a great asset in a dry, sandy garden or in crevices between paving stones, where it will release its aroma when trodden underfoot. It can be cut back after flowering. It is best propagated by dividing in spring, by rooting cuttings in summer, or by raising from seeds sown in a cold frame in spring.

CLOVERS
Trifolium species FABACEAE

Clovers are low-growing plants with distinctive, palmately veined trefoil leaves and densely clustered flowerheads. All have a persistent petal, which conceals the seedpod until it sheds its seeds from the top. They are particularly attractive to bumble bees, which are essential for pollination.

There's a whisper down the field where the year has shot her yield,
And the riches stand grey to the sun,
Singing: 'Over then, come over, for the bee has quit the clover,
And your English summer's done.'
'The Long Trace', Rudyard Kipling (1865–1936)

Zigzag Clover
Trifolium medium FABACEAE

This richly coloured perennial clover is distinguished by its twisting or zigzag stems, reaching up to 50cm/20in in height, and by its long, narrow stipules at the base of the leaf stalk. The leaves are narrower, less hairy and darker than those of red clover and without a clear chevron mark. The stalked, bright reddish-purple flowerheads, up to 2cm/¾in across, are round and slightly flattened at the top, appearing from May to September. The fruiting head has concealed seed pods.

Zigzag clover is found in grassy places and on hedgebanks and woodland margins throughout most of England, but is

Clovers (*Trifolium* species) nourish themselves by taking nitrogen straight from the air and fixing it with the aid of bacteria in the roots. They can in turn feed humans by producing young leaves that can be used to garnish soups and salads.

rarer in East Anglia and the East Midlands; it grows up to 450m/1,475ft in the Pennines.

The young leaves, if picked before flowering, may be added to salads or soups or cooked like spinach.

The nectar-packed flowers attract many insects, especially bees, bee-flies, hoverflies and St Mark's flies. The clustered heads prevent the theft of nectar through the sides of the flowers. The leaves are enjoyed by the caterpillars of garden dart and Hebrew character moths.

This is an attractive plant for covering a bank or for naturalizing in a garden meadow. It prefers a sunny position and moisture-retentive soil. It is best raised from seed, soaked for twenty-four hours in pans, then pricked out into small pots before planting, or it can be divided in spring.

Red Clover
Trifolium pratense FABACEAE

So that my poorest trash, which men call rush and reed,
Doth like the penny grass or the pure Clover show.
Michael Drayton (1563–1631)

Red clover is a sprawling to erect perennial growing up to 60cm/24in tall, with hairy stems, long-stalked leaves and triangular, long-pointed, purple or brown-veined stipules at the base of the leaf stalks. The minutely toothed, dark green, elliptical or inversely ovate leaflets usually have whitish, V-shaped marks across the centre. From May to September the densely clustered, pinkish-purple, globe-shaped flowerheads appear – paler than those of the zigzag clover and up to 1.8cm/¾in across, with two leaves just below the base. The petals later turn brown, hiding the hairless pod with one, notched seed. Cultivated forms can be recognized by their hollow stems and untoothed leaflets.

Red clover is found in a wide range of grassy places and rough ground, on hedgebanks and by roadsides throughout England, from sea-level to nearly 600m/1,970ft in the Pennines.

The fresh flowerheads used to be made into a potent wine and, when dried, they were used as an infusion.

The delicate scent of red clover flowers attracts butterflies, moths and other long-tongued insects, especially bumble bees and hive bees. So valuable is red clover to hive bees that it is sometimes called bee-bread. The leaves are food for the caterpillars of the clouded yellow and pale clouded yellow butterflies and several moths, including the latticed heath, chalk carpet and belted beauty.

Red clover can be naturalized in a garden meadow or used among grasses on a bank. It likes an open site and accepts most soils, except the most acid. The plant is an important constituent of any wild meadow because bacteria in the tiny nodules on the roots help to fix nitrogen in the soil, thus avoiding the need for artificial fertilizers. It can be raised from seed, as for zigzag clover. Hare's-foot clover, *T. arvense*, up to 30cm/12in tall, with attractive, cylindrical, softly hairy, pinkish-white flowerheads, may be a better choice for dry, sandy seaside gardens.

Common Valerian
Valeriana officinalis VALERIANACE

With its bright green, pinnately divided leaves and masses of pink, distinctively scented flowers, the variable common valerian is a handsome and conspicuous perennial. Robust, upright stems grow up to 1.5m/5ft tall, carrying opposite pairs of long leaves divided into pairs of narrowly lance-shaped or narrowly ovate, toothed or untoothed leaflets with a leaflet at the tip. The lower leaves are on grooved stalks, but as the leaves become smaller towards the stem tip they become stalkless. Broad, rounded, branched flowerheads appear from June to August, composed of clusters of tiny pink, tubular flowers, each with five unequal lobes, three protruding white stamens and a calyx, which is at first inrolled and later opens out. The small, dry, ribbed fruit has a feathery parachute at the top to aid dispersal by the wind.

Common valerian grows in rough grassland, scrub and damp woodland throughout England, ascending to over 725m/2,380ft in the Lake District.

Since Roman times it has been used to treat a number of ailments, and extracts from the roots make a sedative used for headaches and insomnia. The genus name comes from the Latin *valeo*, 'to be well'.

Common valerian is one of the most hospitable flowers for insects, attracting hosts of butterflies, moths, sawflies, bees, wasps and other short-tongued insects. Purple nectar-guides on the petals lead them to a small pouch of nectar at the base of each flower. The leaves may be eaten by caterpillars of valerian pug moths.

This is an easily grown, versatile plant, which suits the herbaceous border, the bog garden, the pond margin, a meadow, a shrubbery or a site among trees. It will grow in sun or light shade and will flourish on a wide range of soils (preferably moist), happily competing with taller vegetation. Propagation is by division in spring or autumn, or by sowing seed in April in a sunny position in a light soil.

Great Mullein
Verbascum thapsus SCROPHULARIACEAE

With its tall, tapering spire of light yellow flowers and its soft, grey-green foliage, great mullein is an impressively handsome plant. This rosette-forming biennial is clothed in a woolly covering of thick whitish, branched hairs and its stout upright stem grows to 2m/6½ft in height, with large oval to oblong, stalked basal leaves up to 45cm/18in long. It bears alternate upward-pointing stem leaves, which become smaller and stalkless towards the top. The upper stem leaves have winged

stalks that run down the stem, helping to channel moisture down to the base. A long (up to 75cm/30in high), spikelike raceme of densely packed yellow flowers appears at the top from June to the end of August, each flower having five wide-open, rounded petals. The upper three of the five stamens are clothed in white or yellow hairs, while the lower two are almost hairless. The egg-shaped capsule splits lengthwise to release many tiny, pitted seeds.

Great mullein is common on dry, sunny banks, waste ground and grassy places, especially on light and alkaline soils, throughout most of lowland England.

The Latin genus name *Verbascum* may be a corruption of *barbascum*, meaning 'bearded', because of the plant's hairiness;

Yellow spires and soft green foliage of great mullein (*Verbascum thapsus*) adding stature to a gravel drive where they will happily self-seed.

A favourite flower in medieval times, the easily grown, bright-blue germander speedwell (*Veronica chamaedrys*) often finds its way into gardens without the help of the gardener.

its straight, stafflike appearance explains its alternative common name of Aaron's rod. The dried tops of the plant were once used as flares, hence other common names such as torch-blade and hedge-taper. A distillation of the flowers was formerly used to treat gout, and an infusion made a remedy for coughs and colds.

Beware: most of the plant is poisonous.

The nectar and pollen of the open flowers is easily accessible to both honey and bumble bees as well as to sawflies. The plant's leaves and stems are often damaged by the caterpillars of the mullein moth.

The architectural form and subtle colouring of great mullein make it a highly desirable addition to the garden. It is most effective when grown in groups, either in a sunny border or a gravel bed, or naturalized among grasses. It prefers full sun and well-drained, lean soil, particularly that which is sandy and alkaline. As a biennial, it should be raised from seed annually to ensure some flowering plants every year. The seed should be sown in light soil in April. Once established, great mullein will provide seedlings.

Germander Speedwell
Veronica chamaedrys SCROPHULARIACEAE

The eye-catching, bright azure blue flowers of this enchanting perennial bloom from spring to summer and were a favourite in medieval gardens. They are distantly related to the shrubby hebe from New Zealand. Trailing stems root at intervals and ascend to produce more or less upright flowering shoots up to about 30cm/12in tall. These stems have two vertical lines of white hairs on opposite sides and carry pairs of opposite triangular to ovate, coarsely toothed, bright green leaves, either stalkless or with very short stalks. From the leaf axils, from March to late July, the erect, long-stalked racemes of flowers appear, up to twenty on the spike. Each is up to 1cm/½in across, with four spreading lobes (the lower one being narrower than the others), a central white eye with dark blue radiating veins and two protruding stamens. The hairy, flattened, heart-shaped capsule has a few oblong, flattened seeds.

Germander speedwell is common on hedgebanks, in open woods and grassy places, on all but the most acid soils throughout England.

In the past it was used to treat a number of complaints, including respiratory problems. The name germander is a corruption of the Greek *chamai*, meaning 'on the ground'.

The flowers attract hoverflies and small bees, which are guided by lines on the petals to the nectar, helping to cross-pollinate on the way.

Its long flowering period and jewel-like colour make this a worthwhile plant for the border and the rock garden, for brightening a grassy bank or for naturalizing in a meadow area. It flourishes in full sun or partial shade and in most soils, as long as it is reasonably moist. Control it by cutting away the seedheads before they mature. Propagation is by division in autumn or spring, or by sowing seed in a cold frame in autumn.

Tufted Vetch
Vicia cracca FABACEAE

Tufted vetch is a graceful, climbing perennial with pea-like, bluish-purple flowers, which threads its ladderlike foliage through neighbouring vegetation. From a creeping root with tiny nodules comes a slender, angular stem, which may grow up to 2m/6½ft or more high, scrambling upwards by means of delicate, curling tendrils at the tips of the leaves. These attractive pinnate leaves, up to 2.5cm/1in long, are composed of up to about a dozen pairs of narrowly oblong, downy leaflets. From June to August long racemes of flowers rise from the base of the leaves, each crowded with up to thirty flowers on one side of the stalk. Each flower is up to 1.2cm/½in long, with a large upper petal, pinkish-purple in bud and later turning bright, bluish-violet. The smooth, pea-like pod suddenly splits apart when ripe to eject up to six brown seeds.

Tufted vetch is found in rough grassland, hedgerows and other bushy places throughout England, mainly in the lowlands but reaching nearly 450m/1,475ft on the Welsh border.

The nectar-filled flowers attract pollinating bees, which pick up pollen from a 'brush' on the side of the bent style just below the tip. The leaves provide food for the caterpillars of the wood white butterfly.

This is a delightful plant for weaving through a hedge or growing among grasses, where its colour and form will provide contrast. It grows in sun or semi-shade, preferring broadly neutral soils, and is reasonably tolerant of dry conditions. It can be propagated by division in spring or autumn, but is best raised from the 'peas', soaked for twenty-four hours before being sown in pans, then later planted out.

Sweet Violet
Viola odorata VIOLACEAE

The violet in her greenwood bower,
Where birchen bows with hazel mingle,
May boast itself the fairest flower
In glen or copse or forest dingle.
'The Violet', Sir Walter Scott (1771–1832)

The delicious scent of sweet violet and the appearance soon after winter of its dainty, amethyst-coloured flowers have long made this one of the most treasured English perennials. It is the only native violet with fragrant flowers. From the short, knotty rootstock come tufts of long-stalked, slightly downy, bright green leaves, which are broadly heart-shaped to rounded. From February to May slender flower stalks curve over at the top to carry the nodding, deep violet flowers, sometimes white with a violet spur, up to 2cm/¾in across. Each has the typical pansy 'face' composed of five unequal petals, with a pair on either side and a larger one at the bottom with a long spur holding the nectar. The plant grows up to 20cm/8in high, usually less. The fruit is a rounded, slightly hairy capsule, which remains closed until it falls to the ground and splits into three sections to release small, shiny seeds.

Sweet violet is found in hedgebanks, woodland and scrub, generally on calcareous soils throughout most of lowland England.

Oil from the petals has long been used to make fragrances and flavourings, and both roots and flowers were used in ancient Greece as a sedative and as remedies for a number of ailments.

Bees seeking nectar in the spur land on the 'platform' of the flower's lower lip and as they follow the guide lines on the petals they become dusted with pollen from the stamens, completing pollination when they visit another flower. But in the absence of bee visits, and after spring flowering, the sweet violet has an alternative, economical means of reproduction in the form of budlike, self-fertilizing flowers, which produce abundant seeds. Ants enjoy eating fleshy outgrowths on the seeds and so help dispersal.

Being semi-evergreen, among the first flowers to bloom in early spring and with the added bonus of its scent, sweet violet is a welcome addition to any garden. It will decorate a border, rock garden, container or ground shaded by trees. It grows in sun or shade and moist but well-drained soils (preferably alkaline). The plant spreads by sending out long, creeping runners, which produce new plantlets, and it self-seeds freely. Ripe seed can be grown in a cold frame or the plant may be divided in spring or autumn.

Common Dog-violet
Viola riviniana VIOLACEAE

The snow-drop, and then the violet
Arose from the ground with warm rain wet,
And their breath was mixed with fresh odour, sent
From the turf, like the voice and the instrument.

'And the Spring Arose on the Garden Fair', Percy Bysshe Shelley (1792–1822)

Common dog-violet is usually larger than the sweet violet, but what it gains in size it loses in fragrance, for it is scentless. The leafy perennial grows up to 20cm/8in high with central tufts of long-stalked, usually hairless, heart-shaped leaves with rounded teeth. Where they join the stem there are pairs of lance-shaped stipules fringed with slender teeth. From April to

June long, curving, flowering stalks carry the single, pale blue-violet flowers, each up to 2.5cm/1in across and with a pale patch marked with radiating veins at the base of the lower lip. The backward-pointing spur is pale, never darker than the petals. The three-sided fruit capsule splits to release numerous egg-shaped seeds.

Common dog-violet occurs in deciduous woods, grassland, scrub, on hedgebanks, heaths and rocks (being absent only from the wettest habitats), throughout England from sea-level to 775m/2,540ft in the Lake District. Dwarf forms occur in exposed sites.

The term 'dog' refers to its supposed inferiority compared with sweet violet; the same applies, for example, to dogwood, a tree whose berries are unfit to eat.

Nectar secreted in the flower spur attracts bumble bees, bee-flies and hoverflies. The leaves are the main food of the caterpillars of many species of fritillary butterflies, particularly dark-green and silver-washed.

This is the best native violet for naturalizing in a hedgebank or woodland garden and it can form useful ground cover under shrubs. It is one of the few plants that will tolerate dry shade under lime trees in summer. Dog-violet grows in sun or shade and on most soils, apart from those that are very wet. Stem-tip cuttings can be taken or, more easily, divisions made in spring or late summer, or it can be raised from seed sown in light soil in a cold frame in autumn.

Wild Pansy
Viola tricolor VIOLACEAE

The cheerful, flat-faced flowers of the wild pansy with their varied colouring have for centuries appealed to gardeners, and this annual to short-lived perennial is the forerunner of the modern, cultivated pansy. Its branching stems grow up to about 15cm/6in in height, carrying narrow, elliptical, spoon- or lance-shaped leaves with rounded teeth, long-stalked at the base and short-stalked higher up. At the base of the leaf stalk are large, deeply lobed, leaflike stipules. From April to September the solitary flowers appear on long stalks, differing from other violets by having flatter, broader flowers, each up to 2.5cm/1in across, with the lateral petals angled upwards. As the species name *tricolor* suggests, the flower may be purplish-violet, yellow or whitish, or a combination of all three, but is not often all yellow. All flowers have darker markings at the centre. Annual forms are often blue-violet. The three-angled fruit capsule splits into three parts to release egg-shaped seeds.

Wild pansy is found on cultivated and waste ground, short grassland and occasionally sand dunes, mainly on acid to neutral soils, throughout England, chiefly in the lowlands but ascending to nearly 450m/1,475ft on the Welsh border.

The plant is mainly visited by bumble bees and other long-tongued insects, all directed by a yellow spot in the centre of the flower to the nectar in the spur, giving and receiving pollen in the process.

This viola is a natural candidate for cultivation in gardens, being neat, attractive and colourful. It can be grown at the front of a border, or in a rock garden, raised bed or container. The wild pansy prefers an open, sunny position on well-drained soil that is not too alkaline. The pale blue, yellow or violet perennial form, *V. t.* subsp. *curtisii* – which is native on maritime dunes in the west and on East Anglian heaths – may be preferred in seaside gardens. Wild pansy can be propagated by taking cuttings in late summer and rooting them in a sandy soil in a shaded cold frame. It seeds freely but is quite promiscuous, so if true wild pansies are required they should not be grown near cultivated pansies or the two will hybridize.

RIGHT Wild pansy (*Viola tricolor*) will self-seed to soften the edge of a gravel drive and suits a raised bed or rock garden with well-drained soil.

BELOW Common dog violet (*Viola riviniana*) keeps its leaves over a long period and grows under the shade of a lime tree where little else will.

The densely tufted dwarf sedge (*Carex humilis*) is one of the fashionable grasses in the Cambridge Botanic Garden border. It is also common in short limestone grassland from Dorset to Herefordshire.

Tufted Hair-grass
Deschampsia cespitosa POACEAE

A large plant, this forms dense tufts up to 2m/6½ft high, with stiff stems and wide, ribbed, dark green, sharp-edged leaf blades that are rough to the touch. From June to August the tall flowering stems carry graceful, spreading panicles of a silvery or dull purplish hue.

It is found in wet woods, damp grassland, moorland and marshes throughout England.

Flower arrangers collect the flowering stems for drying.

This is a coarse grass, which is useful in wetter sites with acid soil. Sow seeds as for wavy hair-grass and divide in spring.

Wavy Hair-grass
Deschampsia flexuosa POACEAE

With its airy panicles of delicate flower spikelets on slender stems up to 60cm/24 in high, or even more, wavy hair-grass is one of the most beautiful indigenous grasses. It has narrow, densely tufted leaves, up to 30cm/12in high, and the common name comes from the fine, wavy little branches that hold each spikelet. When in flower in summer, massed groups of this perennial appear as a purplish, brownish or silvery mist.

It is found on moors, heaths and in open woodland, usually in dry places throughout England.

When dried, it is popular with flower arrangers. This grass associates well with flowering plants or shrubs in mixed borders. It likes an open situation and prefers well-drained, sandy or peaty soils, although it will tolerate damp ground. Seeds may be sown *in situ* in late spring; it can also be increased by division in spring.

Common Cottongrass
Eriophorum angustifolium CYPERACEAE

The white, cotton-wool tufted, nodding heads of this perennial grasslike sedge are a striking sight when seen *en masse*. Spreading by creeping rhizomes, it forms clumps of linear, keeled leaves, up to 60cm/24in long, which narrow towards sharp-pointed tips and arch over at one-third to half their height. In May and June the flowering stems carry pendent groups of up to seven, downy white spikelets.

It is found in wet, acid bogs and moors throughout England.

Common cottongrass can make good ground cover on damp soils and is effective in the bog garden or at the margin of a pond. It will grow in shallow water to a depth of about 5cm/2in. It needs sun in order to flower well and, although it prefers acid soils, it will grow in neutral heavy loams as long as there is constant moisture.

Lyme-grass
Leymus (syn. *Elymus*) *arenarius* POACEAE

Gertrude Jekyll admired the glorious, arching, blue-grey leaves of this handsome perennial grass. Sharply pointed, broadly linear, flat or at times inrolled, the leaves grow to about 60cm/24in long from rhizomes that form loose, spreading clumps. From June to August the erect flower spike, up to 2m/6½ft high, bears small, paired blue-grey spikelets, which turn buff-coloured with age.

Lyme-grass is found on dunes round most of the coast of England, where it helps to bind the sand, but is absent from much of the south.

Although this grass is invasive, its beauty makes it worthy of the border if it can be kept in check. In a larger garden it makes strong and attractive ground cover. It needs an open, sunny site and light, well-drained soil. Divide in summer.

Fluffy white seedheads of common cottongrass (*Eriophorum angustifolium*) stretch to the horizon, a striking effect that can be mimicked in the damp soil of a bog garden or pond margin.

Yellow Oat-grass

Trisetum flavescens POACEAE

This elegant, graceful, loosely tufted perennial has a creeping rootstock and sends up smooth, slender stems, up to 80cm/32in in height, with flat, light green leaves that are hairy on the margins. Between May and June, and between August and September, it bears loose panicles with very slender branches, each with roundish, shining yellow spikelets with twisted or bent awns.

It is found in meadows and pastures, especially on chalk.

This grass is not competitive and is useful both for its colour and for its two flowering periods. It makes an ideal meadow grass for calcareous soils. It needs sun and well-drained soils, and is drought-resistant.

FERNS

See you the ferny ride that steals
Into the oak-woods far?
O that was whence they hewed the keels
That rolled to Trafalgar.

'Puck's Song', Rudyard Kipling (1865–1936)

Few foliage plants give as much pleasure as the unfurling fern. Brownish stems with tightly coiled tips, like a bishop's crozier, rise from a dead-looking crown before unfolding to reveal a profusion of feathery green fronds. Once they have fanned open they give the same feeling of lush greenness that they lend to their natural habitat in woodland glades.

Such are the beauty and variety of English native ferns that the Victorians became passionate collectors, scouring the woods for specimens with such efficiency

Yellow oat-grass (*Trisetum flavescens*)

that many species are now rare. The loss of woodland has also reduced the numbers of these primitive plants, so gardens are a welcome refuge. In cultivation ferns provide an interesting green contrast with flowering plants or, better still, they can be grown in a more natural style grouped in a fernery, rock garden or damp, shady border. There they will give a fresh, green display where other plants might struggle. Ferns also stay happily in place for years and need little or no maintenance. They help to form a moist habitat for beetles and other insects.

No one who cares for the countryside would dream of taking a plant from the wild. But gardeners who have friends with good collections of ferns can take advantage of the millions of dustlike spores that cascade from the undersides of the leaves. Ripe spores can be collected by putting pieces of fertile frond into a dry plastic or paper bag. As they dry the spores will be released into the bag.

Ferns are easy to raise, and there are interesting varieties of form, even within a single species. Sprinkle the spores on to a box or tray containing several centimetres/a few inches of seed compost or a mixture of sand and potting compost, then keep warm (not hot) and just moist. Soon the surface will turn green and a magnifying glass will reveal masses of minute, heart-shaped plates known as prothalli. Male gametes swim to the female organs to achieve fertilization and the fern then develops on the prothallus. When the tiny ferns have two or three fronds they should be transferred to a mixture of leaf mould and coarse sand and grown on before planting out. Never plant out ferns in full sun. The base of a wall or hedge is a good site, provided there is room for the fern to spread its roots.

For most ferns, damp, shady conditions are essential for they dislike wind and cannot withstand drought. They can be highly attractive when mixed with white-flowered plants, such as sweet woodruff and wild strawberry, and with shade-lovers, such as solomon's seal and lily-of-the-valley.

The following is a selection of garden-worthy English ferns.

Black spleenwort
Asplenium adiantum-nigrum   ASPLENIACEAE

Black spleenwort is a wintergreen tufted perennial with glossy, leathery, dark green leaves and a short rhizome covered with dark brown scales. The length of the fronds varies from 5 to 50cm/2 to 20in, depending on whether it is growing on stony ground or rich leaf mould. The long, blackish leaf stalk is scaly at the base and the two- or three-pinnate blade has up to fifteen pairs of alternate, triangular pinnae, or leaflets, decreasing in size towards the tip. Oblong sporangia (the spore-producing bodies) cover most of the lateral veins, giving the appearance of a rusty mass, and the spores ripen from June to October.

Black Spleenwort is found in rocky places in woods and on banks and walls throughout England.

This is a fern for the rock garden or for the crevices of a damp stone wall.

Maidenhair Spleenwort
Asplenium trichomanes   ASPLENIACEAE

This is an attractive wintergreen perennial with dense, rosette-like tufts of lance-shaped pinnate leaves composed of fifteen to forty deep green, elliptical pinnae on either side of glossy, blackish stems. It has a short, creeping or erect rhizome covered in dark, narrow scales and the fronds grow up to 20cm/8in long. The oblong or linear sporangia are found on the upper vein branches on the leaf underside. Spores ripen from August to November.

This fern is found in old walls and rock surfaces, mainly on limestone or basic rocks, throughout England, although more common in the west and north.

Maidenhair spleenwort is ideal for vertical or sloping crevices in the rock garden, in a stone wall or in an alpine trough. It needs moist but well-drained soil and is very frost-hardy.

Lady-fern

Athyrium filix-femina ATHYRIACEAE

The graceful, deciduous lady fern grows up to 1m/3½ft high and can look like a miniature version of the exotic tree-fern. The crown of the short, stout, trunklike rhizome is often up to 20cm/8in above the ground and from it spring numerous spreading, pale green filigree fronds with drooping tips. The leaf stalk is reddish, while the leaf axis is green or purplish with scattered scales, bearing a two-pinnate blade with delicate, pointed, deeply toothed pinnae. The conspicuous, elongated J- or C-shaped sporangia are in rows nearer the midrib, and the spores ripen from August to November. It dies back from December to April.

It is found in damp woods and marshes, and on hedgebanks, hillsides and screes throughout England.

This is a useful fern for moist shade, in a border, woodland corner or a shady pond margin.

Male-fern

Dryopteris filix-mas DRYOPTERIDACEAE

More upright and robust in appearance than the feathery lady-fern, the deciduous male-fern grows from a stout, erect rhizome up to 1.2m/4ft in height. The pale brown leaf stalk carries a

broad, mid-green, tapering, pinnate blade with between twenty and thirty-five deeply divided pinnae on each side. About five or six sporangia form rows on each lobe, and the spores ripen from August to November. It dies back in autumn.

The male-fern is commonly found in woods, ditches and on hedgebanks throughout England.

This is a vigorous plant, which can transform the barren areas at the shady base of a wall or hedge; it also looks good in a flower border or among trees, particularly against the silver trunks of birch. It grows in the open or in shade and, unlike other ferns, it flourishes on light, sandy soil and tolerates drier conditions.

Royal Fern

Osmunda regalis OSMUNDACEAE

As its name suggests, this is a truly majestic slow-growing perennial, with clumps of large, striking, bright green sterile fronds (up to 1m/3½ft) and dramatic spires of rust-brown, fertile fronds (up to 2m/6½ft) in summer. The short rhizomes form raised clumps, which in early summer send up sturdy, scale-free, tightly curled stems that unfold to a smooth, pale green. The two-pinnate leaves have up to fifteen pairs of oblong pinnae, the lower ones on the central leaves and the broad outer leaves being sterile. The fertile parts grow at the apex of the central leaves. These look like flowerheads when the sporangia ripen from pale green to orange-brown between June and August.

The royal fern is found in moist woodland, fens, bogs and heaths, and beside lakes, ditches and other water courses, locally throughout England, but it is rare in the east and near populated areas, where collectors have taken it from the wild.

This magnificent fern is an asset to any garden and looks dramatic when grown at the edge of a pond. However, it can equally well be grown in a shady border as long as the soil is moist (preferably peaty) and there is room for its bushy habit. It may be grown in acid or alkaline soils.

LEFT Displaying its fanned, deep-green fronds against grey stone, the maidenhair spleenwort (*Asplenium trichomanes*) is perfect for softening hard rock surfaces. It withstands heavy frosts.

RIGHT Massed male ferns (*Dryopteris filix-mas*) intermingled with other shade loving species flourish in a damp area of a garden in south-east England, originally planted by Gertrude Jekyll.

114

Hart's-tongue *(Phyllitis scolopendrium)*

Polypody *(Polypodium vulgare)*

Royal fern (*Osmunda regalis*)

Hart's-tongue

Phyllitis scolopendrium ASPLENIACEAE

With its wavy-edged, strap-shaped, brilliant green leaves, the evergreen hart's-tongue is a familiar fern in gardens. Its stout rhizome is clothed in brown scales and produces dense tufts of leaves; each of these has a short, scaly, brownish stalk and a narrow, undivided blade, up to 6cm/2½in wide and 60cm/24in long, although often much shorter and heart-shaped at the base and tapering to a curled-over tip. Distinctive diagonal rows of linear spore-producing bodies on the veins of the leaf-underside cover half the blade width, and the spores ripen from August to March.

It is found in old walls, on mossy woodland rocks and banks throughout England, mainly on alkaline ground in wetter areas.

Hart's-tongue is a particularly useful garden fern because it tolerates drier conditions than most and grows on calcareous soils. It can be grown in the rock garden, in the crevices of a stone wall, in a woodland corner or grouped with other ferns in a damp, shady border.

Polypody

Polypodium vulgare POLYPODIACEAE

The slightly leathery, dark green, pinnate leaves of this evergreen fern are usually narrowly oblong, tapering to a point and varying in length, but usually up to about 25cm/10in long. They rise from a rhizome either on or just below the surface and have between twelve and thirty lance-shaped pinnae on each side, the upper ones having two rows of large, round sporangia on the underside. These are yellow at first, turning orange-brown in autumn.

Polypody is found on banks, walls, rocks and in woodland, often on acid soils, throughout England.

As long as the persistent dead leaves are removed, this fern ensures year-round greenness in the rock garden or in the border, where it can be used as ground cover. It forms dense clumps in an open site and is one of the most acid-tolerant species.

Soft shield-fern

Polystichum setiferum DRYOPTERIDACEAE

A 'shuttlecock' crown distinguishes this elegant evergreen fern, whose tufts of soft young, two-pinnate fronds uncoil from a short, scaly rhizome and grow up to 1m/3½ft or more in length. The short-stalked lobes of the toothed pinnae are angled at the base, and the round or kidney-shaped sporangia are found on the leaf-underside.

Soft shield-fern is found in moist woods and hedgebanks, mainly in south and west England.

This is a highly attractive slow-growing fern for the rock garden or border. It needs shade, and will grow even in deep shade, preferring rich, well-drained soil.

Trees, Shrubs and Climbers

And groups under the dreaming garden-trees,
And the full moon and the white evening star.

'Thyrsis', Matthew Arnold (1822–88)

Trees and shrubs form the bones of a garden, providing structure and height and defining its shape and overall appearance. It is the trees and shrubs rather than the fleshing out with herbaceous flowers that, however large or small – and whether there be just one or several dozen – will set the tone throughout the year. They provide fixed points, either in full leaf or as attractive, dark skeletons in winter, and they create living screens against prying eyes, traffic noise and, up to a point, pollution. Trees in particular have a long-lasting impact on the garden and they need to be selected and sited with care. To a certain extent they will dictate the growing conditions for other plants: providing shelter from the wind, casting varying degrees of shade and taking water from the ground.

When planting young trees, people sometimes forget to calculate their ultimate size and put them too close together. Placing large forest trees too near a house can lead to trouble, for in a drought the roots may damage foundations in their search for water. So in small gardens it is sensible to use smaller trees. The rowan and even its larger relatives, the common whitebeam and wild service tree are easy to manage in gardens, as are the crab apple and holly, plus the smaller-growing spindle, juniper,

Beauty and privacy in this tranquil glade are created by the shade of an aged lime tree and the massed green and white native umbellifers and ivy.

119

hawthorn, elder and hazel. The field maple is also modest in growth, has autumnal tints and makes a good hedge.

On an exposed or new site gardeners often want quick-growing trees. Willows and alders grow fast on moist soils, but willows can be competitive with other plants and are easily damaged by wind. Although both willows and alders become large trees, the former happily tolerate cutting back by pollarding or coppicing. This also provides a useful supply of garden sticks, which can be used for stakes, but strip the bark off first so that they do not grow! For a drier, sunny site the silver birch is hard to beat as a fast-growing ornamental.

Climbing plants such as ivy and traveller's joy are extremely versatile, making good cover for walls and fences, trellis work, pergolas and sheds. Especially useful in smaller gardens, climbers take up little root space and allow other plants or container-grown flowers to be positioned at their base.

In the wild or in the garden, each species of native tree or shrub is host to its own array of animal life. Exotic species, on the other hand, may be appealing to human beings but often offer little to the indigenous wildlife. Take the London plane, for instance, which is a fine city tree but a great disappointment to birds, because it does not support the insects on which they rely for protein, especially to feed their young. Sixty different species of conifers are widely grown in England, yet only two – yew and juniper – are indigenous, forming a tiny percentage of the total number in cultivation. Unfortunately, forests of introduced conifers are relative biological deserts compared with the deciduous woods they replaced.

In contrast, one oak tree sustains over 284 insect species, as well as numerous birds and mammals – even the bark nourishes a flora of mosses, liverworts and lichens. Goat willow is not far behind, maintaining

well over 200 different species. The following table shows the numbers of insect species associated with native trees in Britain:

Oak (*Quercus*)	284
Willow (*Salix*)	266
Birch (*Betula*)	229
Hawthorn (*Crataegus*)	149
Blackthorn (*Prunus*)	109
Pine (*Pinus sylvestris*)	91
Alder (*Alnus*)	90
Elm (*Ulmus*)	82
Hazel (*Corylus*)	73
Beech (*Fagus*)	64
Ash (*Fraxinus*)	41
Lime (*Tilia*)	31
Hornbeam (*Carpinus*)	28

Apart from their beauty and their obvious compatibility with the English climate and soil, there is sound reason for growing native trees in order to nurture a rich diversity of floral and animal life.

Field Maple

Acer campestre ACERACEAE

For who would rob a hermit of his weeds,
His few books, as his beads, or Maple dish,
Or do his grey hairs any violence?

Comus, John Milton (1608–74)

The only native maple, this is a picturesque deciduous tree with rugged bark and the brightest autumn foliage of any English tree, the dark green leaves turning from shades of deep golden-yellow to amber. Although capable of reaching 26m/85ft, it is slow-growing and seldom attains much more than 10–15m/33–50ft. The young branches are green at first but later become light brown, and the old branches develop corky wings. The pale, greyish trunk is initially smooth before developing shallow fissures, while the opposite leaves, 5–15cm/2–6in long, are often rose-tinted as they unfurl and have three to five blunt lobes. They are downy underneath, at least on the veins. Upright clusters of a few small, pale greenish-yellow flowers, each with five petals, appear in April and May. Male and female flowers are found on the same tree and the latter develop pairs of seeds, with wings similar to those of its close relative, the sycamore. Field maple wings differ in that they lie in a straight line and are often pink tinged.

The field maple (*Acer campestre*) seen here in flower.

Field maple is found in hedgerows and mixed woodland, mainly on chalk and limestone, in south and east England.

The flowers attract small, pollinating insects, while the leaves produce a honeydew on which hairstreak butterflies may feed. The leaves are the food plant of the maple prominent moth and of sycamore moth caterpillars, and they can become infested by gall-mites or leaf-miners. Tiny red bumps, smaller than a pinhead, on the leaves are caused by insects making a nest for their young.

Its attractive, round-headed shape and interesting bark make the field maple an ideal feature tree. Although it grows fairly quickly at first, it slows down once it is established and may take fifty years to reach maturity. It can also be grown as part of a hedge, as it clips well. It is easily raised from seed, best gathered in the autumn and sown immediately in nursery rows, because germination falls off rapidly if they are stored. After two or three years and thinning out, seedlings can be planted in their permanent sites between October and March.

Silver Birch

Betula pendula BETULACEAE

But now, to form a shade
For Thee, green alders have together wound
Their foliage; ashes flung their arms around;
And birch-trees risen in silver colonnade.

The River Duddon, William Wordsworth (1770–1850)

With its beautiful silvery-white bark, its pendulous branches and its delicate, fresh-looking foliage, this deciduous tree is probably England's most graceful, described by the American poet James Russell Lowell (1819–91) in 'An Indian-Summer Reverie' as 'The birch, most shy and ladylike of trees'. It grows quickly and easily and is a common pioneer of dry soils, reaching a height of around 15m/50ft in twenty years, although within fifty to sixty years some can grow to about 30m/100ft. When young it has shiny reddish-brown bark and erect branches, but with age the bark becomes silver-white and peeling, with black, rough-textured, irregularly shaped patches, and the drooping shoots that justify its Latin name. The slender, whippy juvenile branches are covered in tiny, pale warts but are otherwise hairless. In early spring the scaly winter buds fill out, giving the whole tree a purplish sheen before the light green, hairless leaves unfold on slender stalks in May,

developing into a triangular shape, up to 4cm/1½in long, with a sharp point at the tip and a double-toothed margin. The leaves turn bright yellow before falling in late autumn. Both male and female catkins open on the same tree in April. The yellow male catkins have reddish-brown scales and droop like lambs' tails; once they have shed their clouds of yellow pollen they wither and fall. The smaller, erect female catkins are composed of overlapping green scales and appear with the leaves, ripening and enlarging in summer before breaking up in autumn to release copious quantities of small, winged seeds.

Silver birch grows in woodland and on heathland throughout England but is rarer in the west. It ascends to 550m/1,800ft in the Lake District and prefers dry, acid soils in the open, unshaded by other trees.

Trees in England are not used commercially for timber, but the twigs are cut to make garden brooms.

This is one of the most valuable trees for wildlife, supporting almost 230 species of insects including buff-tip, chevron and pale prominent moths, and the gregarious larvae of the sawfly. Caterpillars that are supported by birch act as a food source for spiders, mites, beetles, bugs, wasps, ants, earwigs, reptiles, amphibians, birds including blue tits, and mammals, including mice and shrews. Pollen is collected by bees in spring and the autumn seeds are an important source of food for a variety of birds, including tits, goldfinches, siskins and redpolls. Birch can support large colonies of aphids, which in turn attract other insects, especially ladybirds.

The fallen leaves also rot quickly to make excellent leaf mould, rapidly giving cover for invertebrates.

The silver birch is a lovely garden tree, giving pleasure throughout the year, from the catkins and the opening of fresh green leaves to its fine silhouette and silvery bark in winter. It can be grown as a single specimen or, if there is space, in a group – the foliage giving light, dappled shade, which allows spring flowers to flourish underneath. It will grow in most well-drained soils in an open position, although on poor, sandy soils its roots can become invasive. Aphid infestation may be a problem, resulting in dripping honeydew, and silver birch also sheds bud-scales, catkins, twigs and seeds, which can be a nuisance. It is easily raised from seed, which can be sown as soon as it ripens in early autumn, then kept moist. Young plants can be grown in beds, as they transplant fairly readily from November to early March.

Hornbeam
Carpinus betulus BETULACEAE

One of the most striking features of the hornbeam is its deeply fluted trunk and smooth, grey bark, which often shines like steel. A slow-growing deciduous tree, it reaches up to 30m/100ft in height but may take 100 years to do so. The ascending branches form a rounded crown and the alternate, oval leaves are similar to those of beech but slightly narrower and longer, 8–10cm/3–4in in length, with double-toothed margins and nine to fifteen pairs of more prominent veins. They are dark green above and paler below and less shiny than beech leaves; they turn yellow and gold in autumn. The minute green flowers are arranged in pendulous, unisexual catkins and appear in April before the leaves have unfurled. The yellowish males with orange anthers are 1.5–5cm/⅝–2in long, a little longer than the leafy-looking green female catkins with narrow, curved-back bracts and red styles. The latter elongate up to 14cm/5½in after fertilization and are composed of clusters of small, ribbed nutlets, each attached to a trilobed 'wing' for wind dispersal.

LEFT The catkin-like flower of silver birch (*Betula pendula*)

OPPOSITE With its silvery bark and lacy, light-green foliage, the 'lady of the woods' (*Betula pendula*) creates a light, dappled shade which is perfect for growing other woodland plants.

The pendulous catkins of hornbeam (*Carpinus betulus*)

The quiet beauty of the dogwood (*Cornus sanguinea*)

Nut clusters of hazel (*Corylus avellana*)

Hornbeam is found in oak or mixed woods, often showing signs of having been coppiced or pollarded. It is a lowland species, native only south of a line from the Wash to the Bristol Channel, and grows well on heavy clays, which is why pollarded hornbeams were a feature of woods on London clay in Middlesex, Hertfordshire and Essex.

The leaves are host to several different miners and the larvae of small moths, including the copper underwing caterpillars and nut-tree tussock caterpillars. The seeds are a staple food of hawfinches in autumn and winter. Like birch, hornbeam is often covered in 'witches-brooms' caused by a small fungus, *Tephrina carpini*.

Hornbeam makes an excellent hedging plant which, when cut, keeps its leaves throughout the winter. As a specimen tree it is attractive and trouble-free, hardier than beech and with leaves that will withstand late spring frosts and provide autumn tints. In a smaller garden it can be controlled by coppicing or pollarding. It grows on clay or lighter soils but not those that are sandy and acid. It is raised from seed gathered and sown in the autumn, which will germinate the following spring. After two or three years seedlings should be planted in position from October to March.

Traveller's-joy or Old Man's Beard
Clematis vitalba RANUNCULACEAE

The cuckoo shouts all day at nothing
In leafy dells alone;
And traveller's joy beguiles in autumn
Last Poems, A. E. Housman (1859–1936)

This sweet-scented, woody climber is a vigorous perennial, which in the wild can develop twisted, jungle-like, trailing stems as thick as a man's wrist. Covered with stringy bark, these stems can grow up to 30m/100ft in length. From late April they carry compound leaves of three to five pairs of well-spaced, oval, pointed leaflets, each 3–10cm/1¼–4in long, with lobed margins. When the stalks of the leaflets feel the pressure of a neighbouring plant they twine around it, using it as a climbing aid. In July and August fragrant clusters of greenish-white, four-sepalled flowers appear, each 2cm/¾in wide and with masses of stamens round the central group of long, hairy styles. These become the glorious, whitish, fluffy fruiting heads that often last until late winter and give the vine its other common name, old man's beard. The long, feathery plume on each seed helps wind dispersal.

Traveller's-joy is found in hedgerows, woodland and scrub, usually on alkaline soils with a pH above 6.0, in the lowlands south of a line joining the Humber and Dee estuaries.

The pollen-rich flowers are visited by numerous insects, including hoverflies and bees, both for pollen and for the nectar at the base of the filaments. The leaves are food for the caterpillars of species of tortricoid moths. The whole plant provides cover for nesting birds and food for insectivores such as birds, shrews, frogs, bats and other small mammals.

This climber can be grown through hedges, along fences or as a covering for a dead tree. But take care that it does not smother young plants or get a grip in open ground, where it will quickly take over. It grows in sun or semi-shade and prefers alkaline soil. It is propagated by taking inter-nodal cuttings in summer, or from ripe seed sown in late autumn and potted out in spring. Seedlings can be planted out the following autumn or spring.

Dogwood
Cornus sanguinea CORNACEAE

With its tall, slender, deep crimson-tinted stems, dogwood lends a vivid splash of colour to the late season and winter scene. Growing up to 5m/16½ft in height, this deciduous shrub has opposite ovate, hairy but smooth edged, short-stalked leaves, 4–8cm/1½–3in long, with three or four pairs of curving veins running from base to tip. The leaves turn from green to a glorious wine colour before falling in October. Flat-topped clusters, up to 5cm/2in across, of small, creamy-white flowers appear in June and July, each with four petals and minute sepals. The black, pea-sized fruits that ripen in September each contain two stones.

Dogwood occurs in hedgerows, scrub and on woodland margins on calcareous soils throughout lowland England, north as far as Durham and south Cumbria.

The flowers have a strong smell, unpleasant to humans but attractive to many pollinating insects. The young leaves provide food for green hairstreak and holly blue caterpillars, while the fruits are eaten – and the seeds spread – by birds.

Dogwood grows fairly quickly and makes a very useful hedging plant, or it can be planted at the back of a large border or fringing a pond where its winter colour will have maximum

impact. The shoots will remain dark red throughout the winter if the plant is trimmed each year. It grows in sun or semi-shade and tolerates a wide range of soils, including those that are cold and wet. Its only disadvantage in gardens is that it suckers readily and may spread into open ground unless checked. But this also makes for easy propagation by taking these suckers and growing them on. A better, though less easy, way is to gather the ripe berries in autumn, stratify them until early spring, then sow them thickly in nursery beds (only 40 per cent will germinate) before planting out in two to three years' time.

Hazel
Corylus avellana BETULACEAE

The shrubby hazel, with its mass of grey-brown twigs and soft green leaves, is the only native tree to produce edible nuts. Hazel usually forms a multi-stemmed deciduous shrub up to 5m/16½ft in height, although as a tree it can reach up to 10m/33ft. The shiny, often mottled, brown bark has light-coloured horizontal pores and can be almost silver-grey on stouter stems, while the alternate, hairy leaves are broad and roundish with double-toothed margins and a short, pointed tip. At any time from January onwards the small, grey-green cylinders of over 100 tiny, clustered male flowers open into the familiar yellow, pollen-filled, 'lambs' tails' catkins up to 8cm/3in long. The female flowers ripen a little later and are far less conspicuous, looking like brown buds with a little crown of bright red stamens. The smooth, rounded, hard-shelled hazel nuts usually occur in groups of one to four, held in leafy, ragged-edged cups of pale green bracts, ripening from green to brown in the autumn and enclosing a sweet-tasting, white kernel.

Hazel is found in hedgerows, woodland and scrub throughout England on a wide range of soils (although not the more acid), and up to 500m/1,640ft in Yorkshire.

It was once a vital part of the rural economy, grown for an astonishingly wide range of uses – from house building, fences and sheep hurdles to basketwork, artists' charcoal and dowsing rods. Hazel twigs can still be extremely useful in the garden, making a natural-looking climbing aid for peas and beans and for climbers or slender-stemmed plants in the border.

Hazel is host to over seventy insect species, its clouds of pollen in early spring providing a feast for foraging bees. The nuts attract the attentions of the long-snouted nut weevil and are collected by squirrels and fieldmice long before they are fully ripe, so owners must be alert and pick early.

This is an attractive and amenable plant for the garden, grown in a shrub border, in a mixed hedge or flanking a path to create a nut walk. The golden catkins are cheering in winter and the leaves turn pale yellow in autumn, often lasting on the tree until late November. Hazel associates well with spring flowers, such as primroses and bluebells. Coppicing every seven years or so will produce straight stems, and hedging hazel can be cut to shape, but for a harvest of hazel nuts it must be left unpruned or just lightly pruned in winter and again in spring when the flowers are visible. It grows in sun or shade, in moist or dry soil and is useful on chalky soils.

Hazel can be propagated by layering or by removing and planting suckers in autumn. It can also be raised from ripe seed sown in a rodent-proof seedbed.

Hawthorn
Crataegus monogyna ROSACEAE

Furth goth all the Courte, both most and lest,
To fetche the flouris freshe, and braunche and blome,
And namely hauthorne brought both page and grome,
With freshe garlandis partly blew and white,
And then rejoisin in their grete delight.

'Court of Love', Geoffrey Chaucer (c. 1345–1400)

May is the common alternative name for hawthorn, and May is indeed the month when this tough deciduous shrub or tree is seen at its glorious best, its dense mass of tangled branches and deeply cut green leaves covered with a mantle of sweet-smelling white blossom. Hawthorn varies greatly in size, but when left uncut it usually becomes a small, rounded tree about 6m/20ft tall, although it can grow to 15m/50ft in height. When young, the bark on the irregular-shaped trunk is smooth greenish-grey or greenish-brown, but when mature the trunk often develops distinct flutes and the bark becomes rough, slightly flaking and a darker, reddish-grey. The zigzag shoots are covered with short spines. In early April the young, bright green leaves unfurl, each becoming dark green above and paler below, up to 5cm/2in long, more or less oval in shape and divided into three to seven lobes, mostly cut more than two-thirds of the way to the midrib. The showy, five-petalled, aromatic, white flowers up to 1.5cm/½in across are carried in flattish clusters, each with up to twenty pink anthers and a single style. The glossy, fleshy, single-seeded fruits, or haws, turn dark-red in the autumn.

Hawthorn is common in hedgerows, woodland margins and scrub throughout England on all but the poorest soils, up to about 500m/1,640ft.

This is one of the most important shrubs for wildlife, providing food for almost 150 insect species, including Duke of Burgundy butterflies, yellow-tail moths, hawthorn shield-bugs and nectar-feeding flies, while the larvae of the small eggar form communes in webs on its leaves. Other insect visitors include beetles, leaf-hoppers and sawflies. The flowers of this ecologically important tree have a smell that is particularly attractive to flies, beetles and some other insects, but less so to butterflies and bees. Some modern cultivars with double flowers have no nectar. The nutlets in the fruit provide winter food for over twenty-three species of birds. From October onwards, the migratory fieldfares, redwings and waxwings arrive and feast on them when not challenged by blackbirds and thrushes. Haws are also important food for woodmice and other small mammals. The dense tangle of thorns provides a safe nesting site for smaller birds.

When clipped and laid, hawthorn was traditionally used to make thorny, stock-proof fences and it can equally make an effective, intruder-proof garden hedge with dark, tangled branches that are attractive in winter. It can also make an appealing specimen tree with year-round interest, and can even be grown in a tub where it takes on an almost oriental, bonsai look. Hawthorn is extremely hardy and may be trimmed at almost any time, although after flowering or autumn are best for hedge trims. It is hardy enough for polluted town gardens, or for exposed inland or coastal gardens. It grows in sun or semi-shade (not in dense shade), and is tolerant of all but the poorest acid soils. It can be raised from seed gathered from the berries in October and sown in a peat substitute/sand mixture in a cold frame in spring. Most seeds take eighteen months to germinate. After one or two years the young trees can be set out in their permanent sites from October to March.

Midland Hawthorn
Crataegus laevigata ROSACEAE

The Midland hawthorn, which is closely related to the common hawthorn, differs in having less thorny stems, leaves with shallow lobes reaching less than halfway to the midrib,

ABOVE With its mantle of sweet-smelling blossom, the hawthorn (*Crataegus monogyna*) lifts the spirits in early summer.

RIGHT Glossy red 'haws', the hawthorn fruit, are an important source of winter food for birds and small mammals.

two styles per flower and two seeds per fruit. It is suitable for heavy soils in south-east and central England and is more successful in shade than common hawthorn.

Broom

Cytisus scoparius FABACEAE

Broom bursts forth in late spring with a bright splash of deep yellow, pea-like flowers held on slender, arching green stems.

An erect, deciduous shrub growing up to 2m/6½ft tall, it has wiry, hairless, five-angled green stems, which bear short-lived leaves, the lower with three leaflets and the upper with one. In May and June it produces a mass of golden flowers, each about 2cm/¾in long and borne singly or in pairs on slender stalks. The black-brown pods ripen by September and noisily explode open to eject the seeds, the two halves coiling up after splitting.

Broom is widespread on light, sandy, acid heaths, scrub and woodland margins throughout England, reaching about 450m/1,475ft in the Lake District.

It produces no nectar but the flowers have a trigger mechanism that sprays pollen on to visiting bees. The leaves are fed on by the caterpillars of green hairstreak butterflies and brocade moths, while the pods are host to a two-winged gall-midge. Ants are attracted to the seeds and help distribute them.

This is a plant for the shrub border, where its cheerful flowers will light up the late spring foliage, or for a gravel bed. It dislikes shade and thrives best in full sun on free-draining, preferably acid, soil. Broom may not survive a very cold winter. It can be raised from seed collected from ripe pods, then sown in spring in a cold frame or greenhouse. Germination, however, may be erratic. In areas where it grows easily, seeds can be sown straight into the ground, but because broom does not transplant easily the young plants must be thinned out before they reach about 30cm/12in. Softwood cuttings can be successful. The shrub is fairly short-lived and after a few years the older branches die back, some falling to the ground and rooting. As young plants develop quickly, making good-sized specimens within five years, it is better to replace old, leggy plants with new ones.

Spurge-laurel
Daphne laureola THYMELAEACEAE

The impressive, broadly spear-shaped leaves of the evergreen spurge-laurel are almost exotic in appearance, with their deep green glossiness and slightly leathery texture. A little like smaller versions of those of the true laurel, *Laurus* (hence the common name), they are 4–11cm/1½–4½in long, splaying out from the top of upright branches; these are usually bare below

Blazing yellow sprays of broom flowers (*Cytisus scoparius*) light up late spring days, as if to prove that this short-lived shrub is well worth propagating. It prefers light soil and dry conditions.

and reach up to 1m/3½ft in height. From February to April the axils of the upper leaves are decorated with clusters of five to ten bright yellow-green flowers that are fragrant in mild, moist conditions. Each tubular flower has four pointed, wide-open lobes. The berries that develop turn from green to black as they ripen in late summer. The shiny, black, egg-shaped fruits each contain one hard seed.

Spurge-laurel is widespread in beech and other open, mixed woods and along woodland margins on calcareous soils throughout England, but is rarer in the west.

Beware: the seeds and berries are highly poisonous.

The sweet-scented flowers attract pollinating moths and humble bees, while the berries, though deadly poisonous to people, are relished by birds such as greenfinches.

Spurge-laurel is one of the most desirable native evergreen shrubs for an open bed or border, providing year-round interest with its bright, early flowers and attractive berries. It flourishes in sun or semi-shade and prefers alkaline soils, although in cultivation it will tolerate acid soils. Keep the plant away from paths, because it does not regenerate easily if it is damaged. It is best propagated by taking cuttings with a heel in late summer, potting them up and growing them on in a sheltered, shady spot, before planting out in the second autumn or the following spring. It may also be raised from seed, but germination is erratic and only a few seedlings may appear. These can be potted singly and grown on in the same way as rooted cuttings.

Bell Heather
Erica cinerea ERICACEAE

Delightful little bright reddish-purple, bell-shaped flowers smother the crown of this compact, evergreen shrub from summer right through autumn. Its numerous erect, branching stems grow up to 60cm/24in high and carry tiny, shiny, dark green linear leaves with rolled-back margins, grouped in whorls of three. From July to the end of September the racemes of flowers, each up to 6mm/¼in long, appear at the ends of the stems. The insignificant seed capsules ripen in autumn inside the dry, dead flowers.

Bell heather thrives only on acid soils with a pH below 6.5, and is found on dry lowland heaths and moors up to 600m/1,970ft in North Yorkshire, but is absent from large areas of the Midlands.

The nectar-filled flowers attract solitary wasps, but if the flowers are too narrow for their heads, they bore in from the side and bypass the pollination mechanism. Bell heather is the food plant of true lover's knot, one of England's most common moorland moths. The low-growing mounds protect ground-feeding birds such as wrens and are less prone to grazing by rabbits than common heather.

With its tight, neat habit and long flowering season, this small evergreen shrub is excellent as ground cover or for forming mounds in the rock garden or a raised bed. It prefers full sun in an open position, but will grow in semi-shade, and it must have free-draining, acid soil. Bell heather is drought-tolerant and thrives in dry conditions. It is easily propagated by layering or from small stem tip cuttings taken in late summer from the current year's growth. Once rooted, these can be set out in a nursery bed the following spring. It is more difficult to raise the plant from seed, because the dead flowers must be dried and rubbed through a fine sieve to extract the seeds before sowing in spring in a greenhouse or cold frame. Different colour forms may be available in garden centres, but beware of sterile cultivars.

Spindle
Euonymus europaeus CELASTRACEAE

Spindle can be a small tree or a large shrub, but either way this pretty deciduous native reaches its spectacular climax in autumn when it becomes ablaze with yellow, russet and red leaves and vivid pink seedpods. Generally growing to a maximum height of about 4m/13ft, it can be recognized by its younger twigs, which are green and distinctly square in cross-section, developing brown, corky ribs along the angles. Older stems become round, with smooth, grey-brown bark. The bluish-green opposite leaves are 3–8cm/1¼–3in long, elliptical or lance-shaped with a pointed tip and finely toothed margin, and from the leaf axils in May come loose clusters of small, four-petalled, greenish-white flowers. By October the female flowers have developed into decorative, four-lobed, deep pink seedpods, which later split open to expose four bright orange arils, each containing a hard white seed.

Spindle occurs in woods and scrub, mainly on calcareous soils, in most of lowland England, but is only occasionally found north of a line joining the estuaries of the Humber and Dee.

Beware: the seeds are poisonous.

Spindle is pollinated by St Mark's flies, which are attracted to the nectar, and the leaves are food for holly blue caterpillars. The fruits provide winter food for birds.

Grown as a specimen tree, as a shrub or in hedge form, this is a rewarding garden plant, easy to grow, not over-large and providing attractive foliage and wonderful autumn colour. It thrives in sun or light shade and most soils, although it prefers lime-rich soils. It can be propagated from seed sown as soon as it is ripe and kept in a cold frame until germination in the second year. Hardwood cuttings may be rooted in autumn.

Alder Buckthorn

Frangula alnus RHAMNACEAE

Alder buckthorn is a charming, slow-growing deciduous shrub that gives a good show of colour in autumn, with yellow leaves and violet-black berries. Despite its name it is actually thornless, its dark grey-brown, ascending branches reaching up to 5m/16½ft in height and bearing hairy brown buds in winter. Shiny oval leaves, 2–7cm/¾–3in long, with parallel veins and untoothed margins, appear in April, followed later by inconspicuous five-petalled, greenish flowers borne in small clusters at the base of the leaf stalk. The two- to three-seeded egg-shaped fruits develop in summer, turning from green through red to black when they are fully ripe in autumn.

Alder buckthorn is found in open woods, scrub and bogs on damp and acid soils throughout most of lowland England, though it is absent from the north-east.

Growing alder buckthorn south of Yorkshire attracts the beautiful yellow brimstone butterfly, because (after buckthorn) this is its main food plant. A tortricoid moth caterpillar lives on the berries in summer, and in winter the black fruits are a valuable source of food for wintering birds. The seeds are stored and eaten by fieldmice.

This can be a useful hedge plant, or it can be grown singly or in groups in a shrubbery. It grows rapidly after coppicing or cutting back and likes moist, but not waterlogged, soils. Alder buckthorn will not tolerate drought or a very exposed site. It is best propagated from seeds gathered in autumn, stratified, then sown in early spring, thinned in autumn and grown on before planting out in a permanent site two years later. Alternatively, semi-ripe cuttings with a heel can be taken in late summer or hardwood cuttings in autumn. Young plants must not be allowed to dry out.

Ivy

Hedera helix ARALIACEAE

And in the warm hedge grew lush eglantine,
Green cowbind and the moonlight-coloured may,
And cherry-blossoms, and white cups, whose wine
Was the bright dew, yet drained not by the day;
And wild roses, and ivy Serpentine,
With its dark buds and leaves, wandering astray;
And flowers azure, black, and streaked with gold,
Fairer than any wakened eyes behold ...
'The Question', Percy Bysshe Shelley (1792–1822)

Ivy, with its glistening, deep green leaves, is our most versatile and vigorous evergreen climber, so ready to scale walls and clothe shady corners that it is treated with scant respect and often cast out in favour of more exotic and tender plants. Yet it will flourish where little else will grow. Its woody stems almost bond themselves to stones and trunks and can climb up to 30m/100ft, but if there is no support for the masses of short rootlets along the stem it will scramble along the ground instead. The glossy stem leaves are 4–10cm/1½–4in across with three to five distinct, triangular lobes and often lighter veins; the flowering shoots that appear when the plant reaches the light, such as at the top of a wall, bear uncut oval or wedge-shaped leaves. From September to November ivy produces attractive yellowish-green, globular, stalked heads of tiny, five-petalled flowers, each 6–8mm/⅜–¼in across with five prominent stamens, which by late spring the following year ripen into clusters of leathery black berries, each containing up to five whitish seeds.

Ivy is found in woodlands and hedges, on banks, rocks and walls, on nearly all types of soil except the most acid and waterlogged, throughout England up to altitudes of about 500m/1,640ft.

Once it has gained height and thickness, ivy is wonderful for wildlife. The dense cover that it creates on trees and walls is invaluable for birds as a nest-site in summer and as shelter in winter. The holly blue butterfly lays its second brood on the flower buds and ivy is the food plant of the swallow-tailed moth. The flowers produce copious nectar and are the last source of food before winter for many insects. By night the nectar is fed on by moths, especially the green-bridled crescent; by day by other insects, such as wasps, hoverflies and

130

butterflies. Brimstone butterflies rely on the nectar before they hibernate. In winter the black berries are relished by blackbirds, thrushes, blackcaps, fieldfares, redwings, robins and wood pigeons.

Few other plants can have so many uses in the garden – ivy can be used as ground cover in dense shade; as a covering for a wall or an old tree stump; as a decorative frieze at the base of stonework; or trailing from a container. As ground cover it can be controlled by mowing with the blades of a rotary mower set high. Although there are many different ivies available to the gardener, *H. helix* is the only form that regularly flowers and fruits in England, and it grows in almost any position and on almost any soil. In town gardens it is resistant to pollution. Contrary to popular opinion, it does not harm healthy trees, as long as it does not cover the crown; nor does it damage walls, as long as bricks or stone and mortar are sound. It is not a parasite and does not damage plants that it climbs, but it should not be planted close to young trees, because it will compete for moisture and nourishment and can overload them while they are becoming established. Overgrown plants can be cut back hard in spring. Flowering shoots may be affected by severe frosts. The easiest way to propagate this robust plant is from naturally formed layers or from cuttings taken in late summer, grown on in a shady spot and planted out a year later. Germination from collected seed can be erratic, but seedlings spread by birds can be grown on. Young plants prefer a short run across the ground before climbing.

Hop

Humulus lupulus CANNABACEAE

The sun in the south or else southlie and west
Is joy to the Hop, as welcomed ghest
But wind in the north, or else northerly east,
To Hop is as ill as a fray in a feast.

Five Hundreth Good Pointes of Husbandrie, Thomas Tusser (*c.* 1520–*c.* 1580)

Twisting clockwise as it goes, the perennial hop can scramble up a tree or through a hedge at tremendous speed, reaching a height of 6m/20ft in a single season. Tendril-like tips and stiff, backward-pointing hairs on the tough, fibrous stem help this climber to make its way through neighbouring foliage, displaying its three- to five-lobed, opposite pairs of sharply toothed, vine-like leaves, each up to 15cm/6in long. From July to August the flowers appear, male and female on separate plants. The green male flowers, 5mm/¼in across with five exposed anthers, are carried in loose, branched clusters, while the tiny green, egg-shaped, female flowers are hidden by scales. After pollination the scales enlarge into the familiar, papery, yellowish-green cones covered in resinous glands that are used by brewers to help preserve and flavour beer. The panicles of cone-like fruiting heads enclose nutlike fruits.

Hop is found in hedgerows, copses and scrub on damp soils in the lowlands of southern England. Being widely cultivated, the plant often occurs elsewhere as an escapee.

Ivy (*Hedera helix*)

Hop flowers (*Humulus lupulus*)

Hop is the only native member of the hemp family, and hop tea was traditionally used by herbalists as a sedative. Young shoots can be cooked and eaten like asparagus, while dried flowering hop is very effective in flower arrangements.

The leaves are the main food of the caterpillars of comma butterflies, of the red admiral and sometimes of peacock butterflies. It is also enjoyed by pale tussock, twin-spotted quaker, pepper and ghost moths.

With its attractive leaves and the pleasantly fragrant fruiting heads of the female plant, this is an excellent native alternative to foreign clematis species for covering a trellis, pergola or garden fence. It can also be grown along ropes or trained on a pole or obelisk to form a shrub. Hop grows in sun or semi-shade and prefers moist, well-drained soil. Propagation is by sowing seed under glass in April and planting out in late May or June, or by division in autumn.

Tutsan

Hypericum androsaemum CLUSIACEAE

The shrubby, semi-evergreen tutsan is a handsome plant with bright yellow, starry flowers sprouting a mass of stamens at the centre and in the autumn a crop of showy fruits. Its woody, branched, two-ridged stems usually reach about 60cm/24in in height and carry pairs of smooth, ovate to oblong, stalkless leaves each up to 9cm/3½in long. From June to August groups of up to nine five-petalled flowers appear in branched clusters at the tops of the stems, each flower up to 2.5cm/1in wide, having five oval, often reddish-tinged sepals and tufts of stamens almost as long as the petals. The rounded, berrylike fruits turn from red to succulent purplish-black when ripe, containing numerous oblong seeds.

Tutsan is widespread in woodland and on hedgebanks on damp, moderately acid to base-rich soils in the lowlands of southern and western England, especially Devon and Cornwall, but is only thinly scattered elsewhere and almost absent from the north-east.

The dried leaves smell sweetly resinous and have been used as scented bookmarks, while the fresh leaves were formerly used to dress cuts and grazes, hence the name tutsan, derived from the old French for 'all healthy'.

Though lacking nectar, the bright colour of the flowers and the abundant pollen produced by the numerous stamens attract many pollen-eating and pollinating beetles and other insects.

Tutsan is a valuable, long-flowering species, which is ideal for a shrub or mixed border in moderate or even fairly deep shade where the soil does not dry out. It tolerates a wide range of soils, provided there is some moisture. Propagate by sowing seed in autumn in a cold frame, by division or by rooting semi-ripe cuttings in summer.

Perforate St John's-wort

Hypericum perforatum CLUSIACEAE

Hypericum, all bloom, so thick a swarm
Of flow'rs, like flies clothing her slender rods,
That scarce a leaf appears …
'The Winter Walk at Noon', William Cowper (1731–1800)

This small, clump-forming perennial shrub up to 90cm/36in has an even longer flowering period than tutsan (*H. androsaemum*), with numerous flowers that are as large as those of tutsan but with smaller leaves and spear-shaped sepals. The hairless, upright, two-ridged stem has a woody base and carries the curiously marked foliage that gives it the Latin species name *perforatum*, for each of the paired, elliptical to narrowly oblong, stalkless leaves is covered with translucent glands that look like punctures. Bright yellow, star-shaped, five-petalled flowers 2.5cm/1in with pincushion stamens appear in widely branched clusters from June to September. They, too, are dotted with glands which show black on the edges of the petals. The almost pear-shaped fruit capsule contains numerous oblong, pitted seeds and splits into three.

Perforate St John's-wort is the most common hypericum in England, found in grassland, open woodland and on hedgebanks, mainly on lime-rich soils.

It was named after St John's Day, 24 June, when it was picked for ritual and medicinal use.

Bee-flies visit the flowers for their accessible nectar.

This plant can be grown in a shrub border, on a dryish bank or naturalized in a meadow area. It is particularly useful for dry shade on chalky soil, one of the most difficult situations in a garden, although in cultivation it tolerates a wide

Ideal for a woodland corner or the shrub border, the tutsan (*Hypericum androsaemum*) is tolerant of a wide range of conditions. Its bright yellow summer flowers are followed by crops of blackish berries.

range of well-drained soils in sun or semi-shade. Propagation is by taking cuttings of the new season's young shoots in late spring or early summer, or by division. Seeds may be sown in a cold frame in early spring or outside in April. The fine seed germinates more readily on damp soil.

Holly

Ilex aquifolium AQUIFOLIACEAE

Heigh-ho! Sing heigh, ho! unto the green holly:
Most friendship is feigning, most loving mere folly:
Then, heigh-ho, the holly!
This life is most jolly.

As You Like It, William Shakespeare (1564–1616)

The intensely dark green, high-gloss leaves of holly, with their undulating margins and sharp spines, make this one of England's most distinctive native evergreens. When grown in an open position the tree can reach up to 23m/75ft in height with a narrow, conical crown, but is more often around 10m/32ft tall. The bark is smooth and steel-grey and the dense, oval to elliptical leaves are tough and leathery in texture, 5–12cm/2–5in long, with a shiny dark green surface and paler underneath. Lower leaves, and those on younger trees, have wavy margins and stout prickles, but upper leaves and those on older trees can be smooth-edged with a pointed tip. In May and June (occasionally also in the autumn) small, fragrant, waxy-white, four-petalled flowers, 6mm/¼in in size, appear in clusters in the leaf axils. Male and female flowers are carried on separate trees, although both sexes do sometimes occur on one tree, and at least one male has to be planted for every six females to ensure pollination. In good years female trees produce an abundance of beautiful scarlet berries, sometimes yellow or orange, which ripen in late autumn or early winter and often last until spring. Each contains up to four black seeds.

Holly is found in woods – often as part of the understorey in oak and beech woods – and in hedgerows and open scrub throughout most of lowland England on a wide range of soils, ascending to 500m/1,640ft in West Yorkshire, but as a native it is absent from much of the East Midlands.

Beware: the berries cause stomach upsets if eaten.

As well as giving cover and shelter to small birds in all seasons, holly produces welcome berries for fieldfares and mistle thrushes in winter. The leaves, which are the favourite food of holly blue caterpillars in spring, are also eaten by two tortricoid moths and are often attacked by a leaf-miner. The red berries remain fresh, with a high moisture content, and last on the tree for almost a year, being resistant to extreme cold. They are a valuable food source when deep snow makes ground feeding impossible, and mistle thrushes defend bushes to keep a long-term food supply throughout the winter. Holly berries are small enough to be swallowed whole by most of the fruit-eating birds and at least nine species have been recorded eating them, especially blackbirds, mistle thrushes, wood pigeons, collared doves, redwings, fieldfares and song thrushes; robins and blackcaps are also consumers.

Native holly makes a very fine garden hedge, always green and shining and an effective barrier against cold winds, noise, pollution, stray animals and burglars. It can also be grown as a specimen tree or in a woodland garden, and is very tolerant of clipping and shaping. Holly accepts sun or shade and a wide range of soils, from clays and peat to sands and chalk, although it grows best in rich, sandy loam. It does not like waterlogged ground but is reasonably drought-proof. The prickly leaves take many years to rot down and, when dried, they can be can be scattered round the base of vulnerable shrubs to repel slugs. Propagation is probably best achieved by taking cuttings with a heel in late summer, planting in a shady cold frame, transplanting after a year, then growing on for a further year or two before setting in a permanent site. Seeds take from eighteen to twenty months to germinate and need stratifying before sowing in a nursery bed protected from birds and small rodents.

Juniper

Juniperus communis CUPRESSACEAE

The Combe was ever dark, ancient and dark.
Its mouth is stopped with bramble, thorn, and briar;
And no one scrambles over the sliding chalk
By beech and yew and perishing juniper
Down the half precipices of its sides, with roots
And rabbit holes for steps …

'The Combe', Edward Thomas (1878–1917)

This evergreen, with its deep green to blue-green, narrow, needle-like leaves, is a versatile and slow-growing plant and the smallest of England's two native conifers. It can make a low, spreading shrub up to 60cm/24in in height, or it can be an erect tree up to 11m/36ft tall. Both may be recognized by the reddish-brown bark and linear leaves borne on young, triangular shoots in whorls of three. Each sharply pointed leaf is 1–2cm/⅜–¾in long, but only about 1.5mm/ ¹⁄₁₆in wide, with a central, greyish-white band underneath. Small, cone-like yellow male flowers and small, greenish female flowers usually appear on separate plants. After pollination the female cones look like green berries, 5–10mm/⅛–½in across, which gradually ripen over three years to glaucous blue and finally black. Each fruit contains up to eight seeds.

Juniper is found on the chalk hills of southern England, on northern limestone and in upland birch woods. The dwarf, prostrate *J. c.* subsp. *nana* occurs only on high mountains in the Lake District, while the compact, shrubby *J. c.* subsp. *hemispherica* is restricted to low cliffs in west Cornwall.

The shoot tips are sometimes infected by gall-midges, which produce a 'whooping gall' – once used medicinally in the treatment of whooping cough. This is the food plant of the Chestnut-coloured carpet, Juniper pug and Juniper carpet moths. The berries are attractive to birds, which swallow them whole and then drop the hard black seeds. The bushes also provide year-round cover for thrushes and goldcrests.

Juniper can be an attractive specimen tree, or it may be grown in the rock garden or shrubbery. The low-growing *J. c.* subsp. *nana* is especially good as ground cover. Junipers prefer an open, sunny site and tolerate a wide range of soils, from calcareous to acid peat, as long as they are not waterlogged. They are very drought-resistant and do not need pruning. Propagate from cuttings of the current year's growth taken with a heel in late summer or early autumn. Pot up in a free-draining mix and keep in a shady cold frame until late the following spring, when they should be sufficiently rooted to plant in a nursery bed. Plant permanently in autumn or spring. Raising from seed is difficult, as the seeds must be stratified and kept in shade for eighteen months before sowing. Alternatively, the berries can be sun-dried and sown straight away in a cold frame, but germination is slow (up to five years).

Wild Privet

Ligustrum vulgare OLEACEAE

The deciduous or semi-evergreen privet is synonymous with hedging, although with its bushy, dark green leaves and pyramid spikes of white flowers it makes an attractive and robust shrub in its own right. Its smooth, dark, wiry stems

Evergreen juniper (*Juniperus communis*)

seldom grow much above 4m/13ft high and the twigs are downy when young. They carry pairs of small, leathery, narrowly oval leaves up to 6cm/2½in long, shiny dark green above and lighter beneath. These develop in March and April, growing darker before falling in winter. Conical clusters of heavily scented, small white flowers appear at the end of the shoots in June and July, followed by shiny black autumn berries with an oily flesh.

Privet is common in hedges, scrub, woodland and downland, mainly on calcareous, soils throughout lowland England.

Uncut hedges and shrubs carry nectar-rich blossom, whose scent attracts bees and other pollinating insects. Untrimmed privet is also a refuge for hibernating brimstone, small tortoiseshell, comma and peacock butterflies. As a hedge plant, it provides good cover for nesting birds and the berries contribute to their winter diet. The leaves are the main food for the caterpillar of one of Britain's most beautiful moths, the privet hawk moth, and for the coronet moth. White letter and black hairstreaks feed on the honeydew on the leaves.

This shrub can be trimmed and used as a hedge, although it has no leaves in winter, or it can be grown in a shrubbery or shrub border, where it will form dense bushes. Like most members of the olive family it has tough, durable wood and wounds heal easily, so it can be shaped, although that will be at the expense of the flowers. Privet withstands pollution and is suited to town gardens. It prefers an open, sunny site in order to flower fully, but will grow in semi-shade; it needs free-draining (preferably alkaline) soil. The shrub is very drought-resistant and will not accept extremely wet ground. Control may be necessary as it suckers readily. Many gardeners grow the Japanese species, *L. ovalifolium*, which is almost completely evergreen and has broader leaves, but offers nothing to English wildlife. Privet can easily be propagated by hardwood cuttings taken from October to December and put straight into the ground or into a nursery bed for a year. It may also be raised from seed collected in autumn, stratified until late winter, then sown in nursery rows before planting out two growing seasons later.

Pyramids of white flowers bloom against the dark green leaves of wild privet (*Ligustrum vulgare*), a shrub with shiny black autumn berries which is often unfairly ignored in favour of the Japanese privet.

Honeysuckle

Lonicera periclymenum CAPRIFOLIACEAE

You've heard them sweetly sing,
And seen them in a round,
Each virgin like a spring
With honeysuckle crowned …
'To Meadows', Robert Herrick (1591–1674)

The beautiful, deliciously fragrant cream and yellow trumpets of honeysuckle are among the great delights of summer as they perfume the evening air. This vigorous, deciduous climber shows its promise early, with green buds emerging in late winter before the spring flowers and full leaves appearing by the beginning of April. Its woody stems twine clockwise up neighbouring plants and can reach a height of 6m/20ft in trees, hence its other common name, woodbine. The opposite pairs of ovate to elliptical leaves, 3–7cm/1¼–3in long, are dark green above and bluish-green below, smooth-edged and usually pointed. Whorls of tubular flowers appear at the end of the stems, mainly in June and July, although some continue right through to September. Each flower is 4.5cm/2in long and 2.5cm/1in wide, with a widely spread, two-lipped mouth with protruding stamens, creamy-white or yellow in colour and often tinged with red or purple. After pollination the flowers change from white to yellow. The round, red berries appear in clusters, each fruit containing up to eight oblong seeds.

Honeysuckle is found in hedgerows, woodlands, scrub, rocks and cliffs on a wide range of soils throughout England, and up to 500m/1,640ft in Teesdale.

Both its scent and the nectar at the bottom of the flower tube attract pollinating moths, especially the large elephant hawk moth, and the leaves are food for the larvae of white admiral and marsh fritillary butterflies. The red berries or seeds from shrivelled fruits are relished by blackcaps, blackbirds, robins, thrushes, blue tits and marsh tits, while the dense tangled stems make excellent nest-sites.

This fragrant climber can be incorporated into a hedge, trained on trelliswork, a pergola or a free-standing support such as an obelisk. It can also be grown over an old shrub or tree trunk or it will flourish in a reasonably large container near the house, where its pervasive evening scent can be enjoyed. It likes full sun but will grow in semi-shade and tolerates most garden soils as long as they are not too dry or too wet. In good open sites it can be vigorous and needs pruning twice a year to keep it within bounds – once after flowering and again in winter. It is more restrained when growing in hedges and through trees. Honeysuckle should not be planted near saplings or other young plants, because it will bind tightly to them, causing damage before they are established. It can be propagated by taking semi-ripe cuttings in late summer and potting them in compost with a cane support, before setting out after a year. It can also be raised from seed collected from ripe berries and stratified, before sowing in boxes in late winter; pot up the seedlings as for cuttings.

Crab Apple
Malus sylvestris ROSACEAE

Covered in clouds of pretty pink blossom in May, crab apple is a small, densely branched deciduous tree, which seldom grows taller than 8m/28ft. This parent of the domestic apple has grey-brown bark that becomes furrowed and flaky when older. From the tangled branches come long shoots that extend the crown, short 'spurs' carrying flowers, and sometimes medium-sized shoots ending in a thorn. The bright green, ovate, short-pointed leaves 3–5cm/1½–2in long are hairless, with a finely toothed margin and stalks up to 2cm/¾in long; they open in late April. Soon afterwards the clusters of dark pink buds unfurl into pale pink or white five-petalled flowers with yellow anthers, up to 3cm/1½in across. These are followed by rounded green fruits, about 2.5cm/1in in diameter, which ripen into a golden-yellow.

Crab apple is found in ancient woods, especially of oak, and in hedgerows and scrub on a wide range of soils throughout lowland England. Escaped cultivated apple trees are often found in hedges, but unlike crab apples these are thornless with hairy shoots and leaves and often with pinker flowers.

Crab apples are adored by birds, which spread the seed in their droppings, while the interweaving branches make good nesting sites. Red admiral butterflies gorge themselves on the sap from the rotting fruit, and the leaves are food for the larvae of figure-of-eight, gothic and pale-shouldered brocade moths.

This small tree is most attractive in both flower and fruit, and is useful for the corner of a medium-sized garden or as a specimen tree in a smaller one. It can also be incorporated into a planted hedge. It prefers an open, sunny site and almost any

soil, except damp peat. It is best propagated by extracting seeds from the fruits in winter, sowing immediately and leaving undisturbed for a year before lining out, 30cm/12in apart, and growing on for two years.

Bog-myrtle or Sweet Gale
Myrica gale MYRICACEAE

And I will make thee beds of roses,
And a thousand fragrant posies;
A cap of flowers and a kirtle
Embroidered all with leaves of myrtle.
'The Passionate Shepherd to his Love', Christopher Marlowe (1564–93)

Bog-myrtle, also known by the prettier name of sweet gale, is a strongly aromatic, grey-green deciduous shrub, which until the nineteenth century was a symbol of love. The plant's tiny yellow resin glands exude a pleasant fragrance that makes it easy to identify. It generally reaches about 1m/3½ft in height, occasionally 2m/6½ft, and the woody, reddish-brown, upright branches carry alternate, inversely lance-shaped, grey-green leaves up to 6cm/2½in long, which are toothed towards the apex. The stiff, golden-brown catkins open in late March, just before the leaves appear, and continue until May, with the male and smaller female flowers usually borne on separate plants. The catkins appear at the tips of twigs of the previous year's growth. The small, nutlike fruits on the female plants each have two narrow wings to aid wind dispersal and contain a waxy resin to protect the seed if it falls into water.

Bog-myrtle is found in wet moorland and heathland, bogs and fens throughout England, up to an altitude of 550m/1,800ft, although it is less common in drier parts of the east.

Bog-myrtle is the food plant of the beautiful brocade, great brocade, dotted clay and rosy marsh moths.

It is an ideal plant for the bog garden, particularly when grown in groups, where it will scent the air on a hot day. It grows in sun or partial shade and prefers acid soil, although it will tolerate some calcareous soils, as long as the ground is wet. Nitrogen-fixing nodules on the roots enable it to flourish in waterlogged conditions. The plant does not regenerate after cutting and should not be pruned. The simplest method of propagation is by layering in spring, but it can also be raised from seed sown in autumn or spring and kept in a cold frame, then lined out in autumn and grown on for two years before planting out. Seeds, seedlings and young plants must be kept moist at all times.

Shrubby Cinquefoil
Potentilla fruticosa ROSACEAE

This small, bushy, deciduous shrub carries its clear-yellow flowers in abundance over a long period from late spring to mid-autumn. Its twiggy stems seldom grow much above 1m/3½ft in height and it has dark green, pinnate leaves, up to 4cm/1½in long, composed of five or seven narrow, oblong leaflets. The saucer-shaped flowers with a prominent centre appear singly or in groups, each up to 1.6cm/⅝in across, with male and female flowers carried on separate plants, although they are difficult to distinguish from one another. The females produce single-seeded fruits in a clustered head.

Shrubby cinquefoil is found on rock ledges and at the margins of lakes and rivers, but is local to only two upland areas in northern England.

The flower is visited by small insects, including picture-winged flies.

This is a valuable, versatile, free-flowering and long-flowering plant, which can be useful for the border, for rock or gravel areas in a water garden or for making a low hedge. It prefers full sun in order to flower well and a light, free-draining soil, although it is tolerant of a wide range of soils. The plant does require moisture and flourishes best where rainfall is dependable. Regular spring pruning of the older shoots will keep the bush compact. It can be propagated from 10–12cm/4–5in-long cuttings of late-summer shoots, potted in sandy compost in a propagator, under polythene or in a cold greenhouse.

Crab apple (*Malus sylvestris*)

Wild Cherry or Gean
Prunus avium ROSACEAE

Loveliest of trees, the cherry now
Is hung with bloom along the bough,
And stands about the woodland ride
Wearing white for Eastertide.

A Shropshire Lad, A. E. Housman (1859–1936)

This is the original cherry, forerunner of the cultivated varieties and a deciduous, white-blossomed tree, which is attractive throughout the year. It grows to about 25m/82ft in height (often less) and in winter shows off its shining, grey or reddish-brown bark banded with rough, orange-brown breathing pores. On mature trees the bark peels off in horizontal strips. The greyish-brown twigs have alternate russet-brown buds and in April and May they release long-stalked, slightly drooping, ovate to elliptical leaves, up to 15cm/6in long with toothed margins and downy underneath. The leaves are initially bronze before turning green, and in autumn the foliage may change to beautiful shades of yellow, orange and red-brown. The fragrant clusters of two to six cup-shaped, five-petalled white flowers, up to 2-3cm/1in in size, on long, grooved stalks bloom at the same time as the leaves unfurl, often covering the crown in blossom before the leaves are fully open. Small shiny fruits, up to 1.2cm/½in across, ripen in July and August through yellow and bright red to dark purplish-red. The taste may be sweet or bitter, but to ensure there is a crop of cherries there must be two or more trees planted to fertilize each other, because they are self-sterile.

Wild cherry is found in lowland woods, often in the understorey layer of oak woods, on fertile, often base-rich soils throughout England.

Pollinating bees flock to the nectar when it flowers. The cherries are larger than most British wild fruits and above the upper size limit for smaller birds. Robins cannot eat them, but they are enjoyed by larger species, such as starlings and wood pigeons. The leaves are eaten by forest bugs, one of England's large shield-bugs, and by the caterpillars of several species of

A spectacle in full flower, wild cherry (*Prunus avium*), is a magnet to bees and has wonderful autumn foliage.

TOP Bird cherry (*Prunus padus*)

MIDDLE Blackthorn or Sloe fruits (*Prunus spinosa*)

BELOW Blackthorn or Sloe flowers *(Prunus spinosa)*

moth. The leaves are galled by the same fungus that causes peach-leaf curl.

Wild cherry is one of England's most attractive native woodland trees, suitable for gardens of all sizes, where it prefers full sun but will tolerate light shade. It requires moist, well-drained soil (preferably neutral to alkaline). *P. avium* is, however, prone to surface rooting, so it should not be planted where the roots might cause problems, such as in lawns and beside paths and paving. Wild cherry is propagated from seed gathered at the same time that the birds arrive to feed on the fruit. With the flesh removed, the stones should be stored in moist sand until the following spring, when they can be sown in nursery beds. Thin out as necessary and plant in a permanent position when two to three years old.

Bird Cherry

Prunus padus ROSACEAE

And manie homely trees were there,
And peaches, coines, and aples bere;
Medlers, plommis, peres, chesteneis,
Cherise, of which manie one faire is …
Geoffrey Chaucer (*c.* 1345–1400)

Bird cherry is at its best in early summer when its white blossom perfumes the air with the scent of almonds. It has a rounded crown and steeply ascending upper branches, and it is often small in stature, although it can grow as tall as 15m/50ft in height. It has smooth, dark reddish-brown bark that peels and smells of bitter almonds, and short horizontal bands of orange breathing pores, while the shiny, pointed winter buds range in colour from yellow to dark brown. The elliptical, finely toothed leaves, which unfold in May, are dull green above, pale green below and up to 10cm/4in long. These are followed later in the month by long, loose, pendent or spreading racemes of up to forty white, five-petalled, almond-scented, self-fertile flowers. The spherical, bitter-tasting, shiny black fruits, up to 8mm/¼in across, ripen in late summer and the leaves often turn gold and red before falling in October.

Bird cherry is found in moist deciduous oak and birch woodland and in scrub throughout northern England, up to 500m/1,640ft in North Yorkshire, although it is much planted and naturalized in southern and central England.

The flowers attract many pollinating bees and flies and the leaves are host to numerous insects. The small cherries are full of tannin and unpleasant-tasting for humans, but, as the name implies, they are relished by birds. As the fruits are smaller than those of the wild cherry, they can be swallowed by robins and thrushes.

This is a good choice for gardens of all sizes and is very hardy, although it does not like exposure to strong winds. It casts light shade, allowing plants to grow underneath, and prefers an open site and damp soil. It is easily propagated from fruits collected in July and stored, with the flesh removed, until the following spring before sowing, thinning and planting out in the same way as for wild cherry.

Blackthorn or Sloe
Prunus spinosa ROSACEAE

How oft, my slice of pocket store consumed,
Still hungering, penniless and far from home,
I fed on scarlet hips and stony haws,
Or blushing crabs, or berries, that emboss
The bramble, black as jet, or sloes austere.

'The Charm of the Country', William Cowper (1731–1800)

Blackthorn's dark tangle of spiny branches is smothered with a mass of tiny, pure-white flowers in spring, but autumn is its high point, when the lustrous bluish-black fruits glow among the foliage. The upright, deciduous shrub or small tree has stiff black, thorny twigs and seldom reaches more than 4m/13ft in height, and on older plants the bark fractures into small, scale-like squares. Its little five-petalled flowers with red anthers blossom in March and April before the small, oval, finely toothed, fresh green leaves appear on reddish stalks. The leaves become longer, up to 4cm/1½in, narrower and a darker, duller green as they mature. In September or October come the almost round fruits, or sloes – each a gleaming purplish-black with a bluish-white bloom.

Blackthorn is widespread in hedgerows, on woodland margins and in scrub on all types of soil except the most acid, throughout the lowlands of England, but up to 400m/1,310ft in the Lake District.

Beware: do not be tempted to bite into the pale green flesh of the sloes, as it is mouth-witheringly acid.

A blackthorn hedge makes an excellent, well-protected nesting site for garden birds, while the flowers produce nectar for bumble bees and early-flying small tortoiseshell butterflies. The leaves are the main food plant of the larvae of black and brown hairstreak butterflies and are host to a gall-midge, which may produce up to sixty blisters around the margin of a single leaf.

This dense, thorny shrub makes a first-class anti-burglar and animal-proof hedge, keeping its green leaves until October or November and providing spring blossom and autumn fruit. It prefers a fairly open position on almost any soil, except the most peaty and acid, and dislikes heavy shade but will protect smaller plants growing underneath. It withstands exposure to strong winds. Blackthorn suckers freely and soon makes dense thickets unless it is controlled, making is suitable only for a large garden. It is propagated from seed treated in the same way as that of wild cherry, and seedlings may be planted out after three years.

Pedunculate Oak
Quercus robur FAGACEAE

Where is the pride of Summer, – the green prime, –
The many, many leaves all twinkling? – Three
On the moss'd elm; three on the naked lime
Trembling, – and one upon the old oak tree!
Where is the Dryad's immortality?

'Ode: Autumn', Thomas Hood (1799–1845)

The sturdy, stately English oak with its massive, spreading branches and distinctive round-lobed leaves is the tree that most readily evokes images of English history and a vanishing landscape. This very long-lived deciduous tree can grow up to 30–40m/100–131ft in height, sometimes with a tall, irregular, open crown, but is more often lower, with a widely spaced, domed crown. The trunk is grey-brown, smooth at first then becoming rough and fissured, and the large branches grow low on the tree, often spreading almost horizontally. Oak's instantly recognizable, pale green, deeply lobed, short-stalked or stalkless ovate leaves, widest above the middle, have three to six rounded lobes each side, tapering to two small earlike lobes at the base. They vary in size, up to about 14cm/5½in long, sometimes bronze or brown when they unfurl in May, while

The pedunculate oak (*Quercus robur*)

Buckthorn (*Rhamnus cathartica*)

the second, summer growth can be tinged with red. Both sexes of pale-green flowers appear at the same time as the leaves, the males in slender, hanging catkins 3–8cm/1¼–3in long and the females in stalked spikes at the tips of shoots. The latter are followed by the familiar acorns, looking like tiny, shiny eggs sitting in a rough-textured cup. Held singly or in clusters of two or three on long stalks, the 'peduncles', which give the tree its name, are green at first but turn brown by autumn.

Pedunculate oak is found in woodland, open ground and in pollarded form in hedgerows throughout England on heavy clays and loams, especially on neutral or lime-rich soils, but rarely above 300m/985ft. Where the soil is suitably deep and rich it is dominant in woods in much of the lowlands.

This is the most important of all English native trees as a habitat for wildlife, attracting 284 insect species. As a 'master tree', it acts as a landmark for gathering colonies of purple emperor butterflies, while the larvae of purple hairstreaks are among the dozens of different caterpillars of butterflies and moths that feed on the leaves. The leaves are also alluring to numerous gall-forming mites and wasps, which produce 'spangles' and 'cherries' on the surface. Invasion of the flowers results in misshapen acorns. The tree also attracts lichens, fungi, bats, squirrels, voles, woodmice, spiders, beetles and a huge variety of birds, including warblers, tits, flycatchers, thrushes, woodpeckers and tawny owls. It is an almost complete ecosystem in its own right.

Fortunate is the gardener with enough space to grow an oak for posterity. It makes a rewarding specimen tree, both impressive and interesting throughout the year. It is tolerant of moderate cutting back and can be pollarded or coppiced from time to time. It grows in sun or semi-shade and likes deep, fertile soils; tolerating those that are damp, but not waterlogged. Oak is reasonably drought-tolerant but does not thrive on dry, shallow soils; nor does it like salty winds in coastal sites. When young, it keeps its leaves through the winter and can be a useful addition to a hedge. Propagate it only from acorns, best collected ripe as they fall and sown immediately in beds protected from mice, with a deep layer of soil over a sawdust marking layer, then removed after germination the following spring. Seedlings should be planted out after one year and replanted every second year until 75cm/30in tall, when they can be placed in their permanent position.

Buckthorn

Rhamnus cathartica RHAMNACEAE

Buckthorn usually makes a bushy deciduous shrub about 5m/16½ft tall with thick foliage growing from near the ground, but it can sometimes be a tree reaching twice that height. The rough bark is grey-brown, almost black on the young twigs, and the shoots are of two kinds: longer growth shoots and short leaf and flower shoots. The latter grow opposite one another, almost at right angles to the stem, and often end in a stout spine. From April they carry dull green, finely toothed, rounded ovate leaves, up to 7cm/3in long, with three or four pairs of lateral veins curving towards the tip. They turn brownish-yellow in autumn. Inconspicuous clusters of tiny, four-petalled, yellowish-green flowers appear at the base of the leaf stalk in spring – male and female on separate plants. From September the female plant carries an abundant crop of pea-sized, three- or four-seeded fruits, green at first but ripening to shiny black and often remaining on the bush after leaf fall.

Buckthorn occurs in woods, scrub and hedgerows on calcareous soils mainly in the south, east and Midlands of England, but is also found as far north as the Lake District and the Tees.

Beware: the berries are purgative but not very poisonous.

Buckthorn is the main food plant of the brimstone butterfly, and the larvae of the green hairstreak also feed on it. The leaves can attract crown rust, which appears as orange specks and, because this attacks cereals, it is best not to plant buckthorn near arable land. The berries are a valuable food for wintering birds.

Buckthorn can be grown as a free-standing tree or as a hedge, but to be sure of the decorative autumn berries one male must be planted to every five or six females. It is generally a problem-free plant that is well suited to small wildlife gardens, particularly in towns. It grows in sun or semi-shade and is fairly tolerant of most soils, although it prefers free-draining, alkaline soil, making it a useful shrub for a dry, chalky garden. It is easily propagated from fruits gathered in autumn, stratified until February and sown in nursery beds. Line out in autumn and grow on for up to two years before planting out permanently. To be sure of the sex, it is better to take semi-hardwood cuttings with a heel in late summer, or the plant may be layered in spring.

Field-rose

Rosa arvensis ROSACEAE

This deciduous, trailing or climbing rose scrambles through hedges and bushes with the aid of hooked prickles. With the support of neighbouring plants it can reach up to 2m/7ft, but in an open spot it forms a low, spreading mound of arching stems. These slender stems are purple on the sunlit side and green in the shade, and the leaves have five to seven oval, shining green toothed leaflets, which are hairy only on the veins underneath. In June and July the scentless clusters of white flowers appear, each up to 5cm/2in across, with five notched petals and a yellow centre featuring a column of joined styles that is as long as the stamens. This persists as a little spike at the top of the small round or oval red fruits, or hips, which ripen in October and often remain after leaf fall.

Field-rose grows in hedgerows, scrub, and in woodland clearings or lightly shaded woods on all but the most acid or waterlogged soils throughout England.

Field-rose may be visited by two kinds of leaflet-rolling insects: gall-midges, which fold the leaf upwards so that the underside encloses flylike maggots, and little black sawflies, which fold the leaflets downwards, with the top side enclosing caterpillarlike larvae. Caterpillars of the small quaker moth may also feed on the leaflets. The hips provide autumn food for birds, woodmice and foxes.

The colour contrast between the two sides of the stem and the persistent red hips in autumn makes this a particularly decorative shrub for running through and over a hedgerow, on a trellis or in a shrub border. Smaller and less vigorous than the dog-rose, it is highly tolerant of cutting back and more suited to a small garden. It will grow in sun or shade, but needs sun in order to flower and fruit; and it grows in most garden soils, preferably deep or clay soils and not those that are very acid or wet. Field-rose can be propagated from hardwood cuttings taken in autumn or from seeds extracted from ripe hips and stored in moist sand outside, protected from mice until late winter. Sow in nursery rows, thin out seedlings in autumn, and plant in a permanent site one or two years later.

Dog-rose

Rosa canina ROSACEAE

Unkempt about those hedges blows,
An English unofficial rose; …

'The Old Vicarage, Grantchester', Rupert Brooke (1887–1915)

Its gracefully arching stems, sturdy prickles and scented, shell-pink flowers combine to give the dog-rose qualities of vigour and delicacy that have inspired English poets for centuries. This beautiful deciduous suckering shrub, the largest of the English roses, has curved spines that enable it to catch on to surrounding shrubs for support, and it can reach more than 3m/10ft in height, but more often up to 2m/6½ft. Each stalked leaf has two or three opposite pairs of usually hairless, oval or elliptical, toothed leaflets with a larger terminal leaflet. The fragrant, pale pink or white five-petalled flowers appear singly or in small groups in June or July, each up to 5cm/2in across, with numerous stamens around a central cluster of separate, hairy styles. Five narrow green sepals usually have a frill of side-lobes. The glossy, scarlet, egg-shaped hips, rich in vitamin C, do not fully ripen until October or November.

Dog-rose is most commonly found in hedgerows, scrub and woodlands on a wide range of soils throughout England up to 550m/1,800ft.

This plant is host to many insects, most notably gall-forming wasps, which produce balls of crimson 'moss' called Robin's pin-cushions on the leaf stalks and smooth or spiked pea-galls on the leaflets. The hips are eaten by blackbirds.

Dog-rose is a strongly growing plant that needs space. It makes a dense and decorative hedge, or it can be grown over an existing hedge where a darker green background will set off the pink flowers and arching stems. It can also be trained on a trellis or over an arbour or decaying tree. It flourishes in full sun, and may grow without flowering in shade. It accepts most garden soils as long as they are not waterlogged or very dry. It is hardy and tolerates cutting back. Propagate as for field-rose.

Burnet Rose

Rosa pimpinellifolia ROSACEAE

This charming, little, bushy deciduous shrub could be called the seaside rose as it flourishes on sand and limestone around the coast. It is low-growing, seldom above 60cm/24in in height, and has upright, much-branched woody stems armed with masses of straight, slender prickles intermixed with stiff bristles. The decorative leaves have from three to five pairs of toothed leaflets and a terminal leaflet, each 5–20mm/⅛–¾in long. From May to July the bushes are smothered in creamy-white (rarely pink) flowers up to 4cm/1½in across, which appear singly at the tips of the stems. Each has five broad, notched petals and numerous golden stamens at the centre. The leathery, round hips are crowned with long sepals and – unlike those of other native roses – ripen to blackish-purple in September.

Burnet rose is found mainly in dunes and sandy places around the coasts of England and locally on inland heaths and downland, ascending to 450m/1,475ft in the Pennines.

The Latin species name and English common name refer to the resemblance of the leaves to those of burnet-saxifrage, *Pimpinella saxifraga*, a member of the carrot family.

The flowers do not contain much nectar but are visited and pollinated by bees, beetles and thrips seeking pollen. The leaf stalks and midrib are attacked by gall-wasps, which produce pea-galls, and the leaflets may be mined by the larvae of small moths.

This is an appealing rose for a shrub border, a dry bank or large rock garden. It prefers an open site and full sun and needs free-draining soil (preferably alkaline). It is useful in that it tolerates very dry conditions. It suckers freely and needs controlling if it is to be kept within bounds, but this can be an advantage if the rose is needed to cover bare ground. It is easily propagated by separating the suckers in autumn. Avoid the double forms of this rose that may be offered by nurseries.

White Willow

Salix alba   SALICACEAE

Willows whiten, aspens quiver
Little breezes dusk and shiver

'The Lady of Shalott', Alfred, Lord Tennyson

When the breeze ruffles its shimmering, silvery foliage the handsome white willow is shown at its best. This shapely, fast-growing deciduous tree reaches a height of 25m/80ft, the grey bark on its stout trunk being closely ridged and fissured. The main branches are erect, carrying smaller, spreading branches with young downy twigs, which become shiny brown, pink or yellow. The long, but short-stalked, alternate leaves (up to 10cm/4in in length) are narrowly lance-shaped with pointed tips and toothed margins; they are pale green

TOP Field rose (*Rosa arvensis*)

ABOVE The shiny, scarlet 'hips' of the dog-rose (*Rosa canina*).

147

above, a beautiful pale bluish-green underneath and covered when young with silky, silvery hairs, which are denser on the underside. In April and May, after the leaves have appeared, the yellow male catkins (up to 5cm/2in long) and the stalkless green female catkins appear on separate trees. The female quickly produces fluffy fruits, distributed by the winds.

White willow is found in wooded river valleys and marshes and by lowland rivers, streams and ponds throughout England, although it is more common in the east Midlands and East Anglia.

Like other willows the leaves are host to many insects, including the Camberwell beauty butterfly and a sawfly that induces the formation of 'bean-galls' on the leaf blade, which tend to be red above and green below.

This is a magnificent tree for the large garden, particularly if grown in its natural habitat beside water. Although it casts light shade itself, it prefers an open site and deep, well-drained, moist loam or peat soils and will not thrive on thin, chalky soils. It copes well in an exposed site and tolerates pollution and cutting back. In the past white willows were frequently pollarded. Owing to its water-seeking roots, the tree should not be planted near drains or close to a house. It is best propagated, like other willows, from hardwood cuttings taken in winter and grown on for a year, or from two-year-old stems inserted *in situ*. By reproducing an individual tree in this way the desired sex or form of this very variable species can be selected. Raising from seed is worthwhile but more difficult, because the seeds must be extracted from the down and sown immediately on to the surface of sterile compost, keeping them moist at all times. Once leaves have appeared the seedlings can be hardened off before growing on.

Goat Willow
Salix caprea SALICACEAE

So many features of this appealing, deciduous shrubby tree are either softly downy or rounded that it cannot fail to charm. The short trunk, with smooth, greenish-brown bark, fissured when old, has many wide branches. These form a rounded outline, usually not more than 5m/16½ft in height

The catkins of goat willow (*Salix caprea*)

although it can reach 10m/33ft, and the young twigs are downy. The alternate leaves of this 'pussy willow', up to 10cm/4in long, are oval with a wavy margin and a short point, dark grey-green above, pale grey with silky hairs on the underside. The catkins, which appear in March and April before the leaves, are also rounded and soft – male and female growing on separate trees. First to open are the slender, light green female flowerheads, which later carry the seed capsules covered in silvery down. Then come the silky, grey, budlike male catkins smothered with showy golden anthers.

Goat willow is found in mixed, broad-leaved woodland, hedgerows and scrub, most often on basic soils, throughout England, ascending to 500m/1,640ft in the Pennines.

Second in importance only to oak as a species for wildlife, goat willow is favoured by beetles, bees, hoverflies, ants and bats, providing food for over 250 different insects. The nectar attracts large tortoiseshell and comma butterflies, while the anthers supply pollen for bees. Purple emperor butterflies pupate on the underside of the leaves, which are also attractive to numerous moths, including the sallow kitten, buff-tip, common quaker and puss, the larvae of which in themselves become food for tits.

This is an attractive, good-natured plant, easy to grow as a tree or shrub or in a mixed hedge. Its grey-green appearance makes an interesting contrast with other trees, and its cheerful catkins appear before most flowers. It prefers a light, sunny spot and grows on most well-drained soils. It tolerates drier conditions than other native willows and withstands pollution and cutting back. Although willows root more easily from hardwood cuttings in winter than any other British shrub or tree, the goat willow is often better propagated from seed or suckers.

Elder

Sambucus nigra CAPRIFOLIACEAE

The shutter of time darkening ceaselessly
Has whisked away the foam of may and elder
And I realize how now, as every year before,
Once again the gay months have eluded me …

'August', Louis MacNeice (1907–63)

Elder is one of the most vigorous and productive English trees, establishing itself with speed and soon laden with great, flat-topped clusters of creamy-white blossom followed by masses of striking, glossy black berries on red stalks. In sheltered spots its deciduous leaves brave the late winter. Often more of a shrub than a tree, it generally grows to around 5m/16½ft, but can be twice that height in a favourable spot. Young shoots arise almost from ground level, smooth at first with marked pores, and the mature tree is covered with thick, ridged, grey-brown bark. Sometimes opening as early as January in a mild winter, the pinnate leaves have five to seven ovate to elliptical leaflets, each up to 9cm/3½in long with toothed margins, and occasionally lasting until December. In June and July the tiny, musky-scented, five-petalled, yellow-white flowers appear at the tips of young shoots in large, flat panicles up to 20cm/8in across, followed in August and September by heavy, hanging bunches of round black fruits, each containing up to five seeds.

Elder is widespread in woods, hedgerows, scrub and rough ground throughout England, commonly on calcareous or nitrogen-rich soils, such as farmland or those that have been manured.

Both flowers and fruit of elder are edible and rich in vitamin C, and they are used for making wine and jam. The flowers can also be dipped in batter and fried, or they make a refreshing cordial; elderflower infusion was once used for treating coughs.

The flowers produce nectar that attracts pollinating flies and beetles, as well as swallowtail moths. The early crop of berries provides a feast for most resident birds, including blackbirds, song thrushes, starlings and greenfinches, as well as summer visitors like blackcaps and garden warblers. Blue tits eat the seeds and comma butterflies enjoy the juice of the fermenting berries.

This adaptable plant can be grown as a shrub or a free-standing tree, in the wild garden or as a hedge, as long as there is sufficient space. It will grow in sun or semi-shade and on most moist but well-drained soils. It may be damaged by very hard frosts, but will regenerate quickly and is extremely tolerant of pruning, which it may require in order to keep it under control. Elder is easily propagated from hardwood cuttings taken with a heel in autumn and then planted out a year later. It can be raised from seeds extracted from the berries. These can be stored outside in moist sand, sown outside in winter, then grown on before setting out the seedlings in a permanent site a year later.

149

Bittersweet or Woody Nightshade
Solanum dulcamara SOLANACEAE

Bittersweet scrambles through hedges and over seaside shingle, displaying its vivid, star-shaped purple and yellow flowers from early summer right through to autumn. Not to be confused with the poisonous deadly nightshade, *Atropa belladonna*, this perennial is also a member of the potato family, with creeping stems, woody below, which grow to around 3m/10ft. Without hooks or twining stems, it relies on neighbouring plants, stones or simply the ground for support. The ovate to lance-shaped, alternate leaves, up to 9cm/3½in long, are pointed and sometimes have two small lobes or leaflets at the base. From June to September the branched clusters of flowers appear on stalks opposite the leaves – each up to 1.5cm/⅝in across with five curved-back, spear-shaped purple petals and five yellow anthers joined to form a pointed cone in the centre. The glossy, bright red, egg-shaped or oval berries, up to 1.2cm/½in long, contain many rounded seeds.

Bittersweet is found in hedges, damp woodlands, rough ground, fens, ditches and pondsides and on shingle beaches throughout lowland England, but is rarer in the northern counties, ascending to 310m/1,020ft in County Durham.

The young stems contain a toxic alkaloid called solanine, which is bitter to the taste at first and then sweet, hence the common name.

Beware: keep the berries away from children because they are mildly poisonous.

Bittersweet has a specialized flower to attract bees, which release the pollen from holes at the tips of the anthers by rapidly vibrating their wings as they hang from the anther cone.

This plant will give a good long show of colour if it is trained on a trellis or sunny wall, or it can be threaded through a hedge, where both flowers and fruit will add interest and colour. It can also be grown over stone walls, twined through hazel twigs in the border or used as ground cover. It likes full sun and moist but well-drained soil. It is best propagated by taking soft or semi-ripe cuttings of short

So abundant are the rewards of growing elder (*Sambucus nigra*) – outstanding flowers, foliage, fruit and ease of maintenance – that if it were an exotic it would be in great demand. It can be used in a hedge or as a shrub or free-standing tree.

side-shoots in summer. Stems will often form roots where they touch the ground and the rooted shoots can simply be removed and grown on.

Common Whitebeam
Sorbus aria ROSACEAE

With leaves that flash silvery-white when rustled by the wind, the common whitebeam is an attractive and eye-catching deciduous small tree or large shrub. It generally grows up to 15m/50ft, but occasionally as high as 25m/82ft, with a compact, densely leafy, round crown, downy young shoots and smooth grey bark marked with pale breathing pores. As the leaves unfold in late April they form pleasing, upright, goblet-shaped groups, glistening white from the felted hairs on the undersides. The mature oval leaves vary in shape and are up to about 12cm/5in long, shiny green above, thickly coated with white hairs below, with many pairs of veins and usually finely toothed margins. They turn yellow and pale brown before falling in autumn. In May and June loose clusters of five-petalled, creamy-white flowers 1.5cm/⅝in appear in broad, flattened heads, followed by round or oblong scarlet fruits spotted with pores.

Whitebeam is found in light woodland and scrub, mainly on chalk and limestone in the southern third of England, but in scattered localities elsewhere, often on inland cliffs. There are many different microspecies of whitebeam in England, some of which are very rare and restricted in range.

The leaves are eaten by the larvae of tortricoid moths and may be tunnelled by leaf-miners and blistered by gall-mites. The fruits are enjoyed by larger birds in winter.

This is an excellent specimen tree for the smaller garden, or – with its neat shape and its attractions throughout the growing season – it would enhance a woodland corner. It is wind-resistant and suits a town garden because it tolerates a smoky atmosphere and regenerates well after light cutting back. It grows in sun or light shade and on most well-drained soils, from dry and chalky to acid. Propagation is best achieved by gathering the fruits, storing them in polythene bags until rotten, then cleaning the seeds and sowing in containers. Germination can be erratic. Seedlings are best pricked out into small pots containing good potting compost, before potting on or planting in nursery beds and growing on for a further season. For small gardens where plants get individual care they

Bittersweet (*Solanum dulcamara*) is effective when trained on a trellis or against a wall. It just as good as the introduced solanums and has a longer flowering period.

may be safely planted in their permanent sites at the end of their second season.

Rowan or Mountain Ash
Sorbus aucuparia ROSACEAE

This graceful, small deciduous tree with elegant, feathery leaves, smooth bark and bright autumn berries has long been a favourite in cultivation. It rarely grows higher than 15m/50ft, with grey bark ringed with pores and greyish-brown twigs, which in winter carry large brown buds covered with white

ABOVE TOP Great clusters of scarlet fruit decorate the compound-leaves of rowan (*Sorbus aucuparia*) in late summer and autumn.

ABOVE Rowan's flat-topped, creamy-white flowerheads.

hairs. The compound-pinnate leaves have five to seven pairs of slender, oblong leaflets and a terminal leaflet, each up to 6cm/2½in long, sharply toothed, deep green above and grey-green below. They often turn gold and red before falling in autumn. In May and June the dense, flat-topped clusters of creamy-white flowers appear, up to 15cm/6in across. The attractive bunches of juicy berries ripen through yellow to orange and finally scarlet by September.

Rowan is found in woodland, moors and scrub on light, free-draining soils in the lowlands throughout most of England, but it is also widespread on rocks and in acid peat on

mountains, where it ascends to over 850m/2,790ft.

The flowers have a heavy scent, which attracts many flies, bees and beetles to feed on their abundant nectar and pollen. The berries provide winter food for larger birds, especially members of the thrush family.

Rowan is one of the most desirable trees for a garden of any size. It does not grow too large; has beautiful foliage, flowers and fruit; and casts only light shade. It prefers a sunny, open position but will grow in semi-shade and in most moist, free-draining soils (preferably neutral to acid). It is wind-resistant and grows fast when young. Rowan is best propagated from seed by gathering the berries just before they ripen and storing them in polythene bags until rotten. The seeds should then be washed and then sown in moist sand; some will germinate the following spring, others may stay dormant for a further year. Thin out the seedlings, grow on and transplant to 1m/3½ft apart, planting in their final position two years later.

Wild Service-tree
Sorbus torminalis ROSACEAE

This deciduous shrub or small tree is unusual in that it shares certain characteristics with three other trees. Growing up to 15m/50ft high, with a broad, domed head, it has bark similar to that of a hawthorn; leaves that at first glance resemble those of a maple; and flowers and fruit rather like those of a rowan. The dark grey bark is smooth at first but becomes lightly fissured and peels in rectangular strips. Winter buds on the twigs are clear green, opening from late April to unfurl variable leaves with five to seven pointed, toothed lobes, the upper ones directed forwards and the more deeply cut lower pair at right angles. They are shiny above and slightly downy below and can turn crimson in autumn. Open clusters of white flowers 1.2cm/½in across appear in May and June, followed by brown oval fruits up to 1.6cm/⅝in long, which ripen in September and have numerous large but inconspicuous rough pores.

The wild service-tree is found in woodland, scrub and hedgerows, but is local and almost confined to clay soils in ancient woods south of a line joining the Humber and Dee estuaries, mainly in the south-east. Towards its northern limits in England it also grows on limestone.

From Roman times the acid-tasting berries were used as a

remedy for colic and dysentery. The name 'service' is a corruption of *sorbus*.

The nectar attracts pollinating flies, and the seeds are often attacked by the grubs of a seed wasp. The whole fruits are relished by birds and mice.

This can be grown as a specimen tree or in a woodland area of the garden. It thrives in sun or semi-shade (although it will fruit and flower best in sun), and in most moist but well-drained soils. It may be propagated in the same way as common whitebeam. Germination is variable.

Yew

Taxus baccata TAXACEAE

Long since, and in some quiet churchyard laid –
Some country-nook, where o'er thy unknown grave
Tall grasses and white flowering nettles wave,
Under a dark, red-fruited yew-tree's shade.

'The Scholar Gypsy', Matthew Arnold (1822–88)

The majestic, slow-growing, very long-lived yew, with its dense, intensely dark green foliage, is one of England's two native evergreen conifers, the other being juniper. It can be low and bushy or a tree up to 20m/66ft high, with a rounded crown and often a massive, fluted trunk. The soft, flaking, reddish-brown bark becomes greyer and deeply furrowed with age. Tough green shoots on the many branches are spirally set with needles, each up to 2.5cm/1in long, and glossy dark green above, paler below. Male and female flowers, which open in February and March, are usually borne on separate trees but can occur on the same tree. Both appear from the leaf axils on the undersides of twigs – the small, round, yellow male cones releasing clouds of pollen and the tiny, acornlike, yellowish-green females swelling to form the fruit. The hard, poisonous, olive-green seed is surrounded (apart from a hole at the top) by a non-poisonous fleshy aril, about 1.2cm/½in in size, which becomes sweet and pinkish-red in August and September.

Yew is widespread in woodland and scrub on chalk and limestone in the south and west of England, but is spread elsewhere by birds. It ascends to 450m/1,475ft in the Lake District.

Beware: the foliage is poisonous to livestock; the seed is also poisonous.

Yew pollen is a valuable food for early-flying honey bees.

Clouds of yellow pollen rise from male yew (*Taxus baccata*) flowers on warm days in spring. With its dense, dark-green foliage the yew makes one of the most dramatic garden hedges, a perfect foil for the colours of herbaceous flowers.

The fruits are eagerly consumed by birds, including mistle thrushes, blackbirds and jays. The dense canopy provides nest sites and cover for birds throughout the year.

Yew makes the most handsome of garden hedges: dense and smart throughout the year, its very dark green a perfect foil for herbaceous plants. A yew hedge can be trimmed in summer or early autumn, and old, overgrown hedges will regenerate well if cut back hard in spring. In a congenial garden site yew can put on growth faster than its reputation suggests; it is also a fine specimen tree for the larger garden. It grows in sun or deep shade and in any well-drained soil, from acid to alkaline, but it does like some moisture in the ground in winter. It is resistant to pollution. Yew can be propagated from cuttings taken with a heel in autumn and grown in a cold frame, but take care not to damage the brittle roots when handling. Growing from cuttings also ensures both male and female progeny. The plant can also be raised from ripe seeds grown in containers and planted out in nursery beds in their second season. They may take up to two years to germinate. Line out and grow for a further two years before planting permanently in autumn or spring.

The flowers of the small-leaved lime (*Tilia cordata*) can be dried to make lime tea; fibres beneath the bark were once used for making rope. These slow-growing trees respond well to coppicing and there is an ancient coppice in Gloucestershire estimated to be 2,000 years old.

Small-leaved Lime

Tilia cordata TILIACEAE

Well, they are gone, and here must I remain,
This lime-tree bower my prison! I have lost
Beauties and feelings, such as would have been
Most sweet to my remembrance even when age
Had dimmed mine eyes to blindness! …

'This Lime-Tree Bower My Prison', Samuel Taylor Coleridge (1772–1834)

This native lime is an elegant deciduous tree growing up to 30m/100ft, with smooth grey bark, which may later become ribbed, and young twigs that soon lose their slightly downy covering. The dark green leaves, too, are hairless except for a few orange-brown tufts in the vein-axils; they are up to 6cm/2½in long, toothed, heart-shaped and tapering abruptly to a fine tip. The leaves turn yellow in autumn. Clusters, 2cm/¾in across, of

four to ten, five-petalled, yellow-white flowers, open in June and July, held above the foliage on long, obliquely upright stalks, each with a leaflike bract at the base. This bract acts as a wing, helping the smooth, rounded, short-beaked fruits to flutter from the tree after they ripen in October.

Small-leaved lime is scattered in woods throughout lowland England, but is most often found on deep, base-rich soils in central England and Essex.

The flowers can be dried to make lime tea.

In summer the trees hum with the sound of myriad bees attracted by the nectar-filled flowers, and many other insects feed on the sugary honeydew produced by aphids, which can be a nuisance when it drips on to paths or cars. The leaves are also food for buff-tip and lime hawk-moth caterpillars.

Small-leaved lime is slow-growing and suitable as a specimen tree, and responds well to pollarding or coppicing if necessary. In large gardens it makes an effective avenue. It grows in sun or semi-shade and fertile, moist, but well-drained soil preferably alkaline to neutral. It is best propagated by collecting seed and sowing thickly in boxes containing seed compost, then leaving for a year and planting out the seedlings 30cm/12in apart in a nursery bed. If grown in quantity they can be transplanted up to two years later, growing on for a further one or two years. When only one or two plants are required, seedlings can be pricked out into small pots initially, then grown on for planting out in their third season.

Gorse

Ulex europaeus FABACEAE

Under the flying white clouds, and the broad blue lift of the sky;
And to halt at the chattering brook, in the tall green fern at the
brink
Where the harebell grows, and the gorse, and the fox-gloves purple
and white …

'Tewkesbury Road', John Masefield (1878–1967)

Gorse is a breathtaking blaze of brilliant yellow in spring, when this densely prickly, dark green deciduous shrub is smothered with coconut-scented flowers. Upright or bushy and rounded, it grows up to 2.5m/8ft in height with an intricate arrangement of numerous strong, deeply grooved spines and small, stiff leaves; these are in groups of three in young plants, but reduced to scales or weak spines on older

shrubs. Abundant deep yellow pea-flowers, up to 1.8cm/¾in long, appear singly or in small clusters from March to June, although in mild conditions gorse can bloom throughout the year. Popping sounds can be heard from the bush on warm summer days when the hairy, blackish-brown, 1.5cm/⅝in-long seedpods burst open to eject the shiny seeds up to 6m/20ft away.

Gorse grows in rough grassland, heaths, open woods and dunes, often on sandy or peaty soils, throughout England, ascending to 500m/1,640ft in the Pennines.

The rich-scented flowers attract honey bees and bumble bees to the pollen, and the thorns are food for caterpillars of the green hairstreak and silver studded blue butterflies. The dense growth makes excellent cover for small birds, while the prickles protect nest sites.

Gorse is an impressive, hardy and trouble-free shrub for the larger garden, which can be planted in the shrub border or used as a thick, intruder-proof hedge. It is useful for coastal gardens and in exposed sites. It likes full sun and will grow in most well-drained soils, tolerating even the poorest and driest, but with a preference for acid to neutral soil. Gorse is wind-resistant but may be damaged by frost, although it will regenerate. Since it is most attractive when young and does not respond well to pruning, it is best replaced when the stems begin to die back. It is easily raised from seed sown in a cold frame soon after ripening: preferably two or three in a pot, selecting the strongest seedling to be planted out the following autumn. Semi-ripe cuttings with a heel can be taken in summer and planted out the following autumn or spring.

Wayfaring-tree

Viburnum lantana CAPRIFOLIACEAE

The wayfaring-tree has an appealing softness, its twigs and buds being felted with greyish hairs, its stems pliant and the underside of its rounded leaves covered by dense, white, silky hairs. A deciduous tree or small shrub, it grows up to 6m/20ft high, but usually less, and has grey-brown bark marked with leaf scars on the older growth. The opposite pairs of thick, ovate, regularly toothed leaves are opaque greyish-green, up to 12cm/5in long, and ridged on the upper surface. They take on deep plum colours in autumn. The loosely domed clusters of five-petalled, creamy-white flowers, up to 10cm/4in across, appear at the tips of the branches in May and June. These are followed by clusters of shiny, slightly flattened egg-shaped or oval berries, which from July to September ripen through red to black.

The wayfaring-tree is found in woodland, hedgerows and scrub, especially on calcareous soils, throughout the southern half of England and north as far as Lincolnshire and Nottinghamshire.

The nectar attracts pollinating hoverflies, and caterpillars of a species of tortricoid moth eat the leaves from June to August. Birds relish the berries, despite their sour smell.

This is an attractive and easily maintained plant for any garden, providing colour and interest throughout the growing season. It can be used in the shrub border, woodland corner or as a free-standing tree. It grows in sun or semi-shade in well-drained soils, preferably alkaline clays, and tolerates dry conditions, but dislikes smoky atmospheres. The shrub is most easily propagated by gathering fruits as they turn black and stratifying them until late winter. Then sow in early spring in a cold frame, thin the seedlings out and leave until autumn before setting out 30cm/12in apart. Grow on for one or two years before planting out in a permanent site. Cuttings with a heel may be taken in late summer and potted up after rooting.

Guelder-rose
Viburnum opulus CAPRIFOLIACEAE

Lovely lacecap flowers are but one of the pleasures of this vigorous deciduous shrub, for they are followed by a heavy crop of brilliant scarlet fruit and tinted foliage. Rarely more than 4m/13ft tall, and usually just half that height, it is spreading and bushy in habit with smooth, slightly angular, greenish twigs and branches that later become reddish-brown. The opposite pairs of young, maple-like leaves soon shed their downy covering, expanding to up to 8cm/3in across, with three to five irregularly toothed lobes. The leaves turn to shades of russet and orange or yellow before falling in late autumn. In June and July the curious, flat-topped clusters of flowers appear at the tips of branches, up to 8cm/3in across; they are composed of an outer circle of showy, pure-white sterile flowers surrounding a central group of small, tubular, creamy-white fertile flowers. By September and October the bush appears to drip with loose, hanging clusters of one-seeded, translucent red berries, which often remain until leaf-fall.

Guelder-rose is found on lowland woodland margins and in hedgerows, scrub and marshes, on moist, moderately acid or alkaline soils throughout England.

Beware: the berries are slightly poisonous.

The plant is an important resource for wildlife. The nectar in the flowers is attractive to hoverflies, while the berries are a good, pre-winter food source for birds.

This is a superb shrub, providing beauty in return for very little effort. Suitable for the shrub border, the woodland corner, a damp hollow, a hedge or simply as a stand-alone shrub, it grows in sun or semi-shade, although it requires sun to flower and fruit well. It thrives on most moist but well-drained soils, except the most acid, and in cultivation tolerates drier, sandy garden soils. It regenerates well after cutting and can be trimmed to shape. It can send out suckers from the roots and colonize open ground if given the chance. Propagation is as for the wayfaring-tree, although guelder-rose does not germinate as readily.

OPPOSITE ABOVE The translucent red berries of the vigorous guelder-rose (*Viburnum opulus*), one of the most desirable of garden shrubs. Easy to grow on almost any garden soil, it provides attractive foliage with handsome autumn colours and it tolerates pruning.

OPPOSITE LEFT The lacecap flowers of guelder-rose.

OPPOSITE RIGHT The domed clusters of creamy-white flowers of the wayfaring tree (*Viburnum lantana*), an attractive garden tree which is valuable to wildlife.

A New Deal for Native Plants

Growing native plants does not mean wholesale conversion to a wild garden. In fact, English flowers with their free-growing habits make a wonderful show when displayed within the confines of a relatively formal setting. The clean, hard lines of clipped hedges, paths, steps, statuary, walls and fences create the perfect stage for the flowing forms and abundant growth of English flowers, shrubs and trees.

They mix happily with imported plants and indeed will often hybridize with related species, so gardeners keen to encourage wildlife should, where possible, propagate their native plants vegetatively to ensure true offspring. Exuberant mixed borders of local species can be established fairly quickly; raised beds and containers are excellent, both for ease of control and for bringing the generally small but exquisite native blooms closer to eye level.

The two plans shown on the following pages combine classical structure with a varied range of native plants, including trees, shrubs and perennials.

A garden for birds

The Flora-for-Fauna garden at the Chelsea Flower Show, sponsored by Christie's and designed by George Carter, features a 7.6-m/25-ft octagonal, three-tiered, trellis tower with nesting sites for different garden birds. The plan combines ornamental gardening with the conservation of England's native plant heritage, showing how to bring new life into the garden by growing England's ancient plants, all of them valuable sources of food for birds. Paths of drought-resistant native grasses divide the area and provide neat blocks of calm between the relaxed planting in the flower beds. These square beds are edged with native box and overflow with herbaceous plants such as wild strawberry, columbine, wood spurge, foxglove, great mullein and sea-holly. A dark blue-green wooden arch draws the eye towards the circular medieval turf seat made of wattle topped with cushions of grass. The seat, which is backed by woodland planting, provides a home for hibernating hedgehogs. Trees and shrubs in the wood and the habitat hedges include hazel, hornbeam, rowan, beech, hawthorn, holly, blackthorn and ivy. In the pool are water-loving natives such as white water-lily, flag iris and marsh-marigold.

Aquilegia vulgaris (Columbine)   *Thymus polytrichus* (Wild thyme)

Caltha palustris (Marsh-marigold)

The plants

Trees
Buxus sempervirens Box
(edging to square borders)
Prunus avium Wild cherry
(on each front corner)
Taxus baccata Yew

Woodland planting
Carpinus betulus Hornbeam
Corylus avellana Hazel
Fagus sylvatica Beech
Salix caprea Willow
Sorbus aucuparia Rowan

Hedges
Crataegus monogyna
Hawthorn
Hedera helix Ivy
Ilex aquifolium Holly
Prunus spinosa Blackthorn

Borders
Aquilegia vulgaris Columbine
Asperula cynanchica
Squinancywort
Crambe maritima Sea-kale
Digitalis purpurea Foxglove
Eryngium campestre
Field eryngo
Eryngium maritimum
Sea-holly
Euphorbia amygdaloides
Wood spurge
Festuca glauca Grey fescue
Fragaria vesca
Wild strawberry
Geranium molle
Dove's-foot crane's-bill
Helianthemum apenninum
White rock-rose
Hippophae rhamnoides
Sea-buckthorn

Knautia arvensis
Field scabious
Leucanthemum vulgare
Oxeye daisy
Linum perenne
Perennial flax
Myosotis arvensis
Field forget-me-not
Primula vulgaris Primrose
Pulmonaria longifolia
Narrow-leaved lungwort

Plan of the garden for birds

Rosa canina, R. pimpinellifolia
Roses
Teucrium chamaedrys
Wall germander
Thymus polytrichus
Wild thyme
Valeriana officinalis
Common valerian
Verbascum thapsus
Great mullein
Viola odorata Sweet violet

Aquatic plants
Butomus umbellatus
Flowering- rush
Caltha palustris
Marsh-marigold
Iris pseudacorus
Yellow iris
Menyanthes trifoliata
Bogbean
Myosotis scorpioides
Water forget-me-not
Nymphaea alba
White water-lily

A period garden

Historical association helped dictate the simple, traditional cruciform shape of the Flora-for-Fauna garden designed by Penny Hart for Hall Place, a sixteenth- and seventeenth-century mansion set in beautiful, award-winning grounds by the River Cray at Bexley, Kent.

The garden was commissioned by the current owners of Hall Place, the London Borough of Bexley, who became the first local authority in England to make a public garden solely of native plants.

Designed on Tudor lines to harmonize with the building, the garden is paved with old, local bricks. Straight edges con-trast with exuberant herbaceous beds brimming with native plants that would have been familiar to the Elizabethan residents of Hall Place. Wild roses clamber up the fence, while the ancient brick wall on one side can be seen through a light covering of wild roses and honeysuckle. Yew and native box are used for boundaries and border edgings, and buckthorn is planted alongside the lower boundary to attract the brimstone butterfly.

A profusion of a great many different species of native flowers grows in the four beds, including foxglove, red campion, field scabious, fleabane and native geraniums. Low-growing plants such as bird's-foot-trefoil, wild strawberry and dog-violet provide ground cover.

ABOVE LEFT *Iris foetidissima* (Stinking iris)

ABOVE RIGHT *Lotus corniculatus* (Bird's-foot-trefoil)

RIGHT *Eryngium maritimum* (Sea-holly)

The plants
Achillea millefolium Yarrow
Aconitum napellus
　Monk's-hood
Adoxa moschatellina
　Moschatel
Agrimonia eupatoria
　Agrimony
Angelica sylvestris
　Wild angelica
Anthoxanthum odoratum
　Sweet vernal-grass
Anthriscus sylvestris
　Cow parsley
Armeria maritima Thrift
Bidens cernua
　Nodding bur-marigold
Briza media Quaking-grass
Carex flacca Glaucous sedge
Carex remota Remote sedge
Centaurea nigra Common
　knapweed
Centaurea scabiosa Greater
　knapweed
Centaurium erythraea
　Common centaury
Chamerion angustifolium
　Rosebay willowherb
Clinopodium menthifolium
Wood calamint

Chrysoplenium oppositifolium
   Alternate-leaved golden
   saxifrage
Daucus carota Wild carrot
Digitalis purpurea Foxglove
Dipsacus fullonum Teasel
Echium vulgare
   Viper's-bugloss
Eryngium maritimum
   Sea-holly
Filipendula vulgaris
   Dropwort
Fragaria vesca
   Wild strawberry
Galium saxatile
   Heath bedstraw
Geranium pratense
   Meadow crane's-bill
Geranium sanguineum
   Bloody crane's-bill
Geranium sylvaticum
   Wood crane's-bill
Geum urbanum Wood avens
Helianthemum nummularium
   Rock-rose
Helictotrichon pratense
   Meadow oat-grass
Hypericum tetrapterum
   Square-stalked St John's
   wort
Iris foetidissima Stinking iris
Jasione montana Sheep's-bit
Knautia arvensis
   Field scabious
Lathyrus pratensis
   Meadow vetchling
Leucanthemum vulgare
   Oxeye daisy
Lotus corniculatus
   Bird's-foot-trefoil
Luzula pallidula
   Woodrush
Lychnis viscaria
   Sticky catchfly

Origanum vulgare Marjoram
Oxalis acetosella Wood sorrel
Pilosella officinarum
   Mouse-ear-hawkweed
Pimpinella major
   Greater burnet-saxifrage
Potentilla erecta Tormentil
Potentilla sterilis
   Barren strawberry
Primula elatior Oxlip
Primula veris Cowslip
Primula vulgaris Primrose
Prunella vulgaris Selfheal
Pulicaria dysenterica
   Common fleabane
Ranunculus acris
   Meadow buttercup
Reseda lutea
   Wild mignonette
Scabiosa columbaria
   Small scabious
Sedum forsterianum
   Rock stonecrop
Silene latifolia
   White campion
Silene dioica Red campion
Silene nutans
   Nottingham catchfly
Silene vulgaris
   Bladder campion
Stachys officinalis Betony
Stachys sylvatica
   Hedge woundwort
Stellaria holostea
   Greater stitchwort
Tanacetum vulgare Tansy
Trifolium ochroleucon
   Sulphur clover
Verbascum nigrum
   Dark mullein
Verbena officinalis Vervain
Vicia cracca Tufted vetch
Viola riviniana
   Dog-violet

Plan of the period garden

Protected from cold easterly winds by an old brick wall (on the right), the four beds are planted with natural-looking drifts of colours. Taller flowers such as teasel, red campion and foxgloves grade down to medium-height plants such as common fleabane and small scabious, while ground cover such as wild strawberry and dog-violet are used for the edging. Scrambling roses cover the fence on the top boundary.

161

Directory of English Native Plants

To encourage the restoration of English plants in English gardens, Flora-for-Fauna commissioned Dr Chris Preston at the Institute of Terrestrial Ecology, Monks Wood – the centre for biological and distribution records in Britain – to compile this native plants directory. This list comprises the plants which are believed by the Botanical Society of the British Isles, who gathered the information for the records, to be native to England. Species formerly recorded in England but now believed to be extinct are marked with an obelus (†).

Some of the plants which we consider particularly gardenworthy are in **bold** type. Species described in this book are preceded by an asterisk *, followed by their relevant page number in **bold**.

English Endemic Plants
(plants found only in England)

Alchemilla minima	Lady's-mantle
Arenaria norvegica subsp. *anglica*	English sandwort
Bromus interruptus †	Interrupted brome
Coincya wrightii	Lundy cabbage
Epipactis youngiana	Young's helleborine
Euphrasia vigursii	Eyebright
Fumaria occidentalis	Western Ramping-fumitory
Gentianella anglica	Early gentian
Limonium dodartiforme	Sea-lavender
Limonium loganicum	Sea-lavender
Limonium recurvum subsp. *recurvum*	Sea-lavender
Sorbus bristoliensis	Whitebeam
Sorbus lancastriensis	Whitebeam
Sorbus subcuneata	Whitebeam
Sorbus vexans	Whitebeam
Sorbus wilmottiana	Whitebeam
Ulmus plotii	Plot's elm

English Native Plants

Acer campestre	**Field maple 121**
Aceras anthropophorum	Man orchid
Achillea millefolium	**Yarrow 33**
Achillea ptarmica	**Sneezewort 33**
Aconitum napellus	**Monk's-hood 33**
Actaea spicata	**Baneberry or herb Christopher**
Adiantum capillus-veneris	**Maidenhair fern**
Adoxa moschatellina	**Moschatel**
Aethusa cynapium	**Fool's parsley**
Agrimonia eupatoria	**Agrimony 34**
Agrimonia procera	**Fragrant agrimony**
Agrostis canina	**Velvet bent**
Agrostis capillaris	**Common bent**
Agrostis curtisii	Bristle bent
Agrostis gigantea	**Black bent**
Agrostis stolonifera	**Creeping bent**
Agrostis vinealis	Brown bent
Aira caryophyllea	Silver hair-grass
Aira praecox	Early hair-grass
Ajuga chamaepitys	Ground-pine
Ajuga pyramidalis	Pyramidal bugle
Ajuga reptans	**Bugle 35**
Alchemilla acutiloba	Lady's-mantle
Alchemilla alpina	**Alpine lady's-mantle**
Alchemilla filicaulis	**Hairy lady's-mantle**
Alchemilla glabra	**Smooth lady's-mantle**
Alchemilla glaucescens	Lady's-mantle
Alchemilla glomerulans	Lady's-mantle
Alchemilla gracilis	Lady's-mantle
Alchemilla minima	Lady's-mantle

Alchemilla monticola	Lady's-mantle
Alchemilla subcrenata	Lady's-mantle
Alchemilla wichurae	Lady's-mantle
Alchemilla xanthochlora	**Intermediate lady's-mantle**
Alisma gramineum	Ribbon-leaved water-plantain
Alisma lanceolatum	Narrow-leaved water-plantain
Alisma plantago-aquatica	Water-plantain
Alliaria petiolata	Garlic mustard
Allium ampeloprasum	Wild leek
Allium oleraceum	Field garlic
Allium schoenoprasum	**Chives**
Allium scorodoprasum	Sand leek
Allium sphaerocephalon	**Round-headed leek**
Allium ursinum	**Ramsons 36**
Allium vineale	Wild onion
Alnus glutinosa	**Alder**
Alopecurus aequalis	Orange foxtail
Alopecurus borealis	Alpine foxtail
Alopecurus bulbosus	Bulbous foxtail
Alopecurus geniculatus	Marsh foxtail
Alopecurus myosuroides	Black-grass
Alopecurus pratensis	**Meadow foxtail**
Althaea officinalis	**Marsh-mallow**
Ammophila arenaria	Marram grass
Anacamptis pyramidalis	Pyramidal orchid
Anagallis arvensis	**Scarlet pimpernel**
Anagallis minima	Chaffweed
Anagallis tenella	**Bog pimpernel**

Anchusa arvensis	**Bugloss**	***Athyrium filix-femina***	**Lady-fern 114**	*Callitriche brutia*	Pedunculate
Andromeda polifolia	**Bog-rosemary**	*Atriplex glabriuscula*	Babington's orache		water-starwort
Anemone nemorosa	**Wood anemone 36**	*Atriplex laciniata*	Frosted orache	*Callitriche hamulata*	Intermediate
Angelica sylvestris	**Wild angelica 38**	*Atriplex littoralis*	Grass-leaved orache		water-starwort
Anisantha sterilis	Barren brome	*Atriplex longipes*	Long-stalked orache	*Callitriche hermaphroditica*	Autumnal
Antennaria dioica	**Mountain everlasting**	*Atriplex patula*	Common orache		water-starwort
Anthemis arvensis	**Corn chamomile**	*Atriplex pedunculata*	Pedunculate	*Callitriche obtusangula*	Blunt-fruited
Anthemis cotula	**Stinking chamomile**		sea-purslane		water-starwort
Anthoxanthum	**Sweet vernal-grass**	*Atriplex portulacoides*	Sea-purslane	*Callitriche platycarpa*	Various-leaved
odoratum		*Atriplex praecox*	Early orache		water-starwort
Anthriscus caucalis	**Bur chervil**	*Atriplex prostrata*	Spear-leaved orache	*Callitriche stagnalis*	Common
Anthriscus sylvestris	**Cow parsley**	*Atropa belladonna*	Deadly nightshade		water-starwort
Anthyllis vulneraria	**Kidney vetch**	*Baldellia ranunculoides*	Lesser water-plantain	*Callitriche truncata*	Short-leaved water-
Apera interrupta	Dense silky-bent	***Ballota nigra***	**Black horehound**		starwort
Apera spica-venti	Loose silky-bent	*Barbarea stricta*	Small-flowered	***Calluna vulgaris***	**Heather**
Aphanes arvensis	Parsley-piert		winter-cress	***Caltha palustris***	**Marsh-marigold 41**
Aphanes inexpectata	Slender parsley-piert	*Barbarea vulgaris*	Winter-cress	*Calystegia sepium*	Hedge bindweed
Apium graveolens	Wild celery	*Bartsia alpina*	Alpine bartsia	*Calystegia soldanella*	Sea bindweed
Apium inundatum	Lesser marshwort	***Bellis perennis***	**Daisy 40**	***Campanula glomerata***	**Clustered bellflower**
Apium nodiflorum	Fool's-water-cress	***Berberis vulgaris***	**Barberry**		**42**
Apium repens	Creeping marshwort	*Berula erecta*	Lesser water-parsnip	***Campanula latifolia***	**Giant bellflower 42**
Aquilegia vulgaris	**Columbine 38**	*Beta vulgaris*	Beet	*Campanula patula*	**Spreading bellflower**
Arabidopsis thaliana	Thale cress	***Betula nana***	**Dwarf birch**	***Campanula***	**Harebell 42**
Arabis glabra	Tower mustard	***Betula pendula***	**Silver birch 121**	*rotundifolia*	
Arabis hirsuta	Hairy rock-cress	***Betula pubescens***	**Downy birch**	*Campanula trachelium*	**Nettle-leaved**
Arabis scabra	Bristol rock-cress	*Bidens cernua*	Nodding bur-marigold		**bellflower**
Arctium lappa	Greater burdock	*Bidens tripartita*	Trifid bur-marigold	*Capsella bursa-pastoris*	Shepherd's-purse
Arctium minus	Lesser burdock	***Blackstonia perfoliata***	**Yellow-wort**	*Cardamine amara*	Large bitter-cress
Arctostaphylos uva-ursi	**Bearberry**	***Blechnum spicant***	**Hard-fern**	*Cardamine bulbifera*	Coralroot
Arenaria norvegica	Arctic sandwort	*Blysmus compressus*	Flat-sedge	*Cardamine flexuosa*	Wavy bitter-cress
Arenaria serpyllifolia	Thyme-leaved sandwort	*Blysmus rufus*	Saltmarsh flat-sedge	*Cardamine hirsuta*	Hairy bitter-cress
Armeria maritima	**Thrift 39**	*Bolboschoenus maritimus*	Sea club-rush	*Cardamine impatiens*	Narrow-leaved
Arnoseris minima	Lamb's succory	*Botrychium lunaria*	Moonwort		bitter-cress
Arrhenatherum elatius	False oat-grass	*Brachypodium pinnatum*	Tor-grass	***Cardamine pratensis***	**Cuckooflower 43**
Artemisia absinthium	**Wormwood**	*Brachypodium sylvaticum*	False brome	*Carduus crispus*	Welted thistle
Artemisia campestris	**Field wormwood**	*Brassica nigra*	Black mustard	*Carduus nutans*	Musk thistle
Artemisia vulgaris	Mugwort	*Brassica oleracea*	Cabbage	*Carduus tenuiflorus*	Slender thistle
Arum italicum	**Italian**	***Briza media***	**Quaking grass 109**	*Carex acuta*	Slender tufted-sedge
	lords-and-ladies	*Bromopsis benekenii*	Lesser hairy-brome	*Carex acutiformis*	Lesser pond-sedge
Arum maculatum	**Lords-and-ladies 39**	*Bromopsis erecta*	Upright brome	*Carex appropinquata*	Fibrous tussock-sedge
Asparagus officinalis	**Wild asparagus**	*Bromopsis ramosa*	Hairy-brome	***Carex aquatilis***	**Water sedge**
Asperula cynanchica	**Squinancywort**	*Bromus commutatus*	Meadow brome	*Carex arenaria*	Sand sedge
Asplenium adiantum-	**Black spleenwort 113**	*Bromus hordeaceus*	Soft-brome	*Carex atrata*	Black alpine-sedge
nigrum		*Bromus interruptus*	Interrupted brome	*Carex bigelowii*	Stiff sedge
Asplenium marinum	**Sea spleenwort**	*Bromus racemosus*	Smooth brome	*Carex binervis*	Green-ribbed sedge
Asplenium obovatum	**Lanceolate spleenwort**	*Bryonia dioica*	White bryony	*Carex capillaris*	Hair sedge
Asplenium ruta-muraria	**Wall-rue**	*Bunium bulbocastanum*	Great pignut	*Carex caryophyllea*	Spring-sedge
Asplenium septentrionale	**Forked spleenwort**	*Bupleurum baldense*	Small hare's-ear	*Carex curta*	White sedge
Asplenium trichomanes	**Maidenhair spleenwort**	*Bupleurum falcatum*	Sickle-leaved hare's-ear	*Carex davalliana*	Davall's sedge
	113	*Bupleurum tenuissimum*	Slender hare's-ear	*Carex depauperata*	Starved wood-sedge
Asplenium trichomanes-	Green spleenwort	***Butomus umbellatus***	**flowering-rush 41**	*Carex diandra*	Lesser tussock-sedge
ramosum		***Buxus sempervirens***	**Box**	*Carex digitata*	Fingered sedge
Aster linosyris	**Goldilocks aster**	*Cakile maritima*	Sea rocket	*Carex dioica*	Dioecious sedge
Aster tripolium	**Sea aster 39**	*Calamagrostis canescens*	Purple small-reed	*Carex distans*	Distant sedge
Astragalus danicus	**Purple milk-vetch**	*Calamagrostis epigejos*	Wood small-reed	*Carex disticha*	Brown sedge
Astragalus glycyphyllos	Wild liquorice	*Calamagrostis purpurea*	Scandinavian small-reed	*Carex divisa*	Divided sedge
		Calamagrostis stricta	Narrow small-reed	*Carex divulsa*	Grey sedge

Carex echinata	Star sedge	*Cephalanthera damasonium*	White helleborine	*Cochlearia anglica*	English scurvygrass
Carex elata	Tufted-sedge	*Cephalanthera longifolia*	Narrow-leaved helleborine	*Cochlearia danica*	Danish scurvygrass
Carex elongata	Elongated sedge			*Cochlearia officinalis*	Common scurvygrass
Carex ericetorum	Rare spring-sedge	*Cephalanthera rubra*	Red helleborine	*Cochlearia pyrenaica*	Pyrenean scurvygrass
Carex extensa	Long-bracted sedge	**Cerastium alpinum**	**Alpine mouse-ear**	*Coeloglossum viride*	Frog orchid
Carex filiformis	Downy-fruited sedge	*Cerastium arvense*	Field mouse-ear	*Coincya monensis*	Isle-of-Man cabbage
Carex flacca	Glaucous sedge	*Cerastium brachypetalum*	Grey mouse-ear	*Coincya wrightii*	Lundy cabbage
Carex flava	Large yellow-sedge	*Cerastium diffusum*	Sea mouse-ear	**Colchicum autumnale**	**Meadow saffron**
Carex hirta	Hairy sedge	*Cerastium fontanum*	Common mouse-ear	*Conium maculatum*	Hemlock
Carex hostiana	Tawny sedge	*Cerastium glomeratum*	Sticky mouse-ear	*Conopodium majus*	Pignut
Carex humilis	**Dwarf sedge**	*Cerastium pumilum*	Dwarf mouse-ear	***Convallaria majalis***	**Lily-of-the-valley 47**
Carex laevigata	Smooth-stalked sedge	*Cerastium semidecandrum*	Little mouse-ear	*Convolvulus arvensis*	Field bindweed
Carex lasiocarpa	Slender sedge	*Ceratocapnos claviculata*	Climbing corydalis	*Corallorhiza trifida*	Coralroot orchid
Carex limosa	Bog-sedge	*Ceratophyllum demersum*	Rigid hornwort	***Cornus sanguinea***	**Dogwood 125**
Carex magellanica	Tall bog-sedge	*Ceratophyllum submersum*	Soft hornwort	**Cornus suecica**	**Dwarf cornel**
Carex maritima	Curved sedge	**Ceterach officinarum**	**Rustyback**	*Coronopus squamatus*	Swine-cress
Carex montana	Soft-leaved sedge	*Chaenorhinum minus*	Small toadflax	*Corrigiola litoralis*	Strapwort
Carex muricata	Prickly sedge	**Chaerophyllum temulum**	**Rough chervil**	***Corylus avellana***	**Hazel 125**
Carex nigra	Common sedge	**Chamaemelum nobile**	**Chamomile**	*Corynephorus canescens*	Grey hair-grass
Carex ornithopoda	Bird's-foot sedge	*Chamerion angustifolium*	Rosebay willowherb	**Crambe maritima**	**Sea-kale**
Carex otrubae	False fox-sedge	**Chelidonium majus**	**Greater celandine**	*Crassula aquatica*	Pigmyweed
Carex ovalis	Oval sedge	*Chenopodium album*	Fat-hen	*Crassula tillaea*	Mossy stonecrop
Carex pallescens	Pale sedge	*Chenopodium chenopodioides*	Saltmarsh goosefoot	***Crataegus laevigata***	**Midland hawthorn 126**
Carex panicea	Carnation sedge	*Chenopodium ficifolium*	Fig-leaved goosefoot		
Carex paniculata	**Greater tussock-sedge**	*Chenopodium glaucum*	Oak-leaved goosefoot	***Crataegus monogyna***	**Hawthorn 126**
Carex pauciflora	Few-flowered sedge	*Chenopodium hybridum*	Maple-leaved goosefoot	**Crepis biennis**	**Rough hawk's-beard**
Carex pendula	**Pendulous sedge 109**	*Chenopodium murale*	Nettle-leaved goosefoot	*Crepis capillaris*	Smooth hawk's-beard
Carex pilulifera	Pill sedge	*Chenopodium polyspermum*	Many-seeded goosefoot	*Crepis foetida*	Stinking hawk's-beard
Carex pseudocyperus	**Cyperus sedge**	*Chenopodium rubrum*	Red goosefoot	*Crepis mollis*	Northern hawk's-beard
Carex pulicaris	Flea sedge	*Chenopodium urbicum*	Upright goosefoot	*Crepis paludosa*	Marsh hawk's-beard
Carex punctata	Dotted sedge	*Chenopodium vulvaria*	Stinking goosefoot	*Crepis praemorsa*	Leafless hawk's-beard
Carex remota	Remote sedge	**Chrysosplenium alternifolium**	**Alternate-leaved golden-saxifrage**	**Crithmum maritimum**	**Rock samphire**
Carex riparia	Greater pond-sedge			***Cruciata laevipes***	**Crosswort 47**
Carex rostrata	**Bottle sedge**	**Chrysosplenium oppositifolium**	**Opposite-leaved golden-saxifrage**	*Cryptogramma crispa*	Parsley fern
Carex spicata	Spiked sedge			*Cuscuta epithymum*	Dodder
Carex strigosa	Thin-spiked wood-sedge	*Cicendia filiformis*	Yellow centaury	*Cuscuta europaea*	Greater dodder
		Cichorium intybus	**Chicory**	**Cynoglossum germanicum**	**Green hound's-tongue**
Carex sylvatica	Wood-sedge	*Cicuta virosa*	Cowbane		
Carex trinervis	Three-nerved sedge	**Circaea alpina**	**Alpine enchanter's-nightshade**	**Cynoglossum officinale**	**Hound's-tongue**
Carex vesicaria	Bladder-sedge			*Cynosurus cristatus*	Crested dog's-tail
Carex viridula	Yellow-sedge	*Circaea lutetiana*	Enchanter's-nightshade	*Cyperus fuscus*	Brown galingale
Carex vulpina	True fox-sedge	*Cirsium acaule*	Dwarf thistle	*Cyperus longus*	Galingale
Carlina vulgaris	Carline thistle	*Cirsium arvense*	Creeping thistle	*Cypripedium calceolus*	Lady's-slipper
Carpinus betulus	**Hornbeam 123**	*Cirsium dissectum*	Meadow thistle	**Cystopteris fragilis**	**Brittle bladder-fern**
Carum verticillatum	Whorled caraway	**Cirsium eriophorum**	**Woolly thistle**	**Cystopteris montana**	**Mountain bladder-fern**
Catabrosa aquatica	Whorl-grass	*Cirsium heterophyllum*	Melancholy thistle		
Catapodium marinum	Sea fern-grass	*Cirsium palustre*	Marsh thistle	***Cytisus scoparius***	**Broom 127**
Catapodium rigidum	Fern-grass	*Cirsium tuberosum*	Tuberous thistle	*Dactylis glomerata*	Cock's-foot
Centaurea nigra	**Common knapweed 44**	*Cirsium vulgare*	Spear thistle	*Dactylorhiza fuchsii*	Common spotted-orchid
Centaurea scabiosa	**Greater knapweed 44**	*Cladium mariscus*	Great fen-sedge	*Dactylorhiza incarnata*	Early marsh-orchid
Centaurium erythraea	**Common centaury**	***Clematis vitalba***	**Traveller's-joy 124**	*Dactylorhiza maculata*	Heath spotted-orchid
Centaurium latifolium	Broad-leaved centaury	**Clinopodium acinos**	**Basil thyme**	*Dactylorhiza majalis*	Western marsh-orchid
Centaurium littorale	Seaside centaury	**Clinopodium ascendens**	**Common calamint**	*Dactylorhiza praetermissa*	Southern marsh-orchid
Centaurium pulchellum	Lesser centaury	**Clinopodium calamintha**	**Lesser calamint**	*Dactylorhiza purpurella*	Northern marsh-orchid
Centaurium scilloides	Perennial centaury	**Clinopodium menthifolium**	**Wood calamint**	*Dactylorhiza traunsteineri*	Narrow-leaved marsh-orchid
Centaurium tenuiflorum	Slender centaury	***Clinopodium vulgare***	**Wild basil 44**		

Damasonium alisma	Starfruit	*Epilobium montanum*	Broad-leaved willowherb	*Euphorbia exigua*	Dwarf spurge
Danthonia decumbens	Heath-grass			*Euphorbia helioscopia*	Sun spurge
Daphne laureola	**Spurge-laurel 128**	*Epilobium obscurum*	Short-fruited willowherb	*Euphorbia hyberna*	Irish spurge
Daphne mezereum	**Mezereon**	*Epilobium palustre*	Marsh willowherb	***Euphorbia lathyris***	**Caper spurge**
Daucus carota	**Wild carrot**	*Epilobium parviflorum*	Hoary willowherb	*Euphorbia paralias*	Sea spurge
Deschampsia cespitosa	**Tufted hair-grass 111**	*Epilobium roseum*	Pale willowherb	*Euphorbia peplis*	Purple spurge
Deschampsia flexuosa	**Wavy hair-grass 111**	*Epilobium tetragonum*	Square-stalked willowherb	*Euphorbia peplus*	Petty spurge
Deschampsia setacea	Bog hair-grass			*Euphorbia platyphyllos*	Broad-leaved spurge
Dianthus armeria	**Deptford pink**	*Epipactis atrorubens*	Dark-red helleborine	*Euphorbia portlandica*	Portland spurge
Dianthus deltoides	**Maiden pink 48**	*Epipactis helleborine*	Broad-leaved helleborine	*Euphorbia serrulata*	Upright spurge
Dianthus gratianopolitanus	**Cheddar pink**	*Epipactis leptochila*	Narrow-lipped helleborine	*Euphorbia villosa*	Hairy spurge
				Euphrasia anglica	Eyebright
Digitalis purpurea	**Foxglove 48**	*Epipactis palustris*	Marsh helleborine	*Euphrasia arctica*	Eyebright
Diphasiastrum alpinum	Alpine clubmoss	*Epipactis phyllanthes*	Green-flowered helleborine	*Euphrasia confusa*	Eyebright
Diphasiastrum complanatum	Issler's clubmoss			*Euphrasia frigida*	Eyebright
Diplotaxis tenuifolia	Perennial wall-rocket	*Epipactis purpurata*	Violet helleborine	*Euphrasia micrantha*	Eyebright
Dipsacus fullonum	**Teasel 49**	*Epipactis youngiana*	Young's helleborine	*Euphrasia nemorosa*	Eyebright
Dipsacus pilosus	**Small teasel**	*Epipogium aphyllum*	Ghost orchid	*Euphrasia ostenfeldii*	Eyebright
Draba incana	Hoary whitlowgrass	*Equisetum arvense*	Field horsetail	*Euphrasia pseudokerneri*	Eyebright
Draba muralis	Wall whitlowgrass	*Equisetum fluviatile*	Water horsetail	*Euphrasia rivularis*	Eyebright
Drosera intermedia	Oblong-leaved sundew	*Equisetum hyemale*	Rough horsetail	*Euphrasia rostkoviana*	Eyebright
Drosera longifolia	Great sundew	*Equisetum palustre*	Marsh horsetail	*Euphrasia scottica*	Eyebright
Drosera rotundifolia	Round-leaved sundew	*Equisetum pratense*	Shady horsetail	*Euphrasia tetraquetra*	Eyebright
Dryas octopetala	**Mountain avens 52**	*Equisetum ramosissimum*	Branched horsetail	*Euphrasia vigursii*	Eyebright
Dryopteris aemula	**Hay-scented buckler-fern**	*Equisetum sylvaticum*	Wood horsetail	***Fagus sylvatica***	**Beech**
		Equisetum telmateia	Great horsetail	*Fallopia convolvulus*	Black-bindweed
Dryopteris affinis	**Scaly male-fern**	*Equisetum variegatum*	Variegated horsetail	*Fallopia dumetorum*	Copse-bindweed
Dryopteris carthusiana	**Narrow buckler-fern**	**Erica ciliaris**	**Dorset heath**	*Festuca altissima*	Wood fescue
Dryopteris cristata	**Crested buckler-fern**	***Erica cinerea***	**Bell heather 129**	*Festuca arenaria*	Rush-leaved fescue
Dryopteris dilatata	**Broad buckler-fern**	**Erica tetralix**	**Cross-leaved heath**	*Festuca arundinacea*	Tall fescue
Dryopteris expansa	**Northern buckler-fern**	**Erica vagans**	**Cornish heath**	*Festuca filiformis*	Fine-leaved sheep's-fescue
Dryopteris filix-mas	**Male-fern 114**	*Erigeron acer*	Blue fleabane		
Dryopteris oreades	**Mountain male-fern**	***Eriophorum angustifolium***	**Common cottongrass 111**	***Festuca gigantea***	**Giant fescue**
Dryopteris submontana	Rigid buckler-fern			*Festuca huonii*	Huon's fescue
Echium plantagineum	**Purple viper's-bugloss**			*Festuca lemanii*	Confused fescue
Echium vulgare	**Viper's-bugloss 52**	**Eriophorum gracile**	**Slender cottongrass**	*Festuca longifolia*	Blue fescue
Elatine hexandra	Six-stamened waterwort	**Eriophorum latifolium**	**Broad-leaved cottongrass**	***Festuca ovina***	**Sheep's-fescue**
Elatine hydropiper	Eight-stamened waterwort			*Festuca pratensis*	Meadow fescue
		Eriophorum vaginatum	**Hare's-tail cottongrass**	***Festuca rubra***	**Red fescue**
Eleocharis acicularis	Needle spike-rush			***Festuca vivipara***	**Viviparous sheep's-fescue**
Eleocharis austriaca	Northern spike-rush	**Erodium cicutarium**	**Common stork's-bill**		
Eleocharis multicaulis	Many-stalked spike-rush	*Erodium lebelii*	Sticky stork's-bill	*Filago lutescens*	Red-tipped cudweed
Eleocharis palustris	Common spike-rush	*Erodium maritimum*	Sea stork's-bill	*Filago minima*	Small cudweed
Eleocharis parvula	Dwarf spike-rush	*Erodium moschatum*	Musk stork's-bill	*Filago pyramidata*	Broad-leaved cudweed
Eleocharis quinqueflora	Few-flowered spike-rush	*Erophila glabrescens*	Glabrous whitlowgrass	*Filago vulgaris*	Common cudweed
		Erophila majuscula	Hairy whitlowgrass	***Filipendula ulmaria***	**Meadowsweet 54**
Eleocharis uniglumis	Slender spike-rush	*Erophila verna*	Common whitlowgrass	**Filipendula vulgaris**	**Dropwort**
Eleogiton fluitans	Floating club-rush	**Eryngium campestre**	**Field eryngo**	***Fragaria vesca***	**Wild strawberry 55**
Elymus caninus	Bearded couch	***Eryngium maritimum***	**Sea holly 53**	***Frangula alnus***	**Alder buckthorn 130**
Elytrigia atherica	Sea couch	***Euonymus europaeus***	**Spindle 129**	*Frankenia laevis*	Sea-heath
Elytrigia juncea	Sand couch			**Fraxinus excelsior**	**Ash**
Elytrigia repens	Common couch			***Fritillaria meleagris***	**Fritillary 57**
Empetrum nigrum	**Crowberry**	***Eupatorium cannabinum***	Hemp-agrimony 53	**Fumaria bastardii**	**Tall ramping-fumitory**
Epilobium alsinifolium	Chickweed willowherb			**Fumaria capreolata**	**White ramping-fumitory**
Epilobium anagallidifolium	Alpine willowherb	***Euphorbia amygdaloides***	Wood spurge 53		
Epilobium hirsutum	**Great willowherb**			*Fumaria densiflora*	Dense-flowered fumitory
Epilobium lanceolatum	Spear-leaved willowherb	**Euphorbia cyparissias**	**Cypress spurge**		

Fumaria muralis	Common ramping-fumitory	*Geranium pusillum*	Small-flowered crane's-bill
Fumaria occidentalis	Western ramping-fumitory	*Geranium pyrenaicum*	Hedgerow crane's-bill
Fumaria officinalis	Common fumitory	*Geranium robertianum*	Herb-robert 62
Fumaria parviflora	Fine-leaved fumitory	*Geranium rotundifolium*	Round-leaved crane's-bill
Fumaria purpurea	Purple ramping-fumitory	*Geranium sanguineum*	Bloody crane's-bill 62
Fumaria reuteri	Martin's ramping-fumitory	*Geranium sylvaticum*	Wood crane's-bill 63
Fumaria vaillantii	Few-flowered fumitory	*Geum rivale*	Water avens 63
Gagea lutea	Yellow star-of-Bethlehem	Geum urbanum	Wood avens
		Gladiolus illyricus	Wild gladiolus
Galanthus nivalis	Snowdrop	*Glaucium flavum*	Yellow horned-poppy 64
Galeopsis angustifolia	Red hemp-nettle	*Glaux maritima*	Sea-milkwort
Galeopsis bifida	Bifid hemp-nettle	*Glechoma hederacea*	Ground ivy 64
Galeopsis segetum †	Downy hemp-nettle	*Glyceria declinata*	Small sweet-grass
Galeopsis speciosa	Large-flowered hemp-nettle	*Glyceria fluitans*	Floating sweet-grass
		Glyceria maxima	Reed sweet-grass
Galeopsis tetrahit	Common hemp-nettle	*Glyceria notata*	Plicate sweet-grass
Galium aparine	Cleavers	*Gnaphalium luteoalbum*	Jersey cudweed
Galium boreale	Northern bedstraw	*Gnaphalium sylvaticum*	Heath cudweed
Galium constrictum	Slender marsh-bedstraw	*Gnaphalium uliginosum*	Marsh cudweed
Galium mollugo	Hedge bedstraw	*Goodyera repens*	Creeping lady's-tresses
Galium odoratum	Woodruff 60	*Groenlandia densa*	Opposite-leaved pondweed
Galium palustre	Common marsh-bedstraw	*Gymnadenia conopsea*	Fragrant orchid
Galium parisiense	Wall bedstraw	*Gymnocarpium dryopteris*	Oak fern
Galium pumilum	Slender bedstraw		
Galium saxatile	Heath bedstraw	*Gymnocarpium robertianum*	Limestone fern
Galium spurium	False cleavers		
Galium sterneri	Limestone bedstraw	*Hammarbya paludosa*	Bog orchid
Galium tricornutum	Corn cleavers	*Hedera helix*	Ivy 130
Galium uliginosum	Fen bedstraw	*Helianthemum apenninum*	White rock-rose
Galium verum	Lady's bedstraw 60		
Gastridium ventricosum	Nit-grass	*Helianthemum canum*	Hoary rock-rose
Genista anglica	Petty whin	*Helianthemum nummularium*	Common rock-rose 65
Genista pilosa	Hairy greenweed		
Genista tinctoria	Dyer's greenweed	*Helictotrichon pratense*	Meadow oat-grass
Gentiana pneumonanthe	Marsh gentian	*Helictotrichon pubescens*	Downy oat-grass
Gentiana verna	Spring gentian	*Helleborus foetidus*	Stinking hellebore 66
Gentianella amarella	Autumn gentian	Helleborus viridis	Green hellebore
Gentianella anglica	Early gentian	*Heracleum sphondylium*	Hogweed
Gentianella campestris	Field gentian	*Herminium monorchis*	Musk orchid
Gentianella ciliata	Fringed gentian	*Herniaria ciliolata*	Fringed rupturewort
Gentianella germanica	Chiltern gentian	*Herniaria glabra*	Smooth rupturewort
Gentianella uliginosa †	Dune gentian	*Hieracium murorum* agg.	Hawkweed
Geranium columbinum	Long-stalked crane's-bill	*Himantoglossum hircinum*	Lizard orchid
		Hippocrepis comosa	Horseshoe vetch
Geranium dissectum	Cut-leaved crane's-bill	Hippophae rhamnoides	Sea-buckthorn
Geranium lucidum	Shining crane's-bill	*Hippuris vulgaris*	Mare's-tail
Geranium molle	Dove's-foot crane's-bill	*Holcus lanatus*	Yorkshire-fog
		Holcus mollis	Creeping soft-grass
Geranium pratense	Meadow crane's-bill 62	*Holosteum umbellatum*	Jagged chickweed
		Honckenya peploides	Sea sandwort
Geranium purpureum	Little-Robin	Hordelymus europaeus	Wood barley
		Hordeum marinum	Sea barley

Hordeum murinum	Wall barley		
Hordeum secalinum	Meadow barley		
Hornungia petraea	Hutchinsia		
Hottonia palustris	Water-violet		
Humulus lupulus	Hop 131		
Huperzia selago	Fir clubmoss		
Hyacinthoides non-scripta	Bluebell 66		
Hydrilla verticillata	Hydrilla		
Hydrocharis morsus-ranae	Frogbit		
Hydrocotyle vulgaris	Marsh pennywort		
Hymenophyllum tunbrigense	Tunbridge filmy-fern		
Hymenophyllum wilsonii	Wilson's filmy-fern		
Hyoscyamus niger	Henbane		
Hypericum androsaemum	Tutsan 132		
Hypericum elodes	Marsh St John's-wort		
Hypericum hirsutum	Hairy St John's-wort		
Hypericum humifusum	Trailing St John's-wort		
Hypericum linariifolium	Toadflax-leaved St John's-wort		
Hypericum maculatum	Imperforate St John's-wort		
Hypericum montanum	Pale St John's-wort		
Hypericum perforatum	Perforate St John's-wort 132		
Hypericum pulchrum	Slender St John's-wort		
Hypericum tetrapterum	Square-stalked St John's-wort		
Hypericum undulatum	Wavy St John's-wort		
Hypochaeris glabra	Smooth cat's-ear		
Hypochaeris maculata	Spotted cat's-ear		
Hypochaeris radicata	Cat's-ear		
Iberis amara	Wild candytuft		
Ilex aquifolium	Holly 134		
Illecebrum verticillatum	Coral-necklace		
Impatiens noli-tangere	Touch-me-not balsam		
Inula conyzae	Ploughman's-spikenard		
Inula crithmoides	Golden-samphire		
Iris foetidissima	Stinking iris 69		
Iris pseudacorus	Yellow iris 69		
Isoetes echinospora	Spring quillwort		
Isoetes histrix	Land quillwort		
Isoetes lacustris	Quillwort		
Isolepis cernua	Slender club-rush		
Isolepis setacea	Bristle club-rush		
Jasione montana	Sheep's-bit		
Juncus acutiflorus	Sharp-flowered rush		
Juncus acutus	Sharp rush		
Juncus alpinoarticulatus	Alpine rush		
Juncus ambiguus	Frog rush		
Juncus articulatus	Jointed rush		
Juncus balticus	Baltic rush		
Juncus bufonius	Toad rush		
Juncus bulbosus	Bulbous rush		
Juncus capitatus	Dwarf rush		
Juncus compressus	Round-fruited rush		

Juncus conglomeratus	**Compact rush**	*Ligusticum scoticum*	Scots lovage
Juncus effusus	**Soft-rush**	**Ligustrum vulgare*	**Wild privet 135**
Juncus filiformis	Thread rush	*Limonium bellidifolium*	**Matted sea-lavender**
Juncus foliosus	Leafy rush	*Limonium binervosum*	**Rock sea-lavender**
Juncus gerardii	Saltmarsh rush	*Limonium britannicum*	Rock sea-lavender
Juncus inflexus	Hard rush	*Limonium dodartiforme*	Rock sea-lavender
Juncus maritimus	Sea rush	*Limonium humile*	**Lax-flowered**
Juncus pygmaeus	Pigmy rush		**sea-lavender**
Juncus squarrosus	**Heath rush**	*Limonium loganicum*	Rock sea-lavender
Juncus subnodulosus	Blunt-flowered rush	*Limonium procerum*	Rock sea-lavender
Juncus triglumis	Three-flowered rush	*Limonium recurvum*	Rock sea-lavender
*Juniperus communis	**Juniper 135**	**Limonium vulgare*	**Common sea-lavender**
Kickxia elatine	Sharp-leaved fluellen		**74**
Kickxia spuria	Round-leaved fluellen	*Limosella aquatica*	Mudwort
*Knautia arvensis	**Field scabious 70**	*Linaria repens*	**Pale toadflax**
Kobresia simpliciuscula	False sedge	**Linaria vulgaris*	**Common toadflax 74**
Koeleria macrantha	Crested hair-grass	*Linnaea borealis*	**Twinflower**
Koeleria vallesiana	Somerset hair-grass	*Linum bienne*	**Pale flax**
Lactuca saligna	Least lettuce	*Linum catharticum*	**Fairy flax**
Lactuca serriola	Prickly lettuce	*Linum perenne*	**Perennial flax**
Lactuca virosa	Great lettuce	*Liparis loeselii*	Fen orchid
*Lamiastrum	**Yellow archangel 70**	*Listera cordata*	Lesser twayblade
galeobdolon		*Listera ovata*	Common twayblade
Lamium album	**White dead-nettle**	*Lithospermum arvense*	Field gromwell
Lamium amplexicaule	**Henbit dead-nettle**	*Lithospermum officinale*	Common gromwell
Lamium confertum	Northern dead-nettle	*Lithospermum purpuro-*	**Purple gromwell**
Lamium hybridum	Cut-leaved dead-nettle	*caeruleum*	
Lamium purpureum	**Red dead-nettle**	*Littorella uniflora*	Shoreweed
Lapsana communis	Nipplewort	*Lobelia dortmanna*	Water lobelia
Lathraea squamaria	Toothwort	*Lobelia urens*	Heath lobelia
Lathyrus aphaca	**Yellow vetchling**	*Lolium perenne*	Perennial rye-grass
Lathyrus japonicus	**Sea pea**	**Lonicera periclymenum*	**Honeysuckle 137**
*Lathyrus linifolius	**Bitter-vetch 71**	*Lonicera xylosteum*	**Fly honeysuckle**
Lathyrus nissolia	**Grass vetchling**	*Lotus angustissimus*	Slender
Lathyrus palustris	Marsh pea		bird's-foot-trefoil
*Lathyrus pratensis	**Meadow vetchling 71**	**Lotus corniculatus*	**Common**
Lathyrus sylvestris	**Narrow-leaved**		**bird's-foot-trefoil 75**
	everlasting-pea	*Lotus glaber*	Narrow-leaved
Lavatera arborea	**Tree-mallow**		bird's-foot-trefoil
Lavatera cretica	**Smaller tree-mallow**	*Lotus pedunculatus*	Greater
Leersia oryzoides	Cut-grass		bird's-foot-trefoil
Legousia hybrida	**Venus's-looking-glass**	*Lotus subbiflorus*	Hairy bird's-foot-trefoil
Lemna gibba	Fat duckweed	*Ludwigia palustris*	Hampshire-purslane
Lemna minor	Common duckweed	*Luronium natans*	Floating water-plantain
Lemna trisulca	Ivy-leaved duckweed	*Luzula campestris*	Field wood-rush
Leontodon autumnalis	Autumn hawkbit	*Luzula forsteri*	Southern wood-rush
*Leontodon hispidus	**Rough hawkbit 72**	*Luzula multiflora*	Heath wood-rush
Leontodon saxatilis	Lesser hawkbit	*Luzula pallidula*	Fen wood-rush
Lepidium campestre	Field pepperwort	*Luzula pilosa*	Hairy wood-rush
Lepidium heterophyllum	Smith's pepperwort	*Luzula spicata*	Spiked wood-rush
Lepidium latifolium	Dittander	*Luzula sylvatica*	**Great wood-rush**
Lepidium ruderale	Narrow-leaved	*Lychnis alpina*	**Alpine catchfly**
	pepperwort	**Lychnis flos-cuculi*	**Ragged-robin 76**
*Leucanthemum vulgare	**Oxeye daisy 72**	*Lycopodiella inundata*	Marsh clubmoss
Leucojum aestivum	**Summer snowflake**	*Lycopodium annotinum*	Interrupted clubmoss
Leucojum vernum	**Spring snowflake**	*Lycopodium clavatum*	Stag's-horn clubmoss
*Leymus arenarius	**Lyme-grass 111**	*Lycopus europaeus*	Gypsywort

Lysimachia nemorum	Yellow pimpernel		
*Lysimachia	**Creeping-jenny 77**		
nummularia			
Lysimachia thyrsiflora	Tufted loosestrife		
*Lysimachia vulgaris	**Yellow loosestrife 77**		
Lythrum hyssopifolia	Grass-poly		
Lythrum portula	Water-purslane		
*Lythrum salicaria	**Purple-loosestrife 77**		
Maianthemum bifolium	**May lily**		
*Malus sylvestris	**Crab apple 138**		
*Malva moschata	**Musk mallow 78**		
Malva neglecta	Dwarf mallow		
*Malva sylvestris	**Common mallow 79**		
Marrubium vulgare	White horehound		
Matricaria recutita	Scented mayweed		
Matthiola incana	Hoary stock		
Matthiola sinuata	Sea stock		
Meconopsis cambrica	Welsh poppy		
Medicago arabica	Spotted medick		
Medicago lupulina	Black medick		
Medicago minima	Bur medick		
Medicago polymorpha	Toothed medick		
Medicago sativa	Lucerne		
Melampyrum arvense	**Field cow-wheat**		
Melampyrum cristatum	Crested cow-wheat		
Melampyrum pratense	Common cow-wheat		
Melampyrum sylvaticum	Small cow-wheat		
Melica nutans	Mountain melick		
Melica uniflora	**Wood melick**		
Melittis melissophyllum	**Bastard balm**		
Mentha aquatica	**Water mint**		
Mentha arvensis	**Corn mint**		
Mentha pulegium	**Pennyroyal**		
Mentha suaveolens	**Round-leaved mint**		
*Menyanthes trifoliata	**Bogbean 79**		
Mercurialis annua	Annual mercury		
Mercurialis perennis	Dog's mercury		
Mertensia maritima	**Oysterplant**		
Meum athamanticum	**Spignel**		
Milium effusum	**Wood millet**		
Minuartia hybrida	Fine-leaved sandwort		
Minuartia stricta	Teesdale sandwort		
Minuartia verna	Spring sandwort		
Misopates orontium	Lesser snapdragon		
Moehringia trinervia	Three-nerved sandwort		
Moenchia erecta	Upright chickweed		
Molinia caerulea	Purple moor-grass		
Monotropa hypopitys	Yellow bird's-nest		
Montia fontana	Blinks		
Muscari neglectum	Grape-hyacinth		
Mycelis muralis	Wall lettuce		
Myosotis alpestris	**Alpine forget-me-not**		
Myosotis arvensis	**Field forget-me-not**		
Myosotis discolor	**Changing**		
	forget-me-not		
Myosotis laxa	**Tufted forget-me-not**		
Myosotis ramosissima	**Early forget-me-not**		

Myosotis scorpioides	**Water forget-me-not**	*Oreopteris limbosperma*	Lemon-scented fern	*Phragmites australis*	Common reed
Myosotis secunda	**Creeping forget-me-not**	**Origanum vulgare*	**Marjoram 84**	**Phyllitis scolopendrium*	**Hart's-tongue 117**
Myosotis stolonifera	**Pale forget-me-not**	*Ornithogalum angustifolium*	**Star-of-Bethlehem**	*Physospermum cornubiense*	Bladderseed
*Myosotis sylvatica	**Wood forget-me-not 80**	*Ornithogalum pyrenaicum*	**Spiked star-of- Bethlehem**	*Phyteuma orbiculare*	**Round-headed rampion**
Myosoton aquaticum	Water chickweed	*Ornithopus perpusillus*	Bird's-foot	*Phyteuma spicatum*	**Spiked rampion**
Myosurus minimus	Mousetail	*Ornithopus pinnatus*	Orange bird's-foot	*Picris echioides*	Bristly oxtongue
*Myrica gale	**Bog-myrtle 138**	*Orobanche alba*	Thyme broomrape	*Picris hieracioides*	Hawkweed oxtongue
Myriophyllum alterniflorum	Alternate water-milfoil	*Orobanche artemisiae- campestris*		**Pilosella officinarum*	**Mouse-ear-hawkweed 86**
Myriophyllum spicatum	Spiked water-milfoil		Oxtongue broomrape	*Pilosella peleteriana*	Shaggy mouse-ear-hawkweed
Myriophyllum verticillatum	Whorled water-milfoil	*Orobanche caryophyllacea*	Bedstraw broomrape		
Najas flexilis	Slender naiad	*Orobanche elatior*	Knapweed broomrape	*Pilularia globulifera*	Pillwort
Najas marina	Holly-leaved naiad	*Orobanche hederae*	Ivy broomrape	*Pimpinella major*	Greater burnet-saxifrage
*Narcissus pseudonarcissus	**Wild daffodil 80**	*Orobanche minor*	Common broomrape	*Pimpinella saxifraga*	**Burnet-saxifrage**
		Orobanche purpurea	Yarrow broomrape	*Pinguicula lusitanica*	Pale butterwort
Nardus stricta	Mat-grass	*Orobanche rapum-genistae*	Greater broomrape	*Pinguicula vulgaris*	Common butterwort
Nartecium ossifragum	Bog asphodel	*Orobanche reticulata*	Thistle broomrape	*Plantago coronopus*	Buck's-horn plantain
Neotinea maculata	Dense-flowered orchid	*Orthilia secunda*	Serrated wintergreen	*Plantago lanceolata*	Ribwort plantain
Neottia nidus-avis	Bird's-nest orchid	**Osmunda regalis*	**Royal fern 114**	*Plantago major*	Greater plantain
Nepeta cataria	**Cat-mint**	*Otanthus maritimus* †	Cottonweed	*Plantago maritima*	Sea plantain
*Nuphar lutea	**Yellow water-lily 81**	*Oxalis acetosella*	**Wood-sorrel**	*Plantago media*	**Hoary plantain**
Nuphar pumila	**Least water-lily**	*Oxyria digyna*	**Mountain sorrel**	*Platanthera bifolia*	Lesser butterfly-orchid
*Nymphaea alba	**White water-lily 81**	*Papaver argemone*	**Prickly poppy**	*Platanthera chlorantha*	Greater butterfly-orchid
Nymphoides peltata	**Fringed water-lily**	*Papaver dubium*	**Long-headed poppy**	*Poa alpina*	Alpine meadow-grass
Odontites vernus	Red bartsia	*Papaver hybridum*	**Rough poppy**	*Poa angustifolia*	Narrow-leaved meadow-grass
Oenanthe aquatica	Fine-leaved water-dropwort	**Papaver rhoeas*	**Common poppy 84**	*Poa annua*	Annual meadow-grass
Oenanthe crocata	Hemlock water-dropwort	*Parapholis incurva*	Curved hard-grass	*Poa bulbosa*	Bulbous meadow-grass
Oenanthe fistulosa	Tubular water-dropwort	*Parapholis strigosa*	Hard-grass		
Oenanthe fluviatilis	River water-dropwort	*Parentucellia viscosa*	Yellow bartsia	*Poa compressa*	Flattened meadow-grass
Oenanthe lachenalii	Parsley water-dropwort	*Parietaria judaica*	Pellitory-of-the-wall	*Poa glauca*	Glaucous meadow-grass
Oenanthe pimpinelloides	Corky-fruited water-dropwort	*Paris quadrifolia*	**Herb-paris**	*Poa humilis*	Spreading meadow-grass
Oenanthe silaifolia	Narrow-leaved water-dropwort	*Parnassia palustris*	Grass-of-Parnassus	*Poa infirma*	Early meadow-grass
		Pastinaca sativa	**Wild parsnip**	*Poa nemoralis*	Wood meadow-grass
Oenothera fallax	Intermediate evening-primrose	*Pedicularis palustris*	Marsh lousewort	*Poa pratensis*	**Smooth meadow-grass**
Onobrychis viciifolia	**Sainfoin**	*Pedicularis sylvatica*	Lousewort		
Ononis reclinata	Small restharrow	*Persicaria amphibia*	Amphibious bistort	*Poa trivialis*	Rough meadow-grass
Ononis repens	**Common restharrow**	**Persicaria bistorta*	**Common bistort 85**	*Polemonium caeruleum*	**Jacob's-ladder**
Ononis spinosa	**Spiny restharrow**	*Persicaria hydropiper*	Water-pepper	*Polycarpon tetraphyllum*	Four-leaved allseed
Onopordum acanthium	**Cotton thistle**	*Persicaria lapathifolia*	Pale persicaria	*Polygala amarella*	Dwarf milkwort
Ophioglossum azoricum	Small adder's-tongue	*Persicaria laxiflora*	Tasteless water-pepper	*Polygala calcarea*	**Chalk milkwort**
Ophioglossum lusitanicum	Least adder's-tongue	*Persicaria maculosa*	Redshank	*Polygala serpyllifolia*	Heath milkwort
Ophioglossum vulgatum	Adder's-tongue	*Persicaria minor*	Small water-pepper	*Polygala vulgaris*	**Common milkwort**
Ophrys apifera	Bee orchid	*Persicaria vivipara*	Alpine bistort	*Polygonatum multiflorum*	**Solomon's-seal**
Ophrys fuciflora	Late spider-orchid	*Petasites hybridus*	**Butterbur**		
Ophrys insectifera	Fly orchid	*Petrorhagia nanteuilii*	**Childing pink**	*Polygonatum odoratum*	**Angular solomon's-seal**
Ophrys sphegodes	Early spider-orchid	*Petrorhagia prolifera*	Proliferous pink		
Orchis mascula	Early-purple orchid	*Petroselinum segetum*	Corn parsley	*Polygonatum verticillatum* †	Whorled solomon's-seal
Orchis militaris	Military orchid	*Peucedanum officinale*	Hog's fennel		
Orchis morio	Green-winged orchid	*Peucedanum palustre*	Milk-parsley	*Polygonum arenastrum*	Equal-leaved knotgrass
Orchis purpurea	Lady orchid	*Phalaris arundinacea*	Reed canary-grass		
Orchis simia	Monkey orchid	*Phegopteris connectilis*	Beech fern	*Polygonum aviculare*	Knotgrass
Orchis ustulata	Burnt orchid	*Phleum alpinum*	Alpine cat's-tail	*Polygonum maritimum*	Sea knotgrass
		Phleum arenarium	Sand cat's-tail		
		Phleum bertolonii	**Smaller cat's-tail**		
		Phleum phleoides	Purple-stem cat's-tail		
		Phleum pratense	**Timothy**		

Rumex maritimus	Golden dock	**Scabiosa columbaria*	**Small scabious 92**	*Silene vulgaris*	**Bladder campion**
Rumex obtusifolius	Broad-leaved dock	*Scandix pecten-veneris*	Shepherd's-needle	*Sinapis arvensis*	Charlock
Rumex palustris	Marsh dock	*Scheuchzeria palustris* †	Rannoch-rush	*Sison amomum*	Stone parsley
Rumex pulcher	Fiddle dock	**Schoenoplectus lacustris**	**Common club-rush**	*Sisymbrium officinale*	Hedge mustard
Rumex rupestris	Shore dock	*Schoenoplectus*	Grey club-rush	*Sium latifolium*	Greater water-parsnip
Rumex sanguineus	Wood dock	*tabernaemontani*		**Solanum dulcamara*	**Bittersweet 150**
Ruppia cirrhosa	Spiral tasselweed	*Schoenoplectus triqueter*	Triangular club-rush	*Solanum nigrum*	Black nightshade
Ruppia maritima	Beaked tasselweed	*Schoenus nigricans*	Black bog-rush	**Solidago virgaurea*	**Goldenrod 96**
Ruscus aculeatus	**Butcher's-broom**	**Scilla autumnalis**	**Autumn squill**	*Sonchus arvensis*	Perennial sow-thistle
Sagina apetala	Annual pearlwort	**Scilla verna**	**Spring squill**	*Sonchus asper*	Prickly sow-thistle
Sagina maritima	Sea pearlwort	*Scirpoides holoschoenus*	Round-headed	*Sonchus oleraceus*	Smooth sow-thistle
Sagina nodosa	Knotted pearlwort		club-rush	*Sonchus palustris*	Marsh sow-thistle
Sagina procumbens	Procumbent	*Scirpus sylvaticus*	Wood club-rush	*Sorbus anglica*	Whitebeam
	pearlwort	*Scleranthus annuus*	Annual knawel	**Sorbus aria*	**Common whitebeam**
Sagina subulata	Heath pearlwort	*Scleranthus perennis*	Perennial knawel		**151**
Sagittaria sagittifolia	**Arrowhead**	*Scorzonera humilis*	Viper's-grass	**Sorbus aucuparia*	**Rowan 151**
Salicornia dolichostachya	Long-spiked glasswort	**Scrophularia auriculata**	**Water figwort**	*Sorbus bristoliensis*	Whitebeam
Salicornia europaea	Common glasswort	**Scrophularia nodosa**	**Common figwort**	**Sorbus devoniensis**	**Whitebeam**
Salicornia fragilis	Yellow glasswort	*Scrophularia scorodonia*	Balm-leaved figwort	**Sorbus domestica**	**Service-tree**
Salicornia nitens	Shiny glasswort	**Scrophularia umbrosa**	**Green figwort**	**Sorbus eminens**	**Whitebeam**
Salicornia obscura	Glaucous glasswort	**Scutellaria galericulata*	**Skullcap 93**	**Sorbus lancastriensis**	**Whitebeam**
Salicornia pusilla	One-flowered glasswort	*Scutellaria minor*	Lesser skullcap	**Sorbus porrigentiformis**	**Whitebeam**
Salicornia ramosissima	Purple glasswort	**Sedum acre*	**Biting stonecrop 94**	**Sorbus rupicola**	**Rock whitebeam**
*Salix alba	**White willow 147**	*Sedum album*	White stonecrop	**Sorbus subcuneata**	**Whitebeam**
Salix aurita	**Eared willow**	*Sedum anglicum*	English stonecrop	**Sorbus torminalis*	**Wild service-tree 152**
*Salix caprea	**Goat willow 148**	*Sedum forsterianum*	Rock stonecrop	**Sorbus vexans**	**Whitebeam**
Salix cinerea	**Grey willow**	*Sedum rosea*	Roseroot	**Sorbus wilmottiana**	**Whitebeam**
Salix fragilis	**Crack-willow**	**Sedum telephium*	**Orpine 94**	*Sparganium angustifolium*	Floating bur-reed
Salix herbacea	**Dwarf willow**	*Sedum villosum*	Hairy stonecrop	**Sparganium emersum**	**Unbranched bur-reed**
Salix lapponum	**Downy willow**	*Selaginella selaginoides*	Lesser clubmoss	**Sparganium erectum**	**Branched bur-reed**
Salix myrsinifolia	**Dark-leaved willow**	*Selinum carvifolia*	Cambridge milk-parsley	*Sparganium natans*	Least bur-reed
Salix pentandra	**Bay willow**	*Senecio aquaticus*	Marsh ragwort	*Spartina anglica*	Common cord-grass
Salix phylicifolia	**Tea-leaved willow**	*Senecio cambrensis*	Welsh groundsel	*Spartina maritima*	Small cord-grass
Salix purpurea	**Purple willow**	*Senecio erucifolius*	Hoary ragwort	*Spergula arvensis*	Corn spurrey
Salix repens	**Creeping willow**	*Senecio jacobaea*	Common ragwort	*Spergularia bocconei*	Greek sea-spurrey
Salix triandra	**Almond willow**	*Senecio paludosus*	Fen ragwort	*Spergularia marina*	Lesser sea-spurrey
Salix viminalis	**Osier**	*Senecio sylvaticus*	Heath groundsel	*Spergularia media*	Greater sea-spurrey
Salsola kali	Prickly saltwort	*Senecio viscosus*	Sticky groundsel	*Spergularia rubra*	Sand spurrey
Salvia pratensis	**Meadow clary**	*Senecio vulgaris*	Groundsel	*Spergularia rupicola*	Rock sea-spurrey
*Salvia verbenaca	**Wild clary 91**	**Seriphidium maritimum**	**Sea wormwood**	*Spiranthes aestivalis*	Summer lady's-tresses
Sambucus ebulus	**Dwarf elder**	**Serratula tinctoria*	**Saw-wort 94**	*Spiranthes romanzoffiana*	Irish lady's-tresses
*Sambucus nigra	**Elder 149**	*Seseli libanotis*	Moon carrot	*Spiranthes spiralis*	Autumn lady's-tresses
Samolus valerandi	Brookweed	**Sesleria caerulea**	**Blue moor-grass**	*Spirodela polyrhiza*	Greater duckweed
Sanguisorba minor	**Salad burnet**	*Sherardia arvensis*	Field madder	*Stachys alpina*	Limestone woundwort
Sanguisorba officinalis	**Great burnet**	*Sibthorpia europaea*	Cornish moneywort	**Stachys arvensis**	**Field woundwort**
Sanicula europaea	Sanicle	**Silaum silaus**	**Pepper-saxifrage**	**Stachys germanica**	**Downy woundwort**
Saponaria officinalis	**Soapwort**	*Silene acaulis*	Moss campion	**Stachys officinalis*	**Betony 97**
Sarcocornia perennis	Perennial glasswort	*Silene conica*	Sand catchfly	**Stachys palustris*	**Marsh woundwort 97**
Saussurea alpina	**Alpine saw-wort**	**Silene dioica*	**Red campion 95**	**Stachys sylvatica*	**Hedge woundwort 98**
Saxifraga aizoides	Yellow saxifrage	**Silene gallica**	**Small-flowered**	**Stellaria graminea**	**Lesser stitchwort**
*Saxifraga granulata	**Meadow saxifrage 92**		catchfly	**Stellaria holostea*	**Greater stitchwort 98**
Saxifraga hirculus	Marsh saxifrage	**Silene latifolia**	**White campion**	*Stellaria media*	Common chickweed
Saxifraga hypnoides	Mossy saxifrage	**Silene noctiflora**	**Night-flowering**	*Stellaria neglecta*	Greater chickweed
Saxifraga nivalis	Alpine saxifrage		catchfly	*Stellaria nemorum*	Wood stitchwort
Saxifraga oppositifolia	**Purple saxifrage**	**Silene nutans**	**Nottingham catchfly**	*Stellaria pallida*	Lesser chickweed
Saxifraga stellaris	Starry saxifrage	**Silene otites**	**Spanish catchfly**	*Stellaria palustris*	Marsh stitchwort
Saxifraga tridactylites	Rue-leaved saxifrage	**Silene uniflora**	**Sea campion**	*Stellaria uliginosa*	Bog stitchwort

Stratiotes aloides	Water-soldier	*Trifolium strictum*	Upright clover
Suaeda maritima	Annual sea-blite	*Trifolium subterraneum*	Subterranean clover
Suaeda vera	Shrubby sea-blite	*Trifolium suffocatum*	Suffocated clover
Subularia aquatica	Awlwort	*Triglochin maritima*	Sea arrowgrass
Succisa pratensis	**Devil's-bit scabious 99**	*Triglochin palustris*	Marsh arrowgrass
Symphytum officinale	**Common comfrey**	*Trinia glauca*	Honewort
Symphytum tuberosum	**Tuberous comfrey 99**	*Tripleurospermum*	
Tamus communis	**Black bryony**	*inodorum*	**Scentless mayweed**
Tanacetum vulgare	**Tansy**	*Tripleurospermum maritimum*	Sea mayweed
Taraxacum officinale	Dandelion	*Trisetum flavescens*	**Yellow oat-grass 112**
Taxus baccata	**Yew 153**	*Trollius europaeus*	**Globeflower**
Teesdalia nudicaulis	Shepherd's cress	*Tussilago farfara*	Colt's-foot
Tephroseris integrifolia	Field fleawort	*Typha angustifolia*	**Lesser bulrush**
Tephroseris palustris	Marsh fleawort	*Typha latifolia*	Bulrush
Teucrium botrys	**Cut-leaved germander**	*Ulex europaeus*	**Gorse 155**
Teucrium chamaedrys	**Wall germander**	*Ulex gallii*	**Western gorse**
Teucrium scordium	**Water germander**	*Ulex minor*	**Dwarf gorse**
Teucrium scorodonia	**Wood sage**	*Ulmus glabra*	**Wych elm**
Thalictrum alpinum	**Alpine meadow-rue**	*Ulmus minor*	**Elm**
Thalictrum flavum	**Common meadow-rue**	*Ulmus plotii*	**Plot's elm**
Thalictrum minus	**Lesser meadow-rue**	*Ulmus procera*	English elm
Thelypteris palustris	Marsh fern	*Umbilicus rupestris*	Navelwort
Thesium humifusum	Bastard-toadflax	*Urtica dioica*	Common nettle
Thlaspi arvense	Field penny-cress	*Urtica urens*	Small nettle
Thlaspi caerulescens	Alpine penny-cress	*Utricularia australis*	Bladderwort
Thlaspi perfoliatum	Perfoliate penny-cress	*Utricularia intermedia*	Intermediate
Thymus polytrichus	**Wild thyme 100**		bladderwort
Thymus pulegioides	**Large thyme**	*Utricularia minor*	Lesser bladderwort
Thymus serpyllum	**Breckland thyme**	*Utricularia ochroleuca*	Pale bladderwort
Tilia cordata	**Small-leaved lime 154**	*Utricularia stygia*	Nordic bladderwort
Tilia platyphyllos	**Large-leaved lime**	*Utricularia vulgaris*	Greater bladderwort
Tofieldia pusilla	Scottish asphodel	*Vaccinium microcarpum*	**Small cranberry**
Torilis arvensis	Spreading hedge-parsley	*Vaccinium myrtillus*	**Bilberry**
Torilis japonica	Upright hedge-parsley	*Vaccinium oxycoccos*	**Cranberry**
Torilis nodosa	Knotted hedge-parsley	*Vaccinium uliginosum*	Bog bilberry
Tragopogon pratensis	Goat's-beard	*Vaccinium vitis-idaea*	**Cowberry**
Trichomanes speciosum	Killarney fern	*Valeriana dioica*	**Marsh valerian**
Trichophorum cespitosum	Deergrass	*Valeriana officinalis*	**Common valerian 102**
Trientalis europaea	**Chickweed-**	*Valerianella carinata*	Keeled-fruited
	wintergreen		cornsalad
Trifolium arvense	**Hare's-foot clover**	*Valerianella dentata*	Narrow-fruited
Trifolium bocconei	Twin-headed clover		cornsalad
Trifolium campestre	**Hop trefoil**	*Valerianella locusta*	Common cornsalad
Trifolium dubium	Lesser trefoil	*Valerianella rimosa*	Broad-fruited cornsalad
Trifolium fragiferum	**Strawberry clover**	*Verbascum lychnitis*	**White mullein**
Trifolium glomeratum	**Clustered clover**	*Verbascum nigrum*	**Dark mullein**
Trifolium incarnatum	**Crimson clover**	*Verbascum*	
Trifolium medium	**Zigzag clover 100**	*pulverulentum*	**Hoary mullein**
Trifolium micranthum	Slender trefoil	*Verbascum thapsus*	**Great mullein 103**
Trifolium occidentale	Western clover	*Verbascum virgatum*	**Twiggy mullein**
Trifolium ochroleucon	Sulphur clover	*Verbena officinalis*	**Vervain**
Trifolium ornithopodioides	Bird's-foot clover	*Veronica agrestis*	Green field-speedwell
Trifolium pratense	**Red clover 102**	*Veronica anagallis-*	
Trifolium repens	**White clover**	*aquatica*	**Blue water-speedwell**
Trifolium scabrum	Rough clover	*Veronica arvensis*	Wall speedwell
Trifolium squamosum	Sea clover	*Veronica beccabunga*	**Brooklime**
Trifolium striatum	Knotted clover	*Veronica catenata*	Pink water-speedwell

Veronica chamaedrys	**Germander speedwell**
	105
Veronica hederifolia	Ivy-leaved speedwell
Veronica montana	**Wood speedwell**
Veronica officinalis	**Heath speedwell**
Veronica polita	Grey field-speedwell
Veronica praecox	Breckland speedwell
Veronica scutellata	Marsh speedwell
Veronica serpyllifolia	Thyme-leaved speedwell
Veronica spicata	**Spiked speedwell**
Veronica triphyllos	Fingered speedwell
Veronica verna	Spring speedwell
Viburnum lantana	**Wayfaring-tree 155**
Viburnum opulus	**Guelder-rose 156**
Vicia bithynica	Bithynian vetch
Vicia cracca	**Tufted vetch 105**
Vicia hirsuta	Hairy tare
Vicia lathyroides	Spring vetch
Vicia lutea	**Yellow vetch**
Vicia orobus	Wood bitter-vetch
Vicia parviflora	Slender tare
Vicia sativa	Common vetch
Vicia sepium	**Bush vetch**
Vicia sylvatica	**Wood vetch**
Vicia tetrasperma	Smooth tare
Viola arvensis	**Field pansy**
Viola canina	**Heath dog-violet**
Viola hirta	**Hairy violet**
Viola kitaibeliana	**Dwarf pansy**
Viola lactea	**Pale dog-violet**
Viola lutea	**Mountain pansy**
Viola odorata	**Sweet violet 105**
Viola palustris	**Marsh violet**
Viola persicifolia	**Fen violet**
Viola reichenbachiana	**Early dog-violet**
Viola riviniana	**Common dog-violet**
	106
Viola rupestris	**Teesdale violet**
Viola tricolor	**Wild pansy 106**
Viscum album	**Mistletoe**
Vulpia bromoides	Squirreltail fescue
Vulpia ciliata	Bearded fescue
Vulpia fasciculata	Dune fescue
Vulpia myuros	Rat's-tail fescue
Vulpia unilateralis	Mat-grass fescue
Wahlenbergia hederacea	**Ivy-leaved bellflower**
Wolffia arrhiza	Rootless duckweed
Woodsia ilvensis	Oblong woodsia
Zannichellia palustris	Horned pondweed
Zostera angustifolia	Narrow-leaved eelgrass
Zostera marina	Eelgrass
Zostera noltii	Dwarf eelgrass

Suppliers of English Native Plants

British Wildflower Plants (Linda Laxton), Burlingham Gardens, Main Road, North Burlingham, Norwich, Norfolk NR13 4TA Tel. 01603 716615

BCTV Enterprises, Conservation Centre, Balby Road, Doncaster, South Yorkshire DN4 0RH Tel. 01302 859522

John Chambers, 15 Westleigh Road, Barton Seagrave, Kettering, Northamptonshire NN15 5AJ

Emorsgate Seed, Limes Farm, Tilney All Saints, Kings Lynn, Norfolk PE34 4RT Tel. 01553 829028

Linda Gascoigne Wild Flowers, 17 Imperial Road, Kibworth, Beauchamp, Leicestershire LE8 0HR Tel. 0116 2793959

Hewthorn Herbs and Wild Flowers, 82 Julian Road, West Bridgford, Nottingham NG2 5AN

Jekka's Herb Farm, Rose Cottage, Shellards Lane, Alveston, Bristol BS35 3SY Tel. 01454 418878

Landlife Wild Flowers Ltd, National Wild Flower Centre, Court Hey Park, Liverpool, Merseyside L16 3NA Tel. 0151 7371819

T & D Marston, Culag, Green Lane, Nafferton, East Yorkshire YO25 0LF Tel. 01377 254487 (Ferns)

Mires Beck Nursery, Low Mill Lane, North Cave, Brough, East Yorkshire HU15 2NR Tel. 01430 421543 (Wild flowers of Yorkshire)

Natural Selection, 1 Station Cottages, Hullavington, Chippenham, Wiltshire SN14 6GT Tel. 01666 837369

Natural Surroundings, Bayfield Estate, Bayfield, near Holt, Norfolk NR25 7JN Tel. 01263 711091

Really Wild Flowers, HV Horticulture Ltd, Spring Mead, Bedchester, Shaftesbury, Dorset SP7 0JU Tel. 01747 811778

Trevor Scott, Thorpe Park Cottage, Thorpe le Soken, Essex CP16 0HN (Grasses)

The Wild Flower Centre, Church Farm, Sisland, Loddon, Norfolk NR14 6EF

YSJ Seeds, Broadenham Lane, Winsham, Chard, Somerset TA20 4JF Tel. 01460 30070

TREE SPECIALISTS

Chew Valley Trees, Winford Road, Bristol BS40 8QE
Tel. 01275 333752

Maelor Nurseries Ltd, Fields Farm, Bronington, Whitchurch, Shropshire SY13 3HZ Tel. 01948 710606
e-mail mike@maelor.co.uk

Trees Please, Low Urpeth Farm, Ouston, Chester-le-Street, Durham DH2 1BD Tel. 0191 4103233

Woodland Improvement and Conservation Ltd, Newent Lane, Huntley, Gloucestershire GL19 3HG Tel. 01452 830344

Index

Page numbers in **bold** refer to photographs

Acknowledgments

PHOTOGRAPHIC ACKNOWLEDGMENTS

The great majority of photographs in this book are by Don Berwick.

For permission to reproduce the photographs, paintings and artwork on the following pages, the publishers thank those listed below:

John Brookes 103 (Denmans, West Sussex); **Christie's International Ltd** 159 (watercolour by George Carter); **Garden and Wildlife Matters** 6, 26; **Geoff Dann © FLL** 37, 67, 68, 122; **Jerry Harpur** 2 (Great Dixter, East Sussex); **Sunniva Harte** 30 (Somerset Lodge, Petworth, West Sussex), 46 (Ramster, Chiddingfold, Surrey), 50 (Brook Cottage, East Meon, Hampshire); **Andrew Lawson** 9 (Denmans, West Sussex) 56, 58–59, 73, 150; © **Osborne & Little** endpapers (*Marlbury Down* fabric from the Wessex Collection), 4 (photograph Fritz von der Schulenburg); **Jean Sturgis © FLL** 161; **V&A Picture Library** 12, 14, 15, 18, 19, 24, 25; **Juliette Wade** 115 (Blaengwrfach Isfa, Bancyffordd, Carmarthenshire, Wales), 118 (The Clock House, Coleshill, Oxfordshire)

BOTANICAL ILLUSTRATIONS

This book contains some of Jacques Le Moyne's delightful, delicate watercolours, which come from the first book illustrating the beauty of English flowers. A French Huguenot refugee, his work was encouraged by his patrons, Sir Walter Raleigh and Lady Mary Sidney, mother of Sir Philip Sidney. During the last 16 years of his life in England he used his acutely observed portraits of plants and butterflies as references for botanical woodcuts in his book *La Clef des Champs*, published in 1586. Le Moyne, who later added the name de Morgues, was born around 1533.

Editor Susan Berry	Editorial Director Kate Cave
Text Editor Anne Askwith	Art Director Caroline Hillier
Art Editor Louise Kirby	Head of Pictures Anne Fraser
Production Natalie Hardick	
Indexer Serena Dilnot	

AUTHORS' ACKNOWLEDGMENTS

We are grateful for the help given by the following: Dame Miriam Rothschild; John Brookes; Mavis Batey; Professor Clive Stace, author of *New Flora of the British Isles* (Cambridge University Press); Dr Chris Preston, Monks Wood, for compiling the checklist of the English flora; the Botanical Society of the British Isles; Professor John Parker and Dr Tim Upson, Cambridge Botanic Gardens; Dr Sally Corbett; Antony Little, Becky Metcalfe and all at Osborne and Little; David Coleman, David Thomas, and members and staff of Bexley London Borough; George Carter; Fiona Crumley and Sue Minter, Chelsea Physic Garden; Dr Brent Elliott; the Royal Horticultural Society Library; the Linnean Society Library; Chelsea Library; the State Library of New South Wales; the Victoria and Albert Museum; Diana Kingham; Jenny Evans, Royal Botanic Gardens, Kew; Maureen Sherriff; Mrs Valerie Simmons; Mrs Jane Berwick; Lynne Frankland, Plantlife; Barry Delves, Hatchards; John Manser; and all who keep Flora-for-Fauna going, both at the Linnean Society and at the Natural History Museum, Dr John Marsden, Professor Gren Lucas, Gina Douglas, Priya Nithianandan, Marquita Baird, Professor Chris Humphries and Mike Sadka.

PUBLISHERS' ACKNOWLEDGMENTS

The Publishers would like to thank Don Berwick for his valuable help with plant identification. They are also grateful to Claudine Meissner for design assistance and to Sarah Mitchell, Tom Windross and Michael Brunström for editorial help.

Quotations from the works of Rudyard Kipling by permission of A.P. Watt Ltd on behalf of The National Trust for Places of Historic Interest or Natural Beauty.